To the
Jackson Family Wines team:

Jess left a legacy of
quality and excellence
in winemaking, as well as
hard work and dedication.

His dream was to start
a family business that endures.
You help to continually
realize his dream.

Thank you for
your commitment.

Warmly,

Barbara R. Banke
and the Jackson Family

A MAN
and
HIS MOUNTAIN

THE EVERYMAN WHO
CREATED KENDALL-JACKSON AND
BECAME AMERICA'S GREATEST
WINE ENTREPRENEUR

EDWARD HUMES

PublicAffairs
NEW YORK

Book design by Pauline Brown
Typeset in 11-point Bauer Bodini by the Perseus Books Group

Library of Congress Cataloging-in-Publication Data

Humes, Edward.
    A man and his mountain : the everyman who created Kendall-Jackson and
  became America's greatest wine entrepreneur / Edward Humes.—First edition.
        pages cm
    Includes index.
    ISBN 978-1-61039-420-8—1. Jackson, Jess Stonestreet, 1930–2011. 2. Vintners—
  California—Biography. 3. Businessmen—California—Biography. 4. Kendall-
  Jackson Wine Estates (Firm)—History. 5. Wine and wine making—California—
  History. I. Title.
  TP547.J22H86 2013
  663'.20092—dc23

                                                                          [B]
                                                               2013020106

First Edition

               10 9 8 7 6 5 4 3 2 1

To Donna, Gaby, and Eben,
Sláinte, Budem, L'chaim,
Cheers!

CONTENTS

Catch Me If You Can

He watches Rachel walk past, mere minutes now before her big moment. Their moment. She doesn't spot him in the crowd, but he is transfixed. For what seems the hundredth time in their still-new relationship, he feels the tightening at the back of his throat at the mere sight of her. Even at his age, his wavy hair reduced to gray stubble, he squares his shoulders and stands a little straighter in unconscious response to her lithe grace, her shining, impossible youth. He can scarcely believe Rachel is his, yet there she walks, dressed in the gold that he picked out for her, exquisite in the afternoon sun.

Jess Stonestreet Jackson is not a man who casually reveals his heart. Even those closest to him—especially those closest to him—know this all too well. This beat cop turned billionaire, this gentlemanly cutthroat wine mogul, has made his friends, his employees, his children, and his wives into Wine Country Kremlinologists. Always they must labor to crack his code, to puzzle out the meaning of a glance or frown or too-broad grin. Only Rachel lays him bare. Years after this morning has passed, recalling how she looked, that perfect moment, Jess's voice will crack. His eyes will well. He had arrived with her certain they would make history that day. Amid a chorus of doubters, he had been sure of it.

And if there was one thing Jess Jackson loved even more than Rachel, it was showing a dubious world that he was right.

THE PREAKNESS STAKES TRANSFORMS BALTIMORE. Once a year this blue-collar port town gives way to the pomp and ritual of one of the oldest sporting events in America, the middle leg of the storied Triple Crown, the Super Bowl of horse racing. Here he would make his stand, an occasion marked by a full week of hot-air balloon races, footraces, pub crawls, parades, live music throughout town, and endless arrangements of bright yellow black-eyed Susans, the state flower and the symbol of the Preakness. Culminating with the legendary stakes race at Pimlico Park, the Preakness has been Baltimore's biggest annual celebration since Ulysses S. Grant called the White House home back in 1873.

In 2008 Jess Jackson brought two things to this party: an impossible horse and a very large bodyguard.

Both horse and guard were results of Jackson's penchant for defying tradition and irritating the rich, powerful, and entrenched. This child of the Depression who worked his way through school as a dishwasher, lumberjack, ambulance driver, fashion model, Teamster, stevedore, and cop had little in common with the gentry of Horse Country, who certainly viewed him as a barbarian. But that hadn't stopped him from using his California Wine Country millions to snap up farms, fillies, and fans. In the same daring, risky, convention-defying way he had built a faltering little winery called Kendall-Jackson into an empire that quite literally put Chardonnay on America's tables, Jackson had, after a few initial disasters, become the most successful new racehorse owner in half a century.

This was not supposed to happen. Corporate scions and other assorted rich guys were always showing up in Horse Country (and Wine Country, for that matter) certain their mad business skills would set them apart. The old guard with the blue grass and blue blood found it highly entertaining because the newcomers invariably skulked away with egos and wallets deflated. And yet here, infuriatingly, was Jess Jackson, transforming a staid and insular thoroughbred industry against its will, as he had previously done in the wine business. He flouted convention. He denounced the corruption others pretended not to see. Worse, he was not just a California winemaking interloper; he was, of all things, a lawyer, too, and he would never be forgiven by the old guard for suing the pants off famous (and, thanks to Jackson, infamous) horsemen for cheating him. Hence the death threats that prompted the bodyguard, along with backroom attempts to block him from entering this marquee race. The obstructionists failed in the end, although Jackson's horse was stuck in the absolute worst starting position possible, a handicap no other horse had ever overcome.

But this time the horse was Rachel Alexandra, a three-year-old filly in the midst of one of the great racing campaigns in the history of the sport. Her previous race just two weeks before, the Kentucky Oaks, had set her apart. That race—a $500,000 contest at Churchill Downs for three-year-old fillies held on the day before the Kentucky Derby—had stunned racing fans as Rachel won by more than twenty lengths, by far the largest margin of victory in the history of that race. Jackson had been a spectator, not an owner, for that one, but after he saw Rachel run, he had to have her. He was one of the four hundred richest men in the world at that point, and no price was really beyond him—a thought that, after so many years, still startled him when he took the time to reflect on it, still etched his broad face not with pride but with something that looked very much like discomfort. He had never lost the poor kid's unease at spending, the idea that thriftiness, not lavishness, was the thing to be admired. This was a guy who still wore his grandfather's hand-me-down boots, after all. "Plenty of wear left in them," he'd grouse when someone asked him about the broken-down old things. So for a long time he wouldn't say how much he had paid for Rachel, pretending it was a secret deal of some sort when in fact he was simply embarrassed. When he finally admitted the price tag had been $10 million, he looked sheepish but confessed no regrets. "She was," he would say in a tremulous tone, as he if he were explaining how he had come to possess the *Mona Lisa* or achieved the summit at Everest, "worth every penny." And to him, Rachel *was* his latest Mona Lisa, and the campaign he had designed for her was his latest mountaintop.

Her previous owner had not planned to enter the Preakness. He didn't believe in running females against stallions, which was a prevailing view among the racing elite. But Jackson had immediately announced his intention to enter the race, notwithstanding the tumult brought on by a new stable, a new trainer, a new jockey, and almost no time left to prepare. The other owners predicted disaster. No way could Jackson prep her in time. And even if he did, there was no way a three-year-old filly, no matter how talented and successful against other females, could stand up to a field of stallions in one of the biggest races in the world. Didn't this outsider, this meddler, understand anything about thoroughbreds? He wasn't just going against tradition. He was going against nature. A filly hadn't won this race since before the Great Depression with good reason. It lay in the female horse's genes, her most ancient instinct, the cardinal rule of the herd: to back down when challenged by a male. Rachel Alexandra would be facing a whole field of the horse-racing game's most alpha males. The old guard of the thoroughbred industry had chortled, delighted at the prospect of Jess falling on his face at last despite his billions, despite his empire of wine and real estate and California hubris, and especially despite his incessant talk of innovation and reform for horse racing. They wanted him to look like a fool. They wanted him to go away.

Rachel is in the gate now, done prancing and snorting, her usual prerace temper replaced by a tense stillness. He had never encountered a horse like Rachel, so anxious to run, so competitive, so focused. It had been eighty-five years since the last filly won the Preakness. And no horse, male or female, had ever won the race from the starting place Rachel had been given: the thirteenth post position, the farthest from the rail, the longest road to victory. That spot had never seen a winner. Never in 134 years.

Just another bit of history to make, Jess figures. He rubs his eyes and raises his binoculars, gazing from the owner's box. He can see she is perfectly still now, a coiled spring at the gate, dark and gleaming in the sun. The unbearable pause after all the horses are in line stretches on for way too many heartbeats. Jess tries to take it all in: the expectant crowd, his wife beside him quietly chanting encouragement to Rachel, the warmth of the sun on his shoulders. This is one of the moments he wants to squeeze tight and hold close and keep vivid. Like the time he perched on his favorite uncle's shoulders as they watched Seabiscuit run back in 1938. There was the first time he saw his firstborn. That disastrous, delicious first Chardonnay he made, the one that almost broke him, then made him rich. And that first case of wine he sold, at the Oyster Bar at Grand Central Station of all places. And the next thing he knew, the First Lady was pouring it at the White House. His wine at the White House: that had been huge. He knows he doesn't have many more moments like that left to him, that he has already probably had more than his share. But he is in the middle of one more first right now, and who the hell cares if it cost him 10 million bucks to get here?

Finally, the bell pulls Jess from his flash of reverie. The gates spring open, and he leans forward in unconscious imitation as Rachel sprints in that light-footed gait of hers, flying into first place, barely seeming to touch the turf as she sets the pace, even though she has to run so much farther than all the other horses just to get to the rail. Yet there she is, first after a furlong. It is the hardest way to win a race from post to finish—to be the pursued rather than the pursuer. But that is Rachel's way, and whether she wins or loses, this is what Jess loves best about her. There for all to see is a style that holds nothing back and contains no artifice, the best and simplest and purest sort of challenge, not just in racing, as Jess sees it, but in business and life as well: catch me if you can.

1

Diving In

JESS JACKSON WRIGGLED INTO HIS HALF-WETSUIT, THREW on an air tank, regulator, and mask, and plunged into the vineyard's dark reservoir. The icy water burned his exposed arms and legs. He could see nothing under the surface; dawn was still hours away. He'd have to feel along the slimy bottom of the pond until he found the weeds and algae clogging the irrigation pumps, then rip them loose so that the reservoir waters could once again flow to the vines.

His big hands reduced to clumsy clubs by the cold, he tried not to panic as he felt around with numbed fingers. He knew time was not on his side. The banks of drippers and sprayers in the fields could protect the grapes from fatal frost. Liquid water soon froze once sprayed on the vines, but that was good: it insulated the fragile fruit, forming a barrier between the grapes and the much colder air temperature that would burn and ruin the crop. But the vital pumps had clogged, the protective waters were not flowing, and there was no one but this middle-aged lawyer and part-time vintner there to do something about the incessant frost alarm. Jackson knew he either could complete this crazy, bone-chilling dive, risking possible hypothermia to save his fledgling vineyard, or he could walk away, go sit by the fire, and lose the farm in a matter of hours. As in, literally lose the farm.

In truth, this wasn't much of a debate for Jackson. In a crisis he preferred offense to defense whatever the consequences—punching rather than rolling with the punches. His years working as a policeman, an ambulance driver, a lumberjack, a gambler, and assorted other risky and dicey careers had convinced him of that much. Years later that résumé would make him a unique entry on *Forbes*'s list of the world's wealthiest men. Not too many former Berkeley cops joined that rarefied company—just one, in fact. So he had raced to rummage through the storeroom where he had stashed the family's sporting gear in old wine barrels. He tore through the tennis rackets, golf clubs, and old volleyballs and finally came up with his diving rig. No one else in the family had been quite sure why he had hauled all this junk up to the farm. Now it seemed there had been a method to the madness as he told his wide-eyed daughter, "I'm going in."

Such was life on Jess Jackson's first mountain. This was long before he acquired another, gentler mountain in Sonoma Valley Wine Country: his prized high ground for the empire he would build of wine, real estate, and horses. But that first freezing, dying, water-starved vineyard was something very different, more trial than trophy. This weekend retreat sat high up in Lakeport, California, a winding, precarious drive three hours north of the house in the San Francisco Bay Area. This property, too, was fertile and beautiful if he squinted hard, but it was also rugged and unforgiving: steamy in summer, achingly cold in winter, the kind of land that looked back at a farmer and dared him to plant. This was not the fashionable, pricey verdancy of Napa and Sonoma to the south, but a far more difficult landscape to tame, a bigger risk, on the far edge of what could reasonably be called California Wine County. It seemed a long-shot start for what would soon be America's most popular wine and one of the country's most successful entrepreneurs—if he survived that cold, dark plunge.

An hour later Jackson staggered out of his black lagoon, and soon enough the pumps were chugging away, the grape harvest had been saved, and Jackson sat wrapped in blankets in the living room as his daughter ferried him mugs of hot tea. Two hours passed before he stopped shaking. This gave him plenty of time to think, to take stock, to realize what an idiot he had been. Hunched there, the warmth slowly returning to his chilled limbs, he couldn't stop thinking that he had taken a very big risk for precious little.

He had been growing grapes for a few years by then, selling the harvest to wineries that always needed extra fruit to round out their crush. This had started out as a nice little sideline to his busy law practice. He wasn't contributing to world-class wine or anything close. But he had wanted to teach his two daughters how to farm, and they had worked hard. They had planted all sorts of veggies, too, along with the grapes and the walnuts. Now in his fifties, the workaholic lawyer could almost imagine a Lakeport retirement in the not-too-distant future. He had found a property that offered him a taste of the farming he had grown up loving and respecting in a way only someone who had known the Depression and poverty could understand: the idea, almost a genetic memory as he imagined it, lodged deep in the human DNA, that if you had a bit of land and could grow a crop, then you'd always be able to put food on the table no matter what else happened. "I'm happiest when I have a lump of dirt in my hand or animals to tend," he told his children more than once—the two he had at the time, as well as the three who would come much later, and then the grandkids, too.

But that wasn't what was going on up in Lakeport by then. Ambition and necessity had gradually tractored over the simple joy of cultivating the earth, of raising a delicate, flavorful tomato that no one would confuse with supermarket fare. He had planted more grapevines, upping his harvest year after year, until the hobby days were over and he needed the grapes to pay their way. Instead, he was getting next to nothing as the once lucrative seller's market for wine grapes had predictably become a buyer's market because everyone had overplanted. Now he was in the no-man's-land between hobby and full-on business—and a failing business at that. Something had to change.

Even though Jackson couldn't have fully articulated it at the time, this moment of desperation and ridiculous stomping around in a wetsuit would mark a turning point, a milestone, and not just for Jackson and the company he was about to create. He would help drive the transformation of the entire sprawling California Wine Country from a sleeping, laughable giant—whose most popular products at the time included $3 strawberry wine that tasted like cough medicine—into what it is today: the center of America's $30 billion wine industry, envy of the world. Jackson would be one of a handful of winemaking pioneers who led this transition, and it happened because this was the moment when he decided it might be time to gamble on a new way of doing business. Why should he sell his grapes to someone else? Why not begin to make his own wine? Why not build his own winery? If he was going to freeze his ass off to save a vineyard and sit shaking and blue by the fire in the middle of the night, he didn't want to do it so that someone else could make wine that came in boxes. Maybe he could make something great, something to be proud of, something that would endure. And a half-formed vision came to him of having a sprawling winery, of growing grapes here and around the state, of amassing bits and pieces of the old estate vineyards that had flourished early in the century, declined during Prohibition, and were now ripe for the taking. This picture made perfect sense to him, though he was at that moment in 1980 just a lawyer with chattering teeth, a few acres of grapes, absolutely no idea how to make great wine, and no previous desire to be a winemaker. But he felt fate had sent him a message: Why not go big, risk everything, try to make something unique and delicious, and see what happens next?

The vision was foolish, impossible, and brilliant, for out of such unlikely dreams an empire arose. Jess Jackson, who had been speaking with his wife, Jane, about retiring from the law and taking it easy, of slowing down and enjoying life, was about to embark on one of the greatest reinventions in American business history. It would take another disaster to finally push him over the edge that divided dreaming from action, but once he did, he would go on to put Chardonnay on America's tables (a wine then barely known to the American public) and make the most popular version of it in the United States for more than a quarter century running. He'd help propel California wines from tasting-room backwaters to world-class vintages, expanding his little wine company's reach from one in which he was CEO, chief counsel, and door-to-door salesman into a global concern making and selling wine on four continents. Yet he would retain the practices and values (and iron control) of a small family business, right down to the traditional handcrafted oak barrels that other global brands abandoned for the sake of efficiency and economy.

And when wine had made him a billionaire several times over, he reinvented himself again as a thoroughbred horseman, rising from the bottom to the top of that bruising business, too, as he moved in the space of a few years from easy mark for con artists to owner of the horse of the year three years in a row.

His decisions and the hard-nosed inspiration that followed that frigid night of the clogged reservoir would make him a leader for the wine industry, regularly emulated and envied because, even his bitterest rivals would concede, he so often seemed to be ahead of the curve. His moves changed the world. Those same moves would also destroy his first marriage, alienate his eldest daughters, drive him repeatedly to the brink of bankruptcy even as he remarried and raised another three children, and embroil him in battles, vendettas, epic lawsuits, and corruption investigations involving some of the most powerful players in wine and horses. And beyond that swirl of events and turmoil, Jackson would end up building something he felt certain would endure: a family business designed to thrive for generations. He longed to make something akin to the great winemaking dynasties of Europe, the Antinoris and the Frescobaldis, who for centuries have passed on the tradition and culture and ancient bonds of the grape, a beverage Jackson saw as unique in symbolism and significance, as old as civilization itself. In the decades that followed that frigid predawn dive, he could have sold out a dozen times over at immense profit to the megacorporations that control most of the rest of the wine industry. Everyone else did: the Fetzers and Mondavis, the family wineries that are now just labels on a corporate spreadsheet. His Kendall-Jackson dynasty is the last of them left standing, a man and his mountain.

He accomplished all of this, for good and ill, after age fifty, one of the greatest second acts in the history of American entrepreneurship.

2

First Pour: Glut and Stuck

WHEN JESS AND JANE JACKSON BOUGHT THE OLD FARM in Lakeport, it was supposed to be his getaway, his career extender. The old pear-and-walnut orchard on the northern edge of Wine Country would, Jess vowed, allow him some breathing space from the San Francisco law practice. It would be his respite from the pressure of managing a busy firm and litigating the high-stakes real estate cases in his esoteric specialty of inverse condemnations. This was a type of law that few knew well but that was in high demand in the seventies, as newly (and belatedly) environmentally conscious state and federal governments were rushing to convert unique coastal properties into parks and preserves before all of California could be paved over. Jackson had no problem with preserving the state's most valuable and fast-disappearing natural resources. In fact, he applauded it, and earlier in his legal career he had even worked the other side. One of his first jobs out of law school had him representing California as it scooped up properties and rights-of-way in the fifties and sixties, though his work then was more about preserving space for freeways than for parks. Now, however, he worked to make sure his clients—mainly large landowners and developers—got maximum compensation for being told their plans to build yet more ocean-view resorts, shopping malls, and subdivisions would have to give way to the occasional national seashore or coastal forest preserve.

Such work could be intense, the trials long and laborious. Jackson, ever the obsessive researcher, immersed in each case, burying himself in evidence, which took the form of minutely handwritten notes on reams of yellow legal pads he consumed by the gross and took everywhere. His daughters' earliest memories revolved around Daddy and his yellow papers; the two were inseparable. When the girls were old enough, he recruited them to join Jane as his office help and researchers, and he always took his work home, where evenings found him surrounded by his piles of legal research. There he would be, ensconced in a living room chair, propped up in bed, or spread out on the table, and calling him to dinner required concerted, frequently loud efforts to get his attention. Usually, Jane would have to dispatch one or both daughters to annoy him into submission before the meal could commence. This was how Jackson seemed to approach everything, whether it was teaching one of his children to swim or arguing some point of property rights in court: intense, consumed, and bent on knowing more than his opponents, seeking out and exploiting weakness.

The results, so far, had been rewarding. His contingency fees often ran to six figures and, once in a while, to seven—tidy sums for trial work in the twenty-first century, a fortune circa 1974. The downside was part of what drove him: lose the case, lose the fee. Little wonder that he started longing for an escape. This all-or-nothing ethic made for a high-pressure existence, one that, he sometimes joked, had more in common with casino gambling than with his once regular paycheck from the state attorney general.

He had intended the farm in Lakeport to be different. It was to be his balm, despite the twisting two- to three-hour drive from the city, because once there, he could dwell in a landscape capped by cold, clear skies with not a legal paper in sight. There were the orchards, a modest farmhouse, a sagging barn sheltering a cranky tractor old enough to be a historic landmark, and a chance to get back to his farming roots. Here, he swore to his wife, he finally could unwind and heal. He could haul his two teenaged daughters up there, and Jenny and Laura could learn how to work the land, as he had done at his grandparents' spread in Colorado as a boy. They'd grow to enjoy, not sell. "It's going to be our Old MacDonald's farm," Jess said, "a little bit of everything, never too much of anything."

He and Jane also considered it as an investment for their retirement, something that, in time, would evolve from a getaway into the place Jess could putter and work when the time came to wind down his practice. He and Jane, his college sweetheart, who had worked as a social worker to support him through law school and then had run his law office from the beginning, were on the same page on this, as they had been with every other big decision that came before.

But then he had planted the grapes. The grapes: those mysterious, demanding, unforgiving, romance-laden clusters. Not to make wine, he assured his wife and himself—no, never. And not even to tend the vines himself. He had someone else to do that because grapes were as much work as the law and even more stubborn, requiring an expertise, both forceful and refined, that his childhood summers shucking corn and tending livestock had not provided. Growing grapes was science. It was art. It was lifestyle. He understood that, and though he strived to learn that alchemy himself, he knew he had to hire out to get the work done. The idea was to sell the fruit to local wineries, which in California of the 1970s needed more grapes than their own vineyards could produce. It would be a nice little supplement to his law practice, with a potential to grow with the market. All part of the retirement plan, he and Jane agreed. At first.

Years later Jess would find it ironic that the grapes had created a final, unbridgeable gap with his wife, for planting them had never been his idea. That inspiration came courtesy of a chance meeting 25,000 feet over the Pacific as he and Jane were returning from a law conference in Hawaii. Hawaii had been a favorite family retreat for years, but this trip had been dispiriting. The pessimistic talk at the conference, the circle-the-wagons mood among his colleagues, had confirmed his own growing fears: Jackson's legal specialty was evolving—and not in a good way. He had built a practice that parlayed a few really good, complex real estate cases a year into big payoffs. This was how he could afford to buy a beautiful house on the peninsula south of San Francisco, along with several investment properties in nearby San Mateo, commercial and office buildings that provided good, steady rental income. But the momentum of appellate rulings of late, the direction of precedent and public pressure, were going against him. The lucrative verdicts that had sustained his career and paid the bills for so long would soon dry up. The straightforward solution, he knew, would be to follow the dollars and shift to a new legal specialty with more promising earnings potential. That would be the obvious, sensible course. Back then there were new areas of practice with plenty in common with his existing expertise: environmental law, privacy law, the enormous shifts in financial law occurring as new electronic investments and records began to supplant paper and ink. The intellectual challenge that had engrossed and satisfied him in his legal practice, but that had begun to fade in recent years, could be renewed. He was only forty-five then, looked ten years younger than that, still in his prime as far as he was concerned: fit, dynamic, energetic.

So why did pushing for new avenues of success in the law seem so much like obsolescence to him? Why did he feel the almost desperate urge to move on to the next big and completely different thing? He had no idea what that might be, other than returning time and again to financially impractical visions of himself working a field in jeans and the worn, treasured leather army boots he had inherited from his grandfather. He had been unable to express this disquiet to Jane, but at this turning point in his career his heart and his head were at odds.

Jackson had been sitting on the plane gloomily contemplating this uncertain future when his daydreams were interrupted by the gentleman sitting across from him. Jess and Jane had treated themselves to first class on this trip, and on this plane the high-end seats were in groups of four, with another couple facing them. The man, balding and pleasant looking, with the weathered face of a fellow who had spent much of his life outdoors, had extended his hand in introduction. "Hank Bartolucci," he said.

Jackson started a moment, then smiled in recognition and took the man's strong, calloused hand. He knew that name. He knew the family. He had represented them in a foreclosure of a winery in Napa Valley years before. The Bartoluccis were a family of winemakers.

Jackson would later say fate had intervened on that flight from Hawaii at the very moment he needed to be shown the way to his next big thing. "Either that, or it was one hell of a coincidence," Jackson would laugh.

It turned out that Bartolucci, sans winery, was still in the wine business, working with a new force in California winemaking by the name of Robert Mondavi, who had been taking Napa Valley by storm. Bartolucci had been scouting out properties in the Lakeport area for Mondavi, seeking farms that the rapidly growing winemaker could buy up and convert to vineyards. Lake County was a fine place to grow wine, Bartolucci confided. Many years ago it had actually been part of Napa County, that most famous slice of California Wine Country, until the municipal lines had been redrawn and the new Lake County created. Indeed, at the dawn of the twentieth century, this region had been the savior of the European wine industry when Old World vineyards were decimated by a parasitic plague, phylloxera, against which American grapes were resistant. Grafting European plants onto American rootstock had been the only thing that staved off extinction for many of those revered lines of Bordeaux and Burgundy and the other fine wine grapes of France, Italy, Germany, and Spain. And while the European vineyards slowly recovered, California wines became the toast of the world—a dominance that lasted right up until Prohibition did what the parasites couldn't. But the area was ready for a comeback, he said. And the property he had lined up was sweet.

"I had found a beautiful place, eighty-four acres of pears and walnuts, perfect for planting grapes," Bartolucci sighed. "But Mondavi decided he didn't want to go into Lakeport after all."

The winemaker noticed Jackson's strange expression then, and Bartolucci's weathered face split into a hopeful grin. "Hey, Jess, you know anyone who might be interested? Why don't you come up and take a look?"

"I know farming," Jackson said. "But I don't know anything about making wine."

Bartolucci shook his head. No need to make wine, he said. Just grow the grapes. Plenty of wineries will want to buy them, he promised. "Come and take a look. If you like it and you decide you want it, my son Ron can help prep the land and get it ready for planting a vineyard."

By the time they got off the plane, Jess and Jane had said yes, they'd drive up to see the property.

They both loved those eighty-four acres off Mathews Road on sight: the isolation, the beautiful old orchards, the quaint house and barn. The property sat very close to the chill waters of Clear Lake, California's largest body of freshwater and the nation's oldest lake, with sediment core samples dated back 480,000 years. Mount Konocti dominated Clear Lake's southern shore, an extinct volcano that had last erupted about 150,000 years before—far enough in the past to be of no worry to residents, but recent enough in geologic time to have left deeply fertile soil throughout the region. European settlers arrived in 1845, but Native Americans had settled Clear Lake as far back as 11,000 years, finding a sheltered place and climate, with abundant fish and game at a time when the rest of Northern California remained in the grip of the last great Ice Age. Jackson would find *matates* and other Native American artifacts in his fields. This was the retreat Jess needed, the place to escape the pressures of work and revel in the soil, in farming. And when he heard the property's backstory from the owner, Donald Covey, it put him over the top, playing on Jess's fascination with history and legend. The Covey family had owned the place since the mid-1800s, when they had come out from Missouri in a wagon train, led by Daniel Boone's brother no less. They had brought the fruit trees and livestock with them. Until fifteen years earlier, two big old cherry trees planted by the settlers had still been there. Old age had finally claimed them, but the land still had a rich heritage that drew Jackson to it.

Within a few months the property was his. But the idea of a quiet retreat soon fell by the wayside. As he would later tell it, the lure of the grape trapped him, deliciously and completely. And permanently.

THERE IS ROMANCE in planting a vineyard, Jess Jackson often said, a participation in something ancient, unique, mystical, and profound. This was why, once he bought the Lakeport land, he felt compelled to replace his perfectly good pears and walnuts with grape vines rather than tomatoes or cows or corn. Wine is the beverage poured to forge bonds with other people, other cultures. Not milk, Jackson would say, not beer or Coke or orange juice. Wine is the elixir. We bring it for luck and for love and on special occasions, from weddings to housewarmings to ship launchings. We make peace with it, toast the living and the dead with it, give it and share it with those closest to us, experience God with it if we're Catholic and seal marriage by breaking a glass for it if we're Jewish. Wine has a deep spiritual significance that no other food or drink possesses. It ties us to the land, to the bounty and gift of nature. It dates back 6,000 years to the *vitis vinifera* grapes clinging to the rocky mountainsides of the Caucasus, where the harsh weather, thin soil, and late springs conspired to make a sweeter, richer, more flavorful grape, the ancestor vine genetically linked to every great vineyard in the world that came after. Planting grapes is embracing the very history of humanity, as Jackson saw it. It is embracing life.

"It's also one helluva a gamble," he liked to add. "It's a trap that, once you begin, never lets you go. I never expected to get into the wine business. But once I was in, there was no way out. It was quicksand to me. Beautiful quicksand."

How is wine a trap? Simple, Jackson said: romance and tribal imperatives aside, the most remarkable thing about planting a vineyard,

the thing that makes it one of the most daunting agricultural projects in the world to undertake, is that for the first five years, four if
you're very good *and* very lucky, all it does is cost. During those first
years, a vineyard earns nothing. It just eats away at your capital and
finds new ways—frosts and pests and diseases and mold and soil
depletion and drought and floods—to suck up great gouts of money,
time, labor, and more money.

But he put up with it, starting small. Jackson would be the first
to admit that he chafed at starting small, preferring his entrances,
gestures, and attacks to be grand and head-on. But for the sake of
family harmony, he acquiesced to his wife's desire to be cautious.
Eventually, he was able to sell his first small harvests of grapes
as Bartolucci had promised. Then he planted some more, and he
sold those, too, and put that money—and some of his law practice earnings—into yet more grapes. Over time he abandoned the
restraint he had promised his wife, upping his investment and risk
in anticipation of greater rewards down the line. Just when he was
on a roll, however, record harvests throughout the state glutted
the grape market. Prices plummeted. This was when he had to
use his scuba gear to rescue his harvests from the frost and he first
began to consider other options. The next year grew worse: his
reliable customers—winemakers he considered friends—said they
were sorry, Jess, but they just could not buy any of his grapes this
time. They could not even use all their own grapes, much less his
Lakeport harvest. That was the way of it, one of his loyal buyers,
Barney Fetzer, told him. The business was cyclical, shortages followed by glut, feast by famine. Maybe next year would be better,
Fetzer said. Maybe not.

Jackson was horrified. He made the rounds of the region's wineries,
worked the phones, cut his prices below his own costs, but nothing
worked. California had more wine grape supplies than demand.

He easily could have retrenched then. He could have eaten his
losses, which would have been substantial but not backbreaking
at that point. He had his practice, his real estate. The family would
be fine, Jane assured him. They hadn't overextended. But Jackson

hated accepting defeat. Would he let fate force him to go belly up? Watch his grapes rot on the vine? Lose all that time and money and effort and limp back to his law books, tail between his legs? That alternative appalled Jackson. But beyond his distaste at admitting failure, he sensed an opportunity waiting to be seized, and he decided it was time not to pull back but to go all in. Instead of walking away, he wanted to build a winery and start turning those grapes into wine himself. He would spare no expense so that those grapes could produce quality wine, vintages that would help pull California out from the bottom shelf and the shadow of France. First cajoling, then bulling ahead against his wife's wishes, he invested heavily in building a new state-of-the-art winery, put up their home and their other properties as collateral to finance the construction, and gambled the family's future on something he swore he didn't really want but clearly could not resist.

For a time it looked like he might pull this gamble off—until a second disaster struck, one potentially far worse than the grape glut that had launched his winery. Nuclear reactors have meltdowns. So do wineries—a kind of winemaking event that threatens to make worthless entire harvests and vintages. The fermentation of his most prized Lakeport grapes had gone awry and stopped cold. His wine, in industry parlance, was stuck.

And so was he.

TO BE FAIR, his had not been a blind and reckless traipse into the wine business. Jackson knew he was risking everything. He knew he was infuriating and alienating his wife when he demanded she sign the papers mortgaging them to the hilt. And he knew he was doing all this to join a California wine industry that was, with good reason, held in low esteem at the time. But he had a plan. As with his legal work, he had done meticulous research on the art, science, and economics of wine and the US market, and he had an insight: the California market was dominated by mediocre, cheap, industrial wines produced in bulk, the grape equivalent of factory tomatoes, flavorless and bland. Then there were the sickly flavored wines and the low-end fortified wines, the throat-scalding Wild Irish Rose and Thunderbird category for the wino set. The high end was dominated by foreign labels perceived by consumers as superior, a distinction based on geography alone. Jackson saw an enormous hole in the market just waiting for someone to come along who could define a new category by making a premium yet affordable California wine. That's what the industry needed, not more screw-top swill or flavored strawberry wine. Someone, some day, was going to produce such a wine in sufficient quantities to have impact. Why not him? But that meant going big. He needed to be able to produce thousands of cases, not hundreds, and so a timid, risk-averse approach just wouldn't cut it.

He had realized that with such a glut of grapes in California, he had suffered needlessly as a seller in a buyer's market. As a winemaker, he could turn that market to his advantage. Then he could use his own grapes and supplement them by buying the finest harvests from the best wine-growing regions in the state—and buy them for a fraction of what they had sold for a few years earlier. Instead of hurting him, the glut would be his perfect opportunity. In his typical obsessive fashion, he systematically researched the different regions of California Wine Country. He read academic papers, historical treatises, and wine journals. He badgered university experts. He showed up in the driveways of his winemaker friends and contacts. And he made a study of the varying and unique qualities that coastal and mountainous areas of California instilled in grapes: the tropical fruit flavors of the Santa Barbara region, the green apple flavors of Anderson valley, the red apple of Sonoma Chardonnay grapes, the floral and pear flavors of his own Lake County. Soon he could taste them and distinguish them and associate them with the land in a way only a tiny percentage of the population could do; an intelligent palate seemed to be a gift he had had without ever knowing it. But instead of focusing on the complex and dry wine that connoisseurs sought out, he tried to develop a palate for what American consumers would embrace in large numbers. He felt drawn to more accessible flavors, though he shared the experts' distaste for the character-free mass-produced wines for which grapes were chosen not by their innate flavors and quality, but by their bulk price. That led to his epiphany: he realized the problem of succeeding in the California wine business was first and foremost a matter of real estate. He needed to control the right vineyards, either owning the land outright or at least contracting for the right grapes from the right places. Everything else would follow. He could create a wine that appealed to consumers not as some mass-produced product, as if wine were no different from juice with a dash of alcohol thrown in, but as the one great "affordable luxury." He would set out to teach America to love good American wine.

The actual mechanics of making such a wine didn't worry him. Now that he knew his target, he felt sure he could find a winemaker to create it for him. He knew there was an entire new generation of hungry, eager winemakers waiting for just this opportunity to turn the industry on its head. All he needed was the winery. "There was a hole in the market big enough to drive a truck through," Jackson would recall. "I knew the opportunity was there. I just had to find a way to seize it."

To turn his ideas into concrete plans, Jackson sought advice from a collection of up-and-coming winemakers he had cultivated, charmed, flattered, befriended, and finally hired as consultants. He had sought out innovators and contrarians and assembled a small group of brash young iconoclasts who were willing to share their expertise and let Jackson test his ideas on them. Though they were technically competitors, winemakers tend to be a collegial bunch, especially in those moribund days in the California wine trade when their purpose was as much about turning around the state's image as it was establishing their own wineries. Success for any of them would pay off for them all in terms of raising the California brand. And so they saw nothing strange in lending a hand to this crazy lawyer in Lakeport whose ideas and passion intrigued them.

A principal member of this Jackson brain trust was the fiercely visionary winemaker Paul Dolan. Back then he had just hired on as new head winemaker at Fetzer, where he was redefining that family-owned company as a source of better-quality California wines. Dolan advised Jackson on features he should consider when building a state-of-the-art winery and, perhaps more importantly, helped him compile a list of top young winemakers in the state— possible recruits for the new brand Jackson hoped to establish. Dolan and Jackson also hashed out what type of wine might be a good signature product to jump-start his brand, and they eventually settled on Chardonnay. This was a risky choice: Chardonnay was not particularly popular with American consumers at that time or even familiar to them. More often than not, it was referred to as "white Burgundy." But other, more popular wine varieties—Cabernet Sauvignon, for instance—had to be aged much longer before they would be drinkable. Two or three years of barrel time would be an eternity for a new winery whose ledgers contained all expenses and no revenues. Chardonnay, in contrast, could be brought to market less than a year after harvest—still a delay between red and black ink, but the shortest one possible. So Chardonnay it would be; this was an economic choice but also a wide-open field. Jackson would have little competition at the outset.

Once that was decided, Dolan and Jackson traveled the state together in search of another elusive quantity: California's best Chardonnay grapes. After several weekends on the road, Jackson had locked up contracts for grapes from two storied vineyards in Santa Barbara and Monterey, gorgeous vineyards that he immediately coveted. He filed away the notion of buying them outright, but buying their harvest would enable him to produce a series of fine Chardonnays. He couldn't rely solely on his own Lake County grapes. They were good, but he did not yet have enough to make the larger volume of wine he needed for a splashy entry into the market.

So he decided to spare nothing on his grapes or on the construction of his Lakeport winery, where he could mass-produce wines using handcrafted and boutique-winery techniques. In late 1981 Jackson brought some papers to his wife to sign. They were for a $500,000 loan to build a large winery with production capacity for up to 100,000 cases of wine and, eventually, expandable to 500,000. This would be a dream winery, not for inching into the winemaking business, as Jane advised, but for launching an empire. Instead of industrial-style wines aged in steel barrels with oak chips thrown in for flavor—the cheap methods used by many big wineries—Jackson envisioned a handmade wine produced on a large scale. He would use real oak barrels for fermenting the Chardonnay, aged with the "lees"—the yeast—left in extra long. This technique generated more flavor and a creamy feel in the mouth, augmented by the deep, buttery oak permeating the wine from the aged wood in the barrel. Such a process required an extra investment in expensive, imported French oak and a process called *sur lees*, a technique of periodic hand-stirring throughout the fermentation process. No large-scale, mechanized winery went to such trouble, but that would be the secret sauce of Jackson's success: handcrafted wine made in industrial quantities, which would enable him to keep the price down.

"We are going to break ground with this," he told Dolan. "We'll be able to sell a $15 bottle of wine for $5.99." It would be costly to build such an operation—which is why no one else was doing it on such a scale—and Jackson and his wife had some of the worst arguments of their marriage over this level of spending. But he refused to cut back on his wine infrastructure investment. For the Jackson family, that meant a year of no vacations, few restaurant meals, and grueling double workdays split between helping with the law practice and working on the winery.

Jackson skimped on only one wine-related area: he hired a neophyte winemaker fresh out of school to save money, figuring the high-powered brain trust would provide the real expertise when needed. This attempt to economize proved to be a terrible mistake: the young winemaker presided over a disaster. At a critical time in the aging and fermenting of the Lakeport Chardonnay grapes, Jess drove up to the vineyard to check on things, and Jackson later recalled finding the winemaker, who lived at the Lakeport house, hosting a rather large, noisy party. The place was a mess, and the winery was in disarray. When Jackson tasted through the various wines in progress—his Lakeport fruit and the other grapes he had bought across the state—the truly bad news became clear: the fermentation of his Lakeport wine was stuck.

A stuck fermentation is one of the great disasters of winemaking. Poor temperature controls can cause it, or a chemical imbalance that impairs the yeast organisms that turn sugar into alcohol. A stuck fermentation leaves wine far too sweet.

For a new, untested winery—where the finances were so tight that the only other employee was one of the founder's daughters on a forced leave from college, her desk a converted Ping-Pong table— a stuck fermentation could mean the end of the dream. Not to mention the end of Jackson's savings.

He fired his winemaker and called Paul Dolan again. Would it be possible to assemble the team of winemaking stars to come in as consultants and help fix the fermentation? Could an "A-Team" develop a plan that might salvage the situation?

Dolan thought that might be possible, and soon a who's who of California Wine Country's young stars had holed up in an old trailer next to the new winery at Lakeport to see if the wine could be saved. This gathering would prove to be an amazing talent pool. There was Dolan, moonlighting from Fetzer, where he would eventually become company president before departing after twenty-seven years and Fetzer's takeover by a conglomerate. He would go on to become a leader of California's organic and sustainable wine movement. Then there was Ric Foreman, one of California's new Chardonnay experts, winemaker at Sterling Vineyards in the Napa Valley town of Calistoga and a former client of Jackson's law practice. Foreman had just made his name in the industry by producing California's first vintage dated Merlot—then an obscure variety in the state, but soon to be one of the most popular. Also on board was Bill Pease, winemaker for Mt. Konocti Winery in Lake County, who was about to move on to the 20,000-square-foot man-made caves of the new Clos Pegase Winery in Napa. Rounding out the team was Chuck Ortman, the only one of the bunch who actually made most of his living at the time as a winemaking consultant. He had also just opened his own winery (which would later become the well-known Meridian Winery) and had begun pioneering some of same innovations Jess wanted to pursue in creating his first Kendall-Jackson Chardonnay: the use of traditional, more natural, and less scientifically controlled French winemaking methods long disdained in the United States. Jackson called this group his winemaking "skunk works."

But despite the talent pool and long nights of experimentation, the team could not jump-start the stuck fermentation. The wine would not budge. It was sweet, the team concluded late one night in the trailer, and it was going to stay that way. The only thing he could do, his consultants told Jess, was to try selling his Lake County juice on the bulk market, where industrial wine companies could blend it into their low-end products and no one would be the wiser. He'd take a loss, but at least he'd recoup some of his costs. But Jackson said that he wouldn't do it, that there had to be some better way to use that wine.

Maybe, several of the winemakers said, Jackson should cut his losses, declare bankruptcy, and walk away.

"That's not going to happen," Jess blustered. In truth, he feared that might be exactly what would happen, a worst-case scenario he would have been a fool not to consider, though he refused to concede it out loud. "Just because I wouldn't admit it to my Dream Team," he'd later recall, "didn't mean I was blind to the possibility."

If he wouldn't sell his wine as bulk and he wouldn't declare bankruptcy, the only other choice was to continue with the grapes he had bought and hope for the best. The team of consultants met at the Lakeport winery trailer regularly for several weeks, making sure that the eight different batches of grapes Jackson had bought from around the state were fermenting properly, which they were.

Next, the young vintners helped Jackson recruit a new winemaker to move onto the farm and take over the day-to-day task of finishing those wines. Jackson drove up to the old Edmeades Winery in the sparsely populated Anderson Valley in western Mendocino County. When he pulled up to an old vineyard in search of the Edmeades's young winemaker, he found the place filled with Dead Heads attending an impromptu outdoor concert by the Grateful Dead. And striding out to meet him was a bearded, mountain-mannish figure, Jed Steele, who had built quite a reputation at Edmeades and who had a personality to match. Steele was an artful blender of wines, and he had developed a small but dedicated following. The two big men hit it off, and they soon agreed that Steele would leave Edmeades and come make wine for Jackson in Lakeport.

Even with Steele taking over day-to-day work on the wine batches, the skunk works team still met every few weeks for blind tastings of each variety, as well as various blends Steele and Jackson concocted. Several of these were well received by the consultants, others not so much. One blend drew harsh words from one of the consultants: he announced it tasted like dog food. Jackson was offended, but the normally prickly Steele surprised the group by saying nothing. At the next tasting, however, he uncorked several new blends, handed one to his critic, then watched stonily as the consultant put it under his nose and began to gag convulsively. Steele had packed the bottle with canned dog food. "That's what you called it, that's what you get," he told the sputtering winemaker. Although the visitors were not amused by Steele's inventive response to an insult, Jackson thought it hilarious, and he would gleefully re-tell the story for years. He and Steele developed a close relationship after that. But everyone who knew them saw the dog food incident as a sign that the two confident, strong-willed men, both of them prideful and thin-skinned, would inevitably clash over some perceived slight, insult, or difference of opinion that neither would back down from. It was only a matter of time.

At last the fermentation was complete, and Jackson's winemaking skunk works team assembled for a final tasting. Jackson's nervousness was soon dispelled: the assembled experts were all smiles as they tasted, quickly agreeing that he and Steele had managed to come up with seven, possibly eight, terrific wines, many, if not most, of them potential gold medal winners. The consensus of the consultants: the winery could do a small bottling of each, a few hundred cases or so per wine, and possibly break even with a series of well-crafted Chardonnays from Sonoma, Monterey, and Santa Barbara. If Jackson could generate some decent sales, he just might stay afloat. The stuck fermentation could be written off, the too-sweet wine poured down the drain.

But Jackson shook his head. That approach wouldn't fly, he said. He had no sales staff, no distribution system. His full-time workforce was an army of two: his daughter Laura and Jed Steele. Jackson himself was only part-time, still running a law practice to pay the bills, including the winery bills. When there were deals to make or break, prices to haggle, or wine sellers to placate, Jackson had to find time to tackle the work. When the irrigation system got clogged and frost threatened to destroy the fruit, it was Jackson who donned his scuba gear in the middle of the night, plunged into the frigid holding pond, and cleared the debris from the pump intakes. There was no one else; he had to do it all. So how could he possibly bring out eight different wines? He'd have eight different products to differentiate, market, and sell. Even if this plan provided a theoretically sound means of producing a passel of good wines, it could easily lead to financial disaster. What he needed was one recipe to rule them all, one wine to bring to market that could encompass all those fine flavors. That, Jackson decided, was the challenge.

"I want to go with a blend," he said. And he pulled out something he and Steele had been working on themselves, a combination of varying portions of all eight of those fine and elegant wines, with a few percent of his own overly sweet Lakeport Chardonnay mixed in. He had wondered if California's most successful Chardonnay maker at the time, Dick Arrowood, might be adding a bit of sweeter wine into his vintages (another old French winemaking trick). Jackson didn't know if that was true or not, but he did know Arrowood couldn't make his $15-a-bottle Chard fast enough. Jackson told his consultants, "That's the market I want to go for."

And he poured each of the winemakers a glass of his "superblend." Before even taking a sip or a sniff, they were to a man horrified. The taste didn't matter. It was the mash-up of all those wines that had them agog. Such blending was not done. And what would he call such a wine? Instead of a specific estate or region—"Napa Valley" or "Russian River" or "Lake County"—the wine would have to bear a nearly generic California appellation. These appellations were strictly governed by the federal Bureau of Alcohol, Tobacco, and Firearms, and even though there were some glaring loopholes (a wine needed to be only 75 percent from a particular appellation to earn its label), the superblend could lay claim only to its state of origin. Such a generic labeling would mean nothing to people. It would confuse everyone. The grapes were from all over.

"That's the point," Jackson exulted. "It will be a blend of the finest coastal Chardonnay grapes in the state—in the nation. Maybe in the world. It's a superblend, something never before presented to the American public."

Jackson thought this a very clever turn: he was taking a disadvantage—a regionless California blended wine—and giving it the cachet of uniqueness, of being an amalgam of the Golden State's very best. This, he argued, was marketing at its very best. And though he didn't say so, he was equally entranced by the fact that marketing such a concept with a single wine and brand would be a great deal easier than marketing eight minivintages. On the back of the label, for the purists and the curious, he would list each of the vineyards that had contributed to the blend, and thus the wine's royal pedigree would be clear. But nonexpert consumers and newcomers to California wine wouldn't notice, care, or understand anything more specific than California anyway, he told his consultants. Such consumers would care only how his superblend tasted. That, at least, would be Jackson's bet. He had learned at an early age how to handicap racehorses with the best of them. Why not handicap a wine? "I'm betting on this," he told his team. "I'm betting everything. Because it's delicious."

Even as his advisers urged him not to do it, they sipped and swished and sniffed his blend and reluctantly conceded that yes, he was right about one thing: the superblend really was delicious. To them, however, that was almost beside the point. It was the flouting of tradition, of the proven paths to success, that most concerned them. Blending across appellations and varieties—not everything in the mix was Chardonnay—broke the unwritten rules of the trade. Jackson shook his head and crossed his arms and said he didn't care, and Steele backed him up.

When Jackson refused to relent on his all-California blend, the skunk works crew next tried to talk him out of including his too-sweet Lakeport wine in the blend. The critics would pillory him, they argued, for sugaring up good wine. Again Jackson overruled the experts. He said that extra bit of sweetness made the wine unique and satisfying to the "midpalate" in a way traditionally drier Chardonnays did not. It would appeal to a much larger segment of the population, Jackson predicted. The French had been goosing various wines with sugar for years, he said; it was the only way they could compensate for the frequently poor weather that regularly forced a harvest before optimum ripeness. He suspected a few California winemakers had quietly done the same without ever admitting it. Jackson, however, would flaunt the practice. The stuck fermentation would be a selling point, giving wine reviewers something to write about, adding drama and triumph to the tale of the upstart winery that made the best of a bad situation.

Most of his consultants disagreed, and even the couple who supported Jackson predicted his superblend would crash and burn anyway because perception driven by snobbish critics so often trumped actual taste in the real-world marketplace. Nevertheless, the group helped him tweak the formula a bit more to achieve the best taste possible. In the end, he and Steele settled on a formula that consisted of roughly 40 percent Santa Barbara grapes, 40 percent

Monterey, and 20 percent Sonoma fruit—a combination that combined grape flavors reminiscent of tropical fruit, lemon, and red apple. Then he shaved 1 percent off each and made up the difference with his sweet, pear-evoking Lakeport Chardonnay—the least of the wines in the blend in both quantity and quality but no less essential.

When he finally bottled this superblend, he dubbed it Kendall-Jackson Vintner's Reserve, Kendall being an ancestral name of his wife's—Jackson's attempt at mollifying Jane for bleeding their finances dry to get them to this point. That first 1982 vintage blending produced a total of 16,000 cases of wine, a pretty good run for a neophyte winery.

Then came the reckoning. It was time to try selling those 16,000 cases, this new type of wine, this unprecedented mixture of disparate Chardonnays with a dash of other varietals thrown in, in an era when blends were for the most part creatures of cheap boxed wine and Chardonnay was both unfamiliar and at odds with the American consumer palate. This was an era when fruity jug wine reigned supreme and actor Orson Welles, with his preternaturally deep and dapper voice, appeared on prime-time TV ads pitching Paul Masson wine by explaining that, though the wine did not come from France, the winemaker did—as if that were what mattered most. It was not the rich, fertile California vineyards that had once ruled the wine world that mattered, Wells assured consumers, but a tenuous French connection. "We will sell no wine before its time" was the company's well-known slogan, given gravitas by Wells's amazing baritone. But it was an odd choice of phrase because the wine was aged barely at all and was packaged in carafes with three-inch tin lids instead of corks, ensuring that the thin white wine inside would go bad in a year or less. The only correct time to sell such wine was as soon as possible.

But that was the marketplace for California wines Jackson had to contend with—a wild west, anything goes environment in which California winemakers were the global underdogs, far behind their French, German, and Italian counterparts, and the pretense of a connection to Europe was seen as the best marketing ploy a winery could adopt. Jackson had his work cut out for him, tasked with creating a new image for a new brand, finding buyers and an all-important distributor to carry his blend to an unknowing public. America was then a nation of beer drinkers, not wine lovers. Jackson had sold a lot of things during his long and varied career. But to that moment he had never sold a single case of wine.

He decided there was only one place to introduce a new wine to the public, only one location that could give him a dramatic entrance and influence other parts of the country. And so he drove to the airport with as many cases of wine as he could get the airline to accept as luggage and booked a flight to New York City.

"If I can sell this wine in New York," he told his skunk works team, "I know it'll sell anywhere."

3

The Street-Smart Farm Boy

IT SEEMED TO JACKSON HE HAD BEEN SELLING SOMETHING or other most of his life. Even the law was about selling himself, his spin on the evidence, his careful culling of reality for the best facts to support his case. He was good at constructing such scenarios, saw how the intersection of scholarship and marketing made a good attorney, one who could sell a judge and jury.

Young Jack Jackson—growing up and extending well into adulthood, he went by Jack, not Jess—took his first job at age nine selling newspapers on a busy street corner in San Francisco. He had done his research and staked out a prime location, not just settling on a spot with heavy foot traffic, but on one with passersby who had money in their pockets. Some days he got to bring home as much as 50¢ for his labors, which was pretty good for a kid during the Great Depression.

He was always big for his age, but bigger kids with bigger fists eventually ousted him from his lucrative corner, scattering his papers and bloodying his nose. A few days later he gave up hawking papers and began selling *Sunset* magazine door-to-door—or trying to sell it. Few people had the disposable income for subscriptions to a glossy lifestyle magazine during those hard times, and those who did subscribe often failed to pay the bill when it came due. Which meant Jack didn't get paid either. And so he moved on to the next job. And the next. He had never stopped working since, Jackson recalled, and he pronounced this one of the main points of pride in his life—not any particular job, but the fact of the work itself as a constant force in his life, regular as gravity, never a break. Four decades later he felt certain that this had prepared him for a new career in wine and that his timing was right, the opportunity as ripe as his grapes in autumn.

In later years Jess Stonestreet Jackson sometimes considered his life a study in timing—but for one glaring exception, a study in impeccable timing. There was his decision to make a Chardonnay that the industry considered too sweet but that arrived just in time to hit a sweet spot with the American public. Later there were the times he quietly bought up fallow coastal hillsides and broken-down vineyards before his competitors realized he was snapping up the California Wine Country's crown jewels just as the state's wine reputation was about to surge. There was his last-minute decision to defy tradition by running a young filly against an all-male field in the Preakness Stakes, a race no girl had won in eighty-seven years. And there were his runs with the dice at the craps tables in Tahoe and Vegas, when he'd win roll after roll, then suddenly step away because he was no longer "feeling it"—a habit he had honed back in the days when a few hundred extra bucks in his pocket would significantly increase his net worth.

At such times Jackson's sense of when (and when not) to make a move became a key to his success, and he came to relish the mystique this good timing conferred upon him, this reputation for being "ahead of the curve," as wine industry analysts sometimes put it. He left it to others to figure out exactly what admixture of hard work, genius, and plain good luck accounted for his success.

The one exception to this penchant for fine (or at least lucky) timing was a pretty big one: his birthday, February 18, 1930.

JESS JACKSON SR. and his wife, Gertrude, learned they were expecting their first child just a few months before Black Tuesday, that day in October 1929 when the bottom fell out of the economy and the Great Depression flattened the country and then the world. Jess arrived four months after that day, a time of hunger, deprivation, and job loss unlike anything the country has experienced before or since. The downturn of the early twenty-first century, bad as it might seem through the self-absorbed lens of the present, could not hold a candle to the world that awaited his birth, Jackson recalled.

"From my parents' point of view, it was a rather inopportune time to find out two were about to become three," he said with a small, sad smile. Then he added, "I was to be an only child."

As if the end of the world ushered in by the Great Depression weren't enough, the world seemed to be coming to an end yet again before Jackson turned twelve. This time it was not the slow starvation of shuttered businesses and failed banks, but the terrifying rise of Adolf Hitler and the Axis and Pearl Harbor. When the twin punches of depression and world war ended, Jess was barely old enough to drive. America had survived the most sustained period of hardship, fear, and danger in the nation's history. Somehow democracy, too, had survived, and America had come through comparatively well, its mainland unscathed by war and its Depression-idled factories restarted and redoubled by the war effort. Is it any wonder, Jackson would later muse, that the generations who passed through that crucible would produce a cadre of driven survivors, the men and women who would go on to build much of what we call America today? Their hard work and achievements became modern America's infrastructure, the highways, bridges, power grids, and dams; the bulwarks of Social Security and the GI Bill and the United Nations; the advancements in medicine, science, and the arts; and the businesses that came to define America's best, from the technology of Silicon Valley to the harvests of Napa and Sonoma Valleys.

The times indelibly marked those who lived through them. Jess Stonestreet Jackson Sr. was crushed by his era. Jess Jr., despite—or perhaps because of—his father's dour, difficult shadow, became one of the restless, the ambitious, the driven.

"When you go to bed hungry, it changes you," Jackson would say more than once, the memory of an empty stomach, the hollow, desperate feel of it, always within easy reach, even a half century later. "You want to be sure, very sure, that you are not hungry again. And that you can provide for yourself and your family. I would take any job to do that. This is what has always driven me."

Jackson's earliest memory—of a specific event rather than general impressions of home or parents—concerned food. He was still a toddler, a year or so before school age. At the time the Jackson family lived in Mill Valley, though it was not much like the affluent Marin County suburb of today just north of San Francisco. Then it was just a small rural enclave recently decimated by a terrible, community-scourging fire, although it subsequently benefited from reconstruction projects funded by the Depression-era Works Progress Administration. These projects would include the erection nearby of the Golden Gate Bridge. When the Jacksons lived there, the bridge had not yet opened and the town's most direct connection to San Francisco was a ferry.

Jack had been playing in his backyard when something caught his attention. It was a splash of color on the other side of the white picket fence separating the Jacksons' rental property from their next-door neighbor's. The boy could see the man who lived next door bending over something in in the yard. It was orange. The man was pulling the thing, wrestling it out of the ground, shaking dirt off whatever it was, then dropping it in a box. Then the man bent and pulled again, repeating the process.

Jack dropped the toy he had been playing with, crawled over to the fence, and peered intently through the pickets. Nearly eighty years later he still could close his eyes and hear the sound of the carrots ripping free from the ground, still recall the heady, sharp smell of bitter green carrot tops mixed with the musky, damp aroma of good garden soil. Beneath the patina of dirt, bright orange carrot skin flashed in the sunlight, and the boy's stomach growled. He was fascinated. Up until then he thought food came from the kitchen, from his mother's pots and stove, from the store. The idea that food could come out of the ground, that good things to eat could be grown right in someone's backyard, seized him like a revelation. And he never forgot that moment.

His neighbor ran a grocery, farming a small vegetable plot at home to raise the produce to sell in his shop. When he looked up, he saw the child staring intently at him—or, rather, at the carrot in his hand. The man smiled and approached the fence where Jack stood, face pressed against the gap in the pickets.

"I must have been looking quite longingly at those carrots he was pulling because he came over and gave one to me," Jackson would later recall. "It was sweet and delicious. That's the first thing I remember doing of my own free will, my earliest memory, taking and eating that carrot, fresh from the ground. And maybe that's where it started, my love of the soil, of growing things, of farms. That carrot amazed me. The beauty of farming *still* amazes me."

Although Jackson spent some of his summers visiting grandparents, aunts, and uncles who maintained the family's long farming tradition, and these times would be among his most influential and memorable childhood experiences, young Jack would be raised a city boy by city parents. He spent most of his early life in the urban core of San Francisco in a succession of apartments and small houses around the Sunset District. The Sunset, once a settlement of squatters living in old streetcars abandoned in a sea of sand dunes, had evolved first into a streetcar suburb of San Francisco, then into a part of the dense, paved-over city proper by the time the Jacksons arrived. There his contact with plants, trees, grass, and other signs of nature was limited to neighborhood playgrounds or the nearby three-mile rectangle of Golden Gate Park.

The family had relocated to the city shortly after that revelatory moment with the carrot so that Jess Sr. could be close to his bookkeeping job at Southern Pacific Railroad. Because money was short, and because Gertrude was adamant that the Jacksons should buy their own family home as soon as they could afford the payments, young Jack's mom went to work full-time as well. She worked for the Electrolux vacuum cleaner company, running its collections department, then later took a job as executive secretary to the vice president of Standard Oil. The latter was an excellent job, particularly given the grim realities of the Depression and the repeated layoffs that left Jess Sr. scrambling for work—and resentful of Gertie's role as the more consistent household breadwinner. When they were both working, they worked six days a week, with only Sundays off. Jackson remembers his father spending many of those days off exhausted on the couch, nursing one of his chronic migraine headaches.

Young Jack became a classic latchkey kid long before the term entered the cultural lexicon. In the morning he'd make his own breakfast, always oatmeal. His mother would kiss him good-bye and leave for work hours before school started; his father departed even earlier. Even in first grade Jack would just walk to school alone and hang out for the next two hours, playing handball by himself against a wall until the bell rang. Rice was the staple of his other meals in those years and occasionally the main course. "Sometimes I went to bed hungry," he recalled. "We were pretty poor. But it was the Depression. Everybody was poor."

Well, not everybody. There was Henry Doelger, who became something of a mentor to young Jack. They met one afternoon when Jack, bored and left to his own devices after classes at Laguna Honda Elementary, irritated a neighbor with his antics. He had been playing noisily on the roof of their apartment building, riding the elevator aimlessly up and down, and when he grew bored of that, he started throwing clods of dirt against the back wall of an office building next door. The occupant of the office emerged to shout at what he took to be a troublesome delinquent. But when Jack answered the stout man in the dark suit politely and apologized, Doelger decided the boy was more lonely than malicious. Doelger made a point of speaking with Jack every day after that, asking him about his schoolwork and interests, and was surprised that the unruly boy so often left unsupervised seemed intelligent and resourceful. Eventually, Doelger ended up paying him a few coins to run errands or to help in the office, where the businessman began instructing the child in some basic principles of real estate. That's when Jackson learned his new friend and benefactor, whom he came to regard as his "Dutch Uncle," was one of San Francisco's most prominent developers.

Doelger would go on to lead the city's postwar suburban building boom, and he was largely responsible for building out the rest of the Sunset District that the Jacksons called home. Decades later Doelger's company would became an important client for Jackson's fledgling law practice. Young Jackson was deeply influenced by Doelger on two fronts: by his real estate acumen, which made him wealthy, and by his gentlemanly, egalitarian demeanor, which remained the same whether he was addressing a millionaire or Jackson's mother, who frequently struggled to pay the rent. If he ever had money, young Jack reflected, he wanted to carry himself like "Uncle Henry."

Another vivid memory from those early years was of the neighborhood Italian and German immigrant families whose kids he'd play with and whose parents made their own wine. Jack would watch, fascinated, the process of mixing, fermenting, and bottling. Family winemaking dated back to the years of Prohibition, and though that era of illegal alcohol had ended before Jack turned four, the homemade wine tradition continued. His fascination ended abruptly when, at age ten or so, he was allowed to taste the cloudy, sediment-filled vintage of the very nice Italian family next door, which he had to struggle not to spit out. The noxious drink gave him a lasting, though not permanent, feeling about the beverage known as wine: he remembered wondering why anyone in the world would want to make—or drink—the stuff. The idea that it would one day make him rich would have made him laugh out loud.

JACKSON'S FRIEND SINCE fifth grade, Carl Mondon, recalled Jack as something of a carefree prankster who gradually became consumed with work and familial responsibilities as they neared graduation from San Francisco's Lincoln High School. The Jack Jackson whom Mondon first met laughed often, a booming bark of a laugh. The boys' favorite activity from ages twelve to their midteens—at least when they could scrape up a couple quarters for admission—was to ride their bikes through the Sunset District to the Sutro Baths, then the world's largest swimming pool complex, for a day of swimming and girl-watching. Sutro, opened in the late nineteenth century, was so impressive that Thomas Edison, inventor of the movie camera, made one of his first films at the place, with its enormous fresh- and saltwater pools of different temperatures, ranging from frigid to steamy. (The once glamorous complex, closed in 1966 and in ruins, is now part of the Golden Gate Recreational Area.)

The two boys also shared a passion for music. Mondon played first violin in the school orchestra, and Jackson studied clarinet, was a self-taught piano player, had a clear, vibrant singing voice, and was able to play even complex tunes from memory after hearing them only once. Jackson played in the San Francisco Youth Orchestra and dreamed of being a composer and a conductor, a career in the arts that would break completely with his family history, legacy, and expectations. Jack and Carl used to practice and jam together after school, imagining futures filled with music, travel, and adventure.

The jam sessions were always at Carl's place. He didn't pay much attention to it at the time, but in retrospect Mondon recalled not having much contact with Jack's dad, which was clearly the way Jack wanted it. During school vacation breaks when Mondon's father enjoyed taking his son on fishing and camping trips, Carl would often invite Jack to come along.

It was on one such trip to Lassen Volcanic National Park in Northern California that the two friends developed a tradition of playing practical jokes on each other. "You ought to check your sleeping bag," Jack had warned Carl before they turned in for the evening.

"Check it for what?" Carl asked.

"I don't know. Sometimes things get in there."

"What kind of things?"

Jackson shrugged. "I don't know. Things."

Carl had looked at the grin on Jackson's face and figured his friend was just trying to spook him before turning in. He ignored the warning and climbed into the sleeping bag—where Jack had stuffed a field mouse he had caught.

"Score one for Jackson," Jack said.

Not long after, Carl's parents gave him a Gilbert Chemistry Set, a wildly popular (and, by modern standards, horrendously dangerous, toxic, and inflammable) boy's toy of the era. Mondon was the science geek of the pair and science became his career; at age eighty-one he was still involved in primary research on the causes of diabetes and other immune diseases. With the chemistry set, he constructed an incendiary smoke bomb and showed it off to Jack, who wanted to light it. Carl said, "Okay, but be careful not to lean too close."

Jack dismissed the warning with a wave, lit the fuse, and stood back, but nothing happened. He finally leaned over to peer at the device, and it went off, singeing his eyebrows. "I told you not to stick your nose in," his friend said. "Score one for Mondon."

Things began to change in high school. Jack's approach to education became as dogged as his pursuit of work. A good student—his grades scored well enough to earn him acceptance and a partial academic scholarship to the University of California at Berkeley—he also became a standout in basketball and football from elementary through high school. He served as president of both his high school freshman and sophomore classes, school treasurer in his junior year, and president, football team captain, and starting quarterback in his senior year. After school hours, having lied about his age, he worked eight-hour shifts on the docks moving cargo, unloading crates of fish at the Ferry Building several nights a week. He did homework during breaks.

Maintaining this schedule left far fewer opportunities for fishing, camping, and secreting mice in sleeping bags. Between his studies, athletics, and work, he had little time for parties, dances, or the other perks and rituals of high school. He dated—Mondon recalled the tall and good-looking athlete had little trouble finding girls happy to go out with him—but he did not have (or seem to want) a serious or steady girlfriend. Jackson realized he was missing out on things other kids took for granted, but he recalled feeling he had little choice in the matter. His father had suffered from a near-fatal strangulated hernia that left him laid up and unable to work full-time for months, which meant the money Jack earned after school became critical.

As close as the two boys were, Jack never discussed his father with Carl, who couldn't help but notice, given how his friend spoke often of his mother. Jack Jackson clearly adored his mom. He re-membered the woman born as Gertrude Brock of Dallas, Texas, as supportive and nurturing despite her grueling work schedule. He loved her cooking and baking, and when she had the resources and the time, her culinary skills were family legend. Many Sundays she'd spend her day off cooking for the whole family—not just her two Jesses, but aunts, uncles, and cousins, too. Young Jack lived for these gatherings and the sense of a close-knit family they conferred one day out of the week.

But Gertrude was out of the house working much of the rest of the time. She seemed wracked with guilt for having to leave her son alone so often. Jack tried to reassure her with his resourcefulness and self-sufficiency, a solemn grade-school student taking care of himself and the house in her absence. He told her not to worry—he didn't mind. He realized many years later this probably broke her heart even more than if he had complained and pestered.

His early relationship and memories of his father were not so warm. In later life the most positive adjectives he could mus-ter in summing up the father he knew then were "professional," "reserved," and "conscientious when it came to discipline." Even Jackson recognized this as a rather sad description of the most im-portant man in a boy's life. In truth, Jess Sr. was an angry, distant man who thought it was perfectly appropriate to spank Jess for wetting himself. Jackson was not yet one year old at the time. Such "whippings" were a regular feature of Jackson's childhood for even the most minor infractions.

Although young Jack rarely spoke of his father to friends or his other relatives, later in life there was one story stretching back to when he was eight that he recounted often to his own children. His mother had made a birthday dinner for Jack's uncle Luke, and Gertrude had made a huge and fabulous Texas chocolate cake that had young Jack's mouth watering, for it was an old family recipe he had sampled only once before while visiting relatives. But Jess Senior was in a dark mood that night, his gaiety at the birthday dinner a mask that couldn't quite fool his son. Jack knew something bad was coming. When the cake was brought out and Luke had blown out the candles, Jess Senior turned to Luke and said, "I bet you I could eat that whole thing myself." Everyone thought that he was joking, that it was just a way of complementing his wife's baking skills. Luke laughed and said, "Bet you can't." Jess Sr. pulled the cake toward himself, said, "Let me show you," and, as everyone watched in stunned silence, proceeded to wolf down the entire cake. He offered no one else even a taste, least of all the disappointed eight-year-old who had been waiting all night for a slice. This is the story Jess chose to tell about his father. The other stories, much worse, he tended to keep to himself.

The darkest of these was the story of Rosie. During the height of the Depression, the Jacksons kept chickens in their backyard, primarily for eggs but also for the occasional chicken dinner. Gertrude was an animal lover, and she instilled this love in Jack, too, who cared for the chickens and was allowed to keep all sorts of other animals as pets: a procession of stray dogs, birds, a favorite black-and-white cat named Bootsie. Jess Senior barely tolerated the pets, resentful of the attention and time they absorbed and of the bond between mother and son they represented—from which he seemed to feel excluded. Jack loved caring for the chickens, and he had made a beloved pet out of one hen, Rosie, their best egg layer. She followed the boy everywhere when he came out back to tend the birds. One day Jack came home from school to find his mom had prepared a chicken dinner. As he did every day, he went out in the yard to feed the chickens before coming to the table, then raced back in the house, asking, "Where's Rosie?" His father's eyes slid to the roasted bird on the table. Jess Senior didn't say a word. He just smiled at his son, nodding. Gertrude was horrified. Her husband had brought in a chicken that afternoon, headless and plucked and ready for the oven; she had no idea it was Rosie. She never would have cooked and served Jess's favorite pet. Neither of them ate that night, but Jess Senior professed to enjoy the meal immensely.

Jess Senior, who had run away from home as a teenager because of his own abusive father, took a hand or a leather shaving strop to Jack for even the most minor offenses. This took a toll on his mother, too, as Gertrude repeatedly tried to intervene. Jackson vividly recalled the occasion she shamed Jess Senior into stopping a beating by shouting, "Just because somebody did it to you doesn't mean you can do it here!" Young Jack long remembered the stunned look on his father's face, as if it had never occurred to him he was behaving like the father he had despised and run from back in Texas. Nor did Jack forget what his father did next: he struck his wife instead, without a word. It was over before Jack could say or do anything but stare at the livid red patch on Gertrude's cheek. But on other occasions after that when Jess Senior hit his wife, Jack raced between them and took the blows himself. The violent punishments did not stop until Jack, at age thirteen, realized he was as tall and strong as his father. Seizing Jess Senior's arm as it was about to strike Gertrude over some imagined slight, Jack said, "You're not going to hit her or me anymore." His father looked at him coldly, and instead of raging or lashing out as Jack had expected, he made his expression blank and then turned away. Their relationship was peaceful after that, Jackson recalled—peaceful but even more cold and distant.

Still, the tension, financial strain, six-day workweeks, and legacy of violence had worn down the once cheerful Gertrude until she had what the family would call her "nervous breakdown." Jackson, who was in his early teens at the time, never knew exactly what ailment beset his mother or what the modern psychiatric diagnosis would have been—severe depression, he supposed—but her condition was deemed sufficiently dire to land her in Stockton State Hospital. There she received the state-of-the-art mental health care of the era: debilitating bouts of electroshock therapy. She ended up confined at Stockton for more than two years.

The Sunday ritual at the Jackson household changed from Jess Senior nursing his chronic headaches on the couch and Jess Junior making himself scarce to the pair of them trudging off together for weekly afternoon visits to see Gertrude at Stockton, the one thing they reliably did together. Jack wanted to see his mother, but he dreaded the visits to the imposing red brick edifice of Stockton, which would gain notoriety many years later for being part of California's grotesque eugenics program and forced sterilizations of thousands of men and women. Even as a child, Jess sensed that his mother's treatment at the hospital, particularly the shock therapy, was barbaric and only made her worse. "But I didn't have enough gumption, courage, or knowledge to say so," he recalled. "If only I had said to knock it off. Mom was never the same after that."

Jack threw himself into school and work more than ever, laboring as many hours as he could because the family needed the money without Gertrude working full-time. His daily life became school, his obligations to his teams and coaches, work, and a few hours of sleep at night—all of this punctuated by those terrible visits to Stockton once a week and the haunted expression on his mother's face. When she finally came home, she was too frail to return to her old job, so Jack kept the same brutal schedule. Gertrude taught piano lessons out of the Jackson home, but her earnings were much smaller than they had been. These were the leanest times for the family.

This was the period in Jess's life when he learned to escape from his sadness and stress by withdrawing emotionally, his natural warmth and charisma masked as often as not. "I would be involved, and trying my best at whatever I was doing, but I would detach, so I could observe as if I was looking down at myself from above," Jackson recalled. "I'd tell myself, it'll be interesting to see how it turns out. That's how I handled the stress."

Life, in other words, could be reduced to a thought experiment, he recalled, like a science lab test at school. This ability served him well as a trial lawyer and a businessman. But this sort of detachment became a lifelong habit, a kind of default position for Jackson in all sorts of situations and relationships. Many people might want their attorney to assess every witness and argument in just such a cold and calculating manner, Jackson would later say, but this defense mechanism could be a more problematic trait for a husband and father.

"It became a part of me," Jackson said simply. "For better and for worse."

And yet, even as he despised himself for it, the son still sought some sort of approval from the father. In high school Jack would invite Jess Senior to every sporting event and would describe his accomplishments in detail afterward. But Jess Senior never agreed to come. Jack would look in the stands every game, hoping to see his father, but never spotted him. His uncle Luke Jackson, the head disciplinarian in the San Francisco school system, came to many of Jack's games, however, and the nephew and uncle formed a close bond throughout Jack's childhood. Luke took him on regular outings, and Jackson vividly remembered sitting on his uncle's shoulders at age eight at Bay Meadow racetrack near San Francisco, watching the legendary Seabiscuit run and win. His uncle, quite short in stature, barely over five feet, two inches, couldn't see over the heads and hats of the crush of spectators near the rail, so he demanded that Jack tell him what was going on. "Call the race, call the race!" Luke cried, and so the boy did, doing his best imitation of a racetrack announcer, shouting into his uncle's ear over the noise of the cheering, shouting crowd. When he reported that Seabiscuit was charging up from behind and challenging the early leaders, Luke started jumping up and down, and Jack had to hold on tight to avoid falling off and being trampled by the mob. Seeing the wildly popular thoroughbred, the greatest stakes horse (and one of the best-liked sports figures) of the era, ignited in the boy a fascination with horseracing that stayed strong his whole life.

Jack played quarterback in his senior year, but it was as a junior, playing the flanker position on Lincoln High School's football team, that he reached the San Francisco city championship and was a star of the game. Over the course of an hour, Jack recovered a fumble, blocked a kick, caught a forty-yard pass (but fumbled it), and, on defense, sacked the opposing quarterback. Cheering him on was his uncle Red Kemp, his mother's brother-in-law, who had been a boxer and a football player as a student and came often to see Jack play.

After the championship game, Uncle Red climbed the goal post and rocked it to the ground, whooping and cheering the Lincoln team and his nephew's performance. Red had convinced Jess Senior to come to this game, too, the only one of Jack's sporting events his father ever attended, but he did not take part in the postgame celebration and had no comments about his son's performance afterward. Red tried to make up for this with his own wild display of enthusiasm, but Jack felt crushed. That was the day, Jackson recalled many years later, that he finally gave up trying to impress his father.

JACK'S RESPONSE TO his mother's decline and his father's combination of cruel uninterest and violent punishments was to throw himself into ever more work and jobs after school. He found an old lawnmower and started cutting grass for quarters, cash on delivery, and took a newspaper route. Then he worked as a grocery store bagger and a part-time soda jerk at a neighborhood pharmacy, clad in a white apron and mixing Cokes and egg creams. He delivered prescriptions on his bicycle, too, until his bike was stolen, a major trauma. In high school he took jobs at a furniture warehouse, he worked as a temp mail carrier during the Christmas rush, he worked for a candy maker and a fish monger, and he modeled clothes for Macy's advertisements. The modeling was a departure for him, but he was a natural: Jack was a tall, ruggedly good-looking kid who topped six feet by age fifteen.

Mostly, though, young Jack found jobs that put his strong hands and back to work. Those were the jobs he could get, and he rarely turned one down. In later life he would call his blue-collar, manual labor pedigree a blessing and an asset. He said it taught him how to find little tricks that rendered mundane and repetitive tasks a bit more pleasant. "At the candy company, I'd say to myself, how many one-hundred-pound sacks of sugar can I unload in an hour? I'd keep track of my time and make a game of it. That overcame the boredom for me. The same with my other jobs. I thought I had a pretty good mind and might be able to find something better, but in those days I never had any idea what I would end up doing in life or where I was going to end up. But working all those jobs gives you confidence that you'll be okay. I knew no matter what, I could always find a way to support myself and my family. I could always find a way."

In all, Jackson recalled having some sort of job, even if it was part-time, continually from age nine, which meant he was a working man (or boy) for seventy-two straight years. "As a child, I needed money. The family needed money. This was how my work ethic began, and it meant working hard and long and as much as I could without ignoring my other responsibilities at home and school. We call this a 'work ethic' now, and that certainly carried through for the rest of my life, but at the time it was more basic than that. It taught me self-reliance. It taught me to recognize that if you wanted something, you'd better find a way to save up for it and get it yourself."

Given that background, Jackson later reflected, he flew off to New York in 1982 almost ludicrously confident that he would be able to prove to the toughest merchants and restaurateurs in the world that he had just bottled the next big thing in wine. "Oh, naturally I believed I was right," he recalled years later. "But so has every other person who ever drove off a cliff."

4

The Oyster Bar
and
Nancy's Wine

"ALL RIGHT, I'LL TAKE A CASE," THE RESTAURANT owner growled, slamming down the wineglass he had just drained. "Now get the hell out of here."

Jess Jackson had to smile. This was New York City, after all, and the famous and famously busy Oyster Bar at Grand Central Station at that. The rude dismissal was as good as a winning lottery ticket as far as the neophyte California winemaker was concerned. All that mattered to him was the first part of the sentence: he had sold his first case of Kendall-Jackson Chardonnay.

"I'll be back," he told the Oyster Bar owner and, gripped by an irrational optimism, hit the street in search of sale number two. Only ninety-nine more to go by the end of the day in order to avoid financial ruin.

And to think, he muttered to himself, he had decided to grow wine grapes as a relaxing hobby. No one, least of all Jackson, imagined then that this buttery soft Chardonnay he was lugging around Manhattan would neither break nor relax him but would instead make him a billionaire.

This quest had begun earlier that day with the all-important search for a distributor. As authors needed literary agents and investors needed brokers, winemakers needed distributors, the infuriatingly indispensable middlemen who controlled whole cities, states, or regions in the tightly regulated alcoholic beverage trade. Distributors served as the conduits—or the blockades—between a winery and the retailers that sold booze to the public. Jackson had to have distributors—a whole network of them—to make a go of it in the wine business. Sure, he could sell directly to some resellers—restaurants, for instance, which were a tried-and-true means of getting the word out to the wine-drinking public—but to move meaningful quantities, to get on the shelves of groceries and liquor stores where the real sales happened, he needed distributors.

The problem was, no distributor in the city would even take his call. No one had heard of Kendall-Jackson or Jess, and the prevailing attitude was that no one needed yet another no-name California wine to gather dust along with all the others no one wanted to buy. Unable to score an appointment, Jackson and the young helper he had hired for this trip, a California wine salesman named Dennis Canning, drove out to a small, new operation in the Jersey suburbs called WineBow. They showed up on the doorstep unannounced and not particularly welcome, but they were admitted to face off in a cramped office with the impatient boss. WineBow had never sold a California wine before; the company specialized in imported Italian vintages. But Jackson browbeat the owner, insisting he wouldn't leave until he had poured a taste, his sales pitch hyperbolic and unrelenting: "You don't know what you're missing; you have to have this product. Instead of imports, you can now represent one of the best wines in America."

The distributor rolled his eyes but finally sipped the wine. Yes, he grudgingly admitted, it was good. "But the answer is still no. I can't sell what I've got. Why should I gamble on some California wine no one's ever heard of?"

Jackson stared at the distributor, his lawyer's sensibilities detecting a loophole in that question where others would have heard only refusal. "How about we gamble on dinner instead?" Jackson shot back. And he proceeded to bet the future of his little winery with the bemused distributor.

"I'll make you a dinner bet," Jackson said. "I'll take midtown, and Dennis will take downtown. Give me your least competent salesman for the day—I don't care if he's a drunk—and give me your newest salesman, who doesn't know the ropes yet. I'll put the new one with Dennis, and I'll take the drunk, and if we each sell a hundred cases of wine by the end of the day with these people, you owe me dinner. And you'll distribute our wine. And if we don't, you can bring your entire staff and I'll pay for everybody's dinner but yours. And you won't see me again."

The distributor, figuring the you'll-never-see-me-again scenario to be the most probable, waved him off, saying, "Fine, fine, it's a bet." Then the distributor added what would soon become a familiar refrain: "Now get the hell out."

It was noon before Jackson got back to the city to make his first sale at the Oyster Bar. A long procession of Manhattan wine shops, liquor stores, and restaurants followed, and each presentation was the same. He'd squeeze his six-foot-two-inch frame up to the crowded bar, watch the owner's or manager's hand disappear inside his own larger paw, raise a bottle of Chardonnay in his free hand, and say in a rush, "I'm Jess Jackson, I'm from California, I'm very proud of this wine, all I want you to do is taste it, and I'll get out of your hair." If he wasn't kicked out immediately—which happened nearly half the time—he'd pour, watch the nod of approval, then ask, "What do you think it's going to sell for?" At the Oyster Bar the manager had squinted at him and said, "$13." Jackson responded, "You can have it for $4.95 a bottle delivered and keep the difference." He offered the same deal to everyone else willing to try his wine, as he and Canning trudged from liquor store to restaurant to market to cocktail lounge, one after another. Canning landed another signature New York eatery, Central Park's historic Tavern on the Green, and with that coup, Jackson knew they'd pull it off.

By the end of the day the two hundred cases had been sold, Jackson had a free dinner, and his winery had its first distributor.

CELEBRATION OF THAT sales milestone was short-lived. Making deals with distributors only *enabled* sales. It didn't guarantee them. With only himself and one salesman making calls and pounding the bricks, selling an unknown wine and unfamiliar brand one market, liquor store, and restaurant at a time, sales grew at a snail's pace. Restaurants were a mainstay, where the economics of wine-by-the-glass made a fine wine at a cheap price particularly attractive to restaurateurs, but that area of sales remained slow going, too. It required a huge commitment of time and energy to get busy restaurant owners and sommeliers to drop what they were doing to taste the Vintner's Reserve.

Meanwhile, the Kendall-Jackson Winery project faced a financial cliff. In a year's time the $500,000 construction loan Jackson had taken out to build the winery would come due—with the family home and other properties put up as collateral against Jane Jackson's wishes. If revenues from wine sales failed to cover the debt, the consequences for the business, and the Jackson family, would be dire. "Cash flow is king," Jackson would recall ruefully, "and at that point all our cash was flowing the wrong way."

Mired in red ink, Jess had to put his commercial properties up for sale one by one to finance his big gamble. Then he gave up his law office in San Mateo and dropped his staff, renting office space as a sole practitioner from a large San Francisco law firm with which he frequently collaborated. When the $3,000 monthly cost for that arrangement proved too much, he packed up and opted for a less expensive little office space near the Embarcadero in San Francisco, not too far from his childhood stomping grounds.

Through 1982 and much of 1983, Jackson split the wine business between Lakeport, where Jed Steele ran the winery and lived in a double-wide trailer, and the Jacksons' suburban San Francisco home, where Jackson's younger daughter, Laura, pulled out of college and kept the books, payroll, and accounts from her Ping-Pong table workstation in the basement. There were times when the meager payroll couldn't be met or some supplier's bill would have to be left unpaid. Laura would have to call up and apologize and ask for a little more time, and the response would often be testy, she recalled. More than once she hung up the phone in tears. "We were on a tightrope," Laura recounted. "Dad wanted to expand and grow, but we were trying not to tip over at the same time."

Other times she would have to load up and deliver cases of wine with the family car, an old Cadillac dubbed "the Yellow Banana" that Jess had accepted from a client in lieu of cash for legal fees. One time Laura was dispatched to a shabby dockside warehouse in Oakland, where two heavy French oak wine barrels were loaded into the Cadillac, its old shock absorbers groaning. She had to drive the casks all the way up the winding road to Lakeport.

As the winery construction loan came due and other bills mounted, Jackson came home one evening looking grim. A major case he had hoped would bring in hundreds of thousands of dollars in fees was buried in the court bureaucracy, his payments frozen and unavailable to bail out the winery. "We have to sell the house," he told his stunned wife and daughters in the fall of 1983—the beautiful, sprawling home they had bought a decade earlier in affluent suburban Hillsborough. And he would have to price the house to sell quickly, ultimately agreeing to let it go for $600,000, well under market prices at the time. Jane was furious. Her fears that the winery would consume everything they had worked for during the previous thirty years seemed to be coming true. The girls were devastated, and Jackson was torn, too. They all had loved that house, with the thick stand of oak trees, the rosewood study, the broad terrace and spaciousness. Buying that place, in a neighborhood filled with wealth and celebrity, had marked the Jacksons' passage into the good life. Now they had to move into a modest rental house in San Mateo. Jane told her daughters that she was going to work hard to help Kendall-Jackson succeed and to see if this new rift between her and their father could be repaired. A few months later Jane and Jess celebrated their thirtieth wedding anniversary in that rental house, a quiet meal at home, accompanied by generous pours of a certain buttery smooth Lakeport wine that the rest of the world seemed intent on ignoring. But the mood had lightened in the household as a gradual turn in fortunes for the struggling family winery seemed to be in the offing.

The first favorable turn of events for Kendall-Jackson Vintner's Reserve came in the guise of young woman, Teresa Mattingly, who lived near the winery. With the construction loan dealt with and the financial pressure eased for the moment from the sale of the family home, Jackson decided he could afford another staffer. He had placed a classified ad in the tiny *Lake County Record-Bee* for the position of manager of the Kendall-Jackson Winery tasting room. Jackson was disappointed when no one applied, though slightly relieved, as he did not actually have a tasting room. But Mattingly had spotted the ad after the application deadline in the listing had already passed and decided that instead of formally applying, she would just stop by to introduce herself to her new neighbor.

When she knocked at the little yellow ranch house near the massive winery building, the door flew open and she was flustered at being greeted enthusiastically not by some anonymous employee but by an ebullient Jess Jackson. She hadn't expected the owner to be there or to be so warm and welcoming—or handsome enough to spark a bit of a crush then and there. "Come in, come in," he said, and they ended up chatting for nearly two hours. He had arrived for a few days to work at the winery, where he shared a small office in the house with Jed Steele. Mattingly found Jackson charming. He waved off the application deadline as a mere formality and asked about her background. Mattingly explained that she had previously worked at a winery owned by her husband's family where she had handled contest entries and public relations. Jackson grew excited. He told her he needed his tasting-room manager to perform those duties, too. Kendall-Jackson was a start-up, and everyone wore multiple hats, he said—even the owner. "I prune, I tie, I drive the tractor, I sell wine," he said. "We work hard here. Everyone pulls more than his weight."

He looked at her intently, a big smile on his face. With strangers and visitors, Jess found it easy to be warm and welcoming rather than detached. Mattingly found herself nodding, wanting not just a job from this big, silver-haired man, but his approval. How, she would later wonder, had he done that? As their visit drew to a close, Jackson didn't offer her the job, didn't turn her down, didn't give any indication when or what he would decide. He just handed her four bottles of wine with no labels on them, just numbers, and told her to take them home. Mattingly gave him a confused look. "Taste them," he said, "and then tell me what you think." Then he added, "When you come to work tomorrow."

The next day Mattingly and Jackson set up a simple tasting room in a wine barrel storage area. When visitors stopped by for a taste, she would pour samples right on top of the barrelhead. Eventually, Jackson planned to renovate the barn into a proper tasting room. But the impromptu barrel pours were fine for the moment, as Lakeport was a long drive north from the beaten trail of winery tourists plying tastes in Napa Valley. There was, at best, only a trickle of tasters wandering into the remote winery.

One of Mattingly's responsibilities was doing something about that. So she began an energetic campaign to enter Kendall-Jackson wines into national competitions, a tried-and-true method for a new winery to garner recognition and publicity at relatively low cost if a prize could be won. She had no trouble identifying the different wines Jackson gave her to blind-taste prior to her first day on the job: a Chenin Blanc, a Riesling, and a Gamay Blanc, all produced in relatively small bottlings at the winery with its own grapes, and the Vintner's Reserve Chardonnay blend. "Even then, before anyone had heard of it, I thought it was fabulous," she recalled. That was the wine, she told Jackson, that had to be entered into as many competitions as possible. That was the wine that could surely, at the very least, pull in a bronze medal. Maybe a silver. Jackson was pleased.

But there was a problem: Jackson had waited too long. With loans and home sales and his law practice and his deadbeat clients and his sales trips to New York filling his days and nights, entering contests had been the last thing on his mind. By the time he hired someone to take care of it, the deadlines for most of the major competitions had already come and gone. Jackson shrugged. It was Mattingly's responsibility now. "You'll figure something out," he told her, and the charismatic smile was gone, replaced by a hard stare, then a view of Jackson's back as he stomped off to see the winemaker. His words came out sounding more like a command than an expression of hope, Mattingly thought, and she (as would Jackson's other employees in years to come) soon learned that this was the essence of the Jess Jackson method of motivational leadership: something as trivial as a deadline should not impede success and excellence. She would have to figure out what to do, regardless of whether it was possible. Nothing else would be acceptable.

Mattingly started sifting through stacks of trade journals and industry publications in search of a contest deadline that had not yet lapsed. All the well-known competitions, big and small, from national contests to county fairs, had passed. At last, she came across a relatively new tasting contest then sponsored by the Beverage Institute: the American Wine Competition. The deadline was so close she had to send the cases of wine for the tasting to Chicago by overnight express. As she watched the United Parcel Service truck depart, she shook her head, thinking, "There goes half my budget for the year." But she had got the wine into play.

Weeks later a call from the Beverage Institute came in to the law office. Jackson's confused secretary wasn't sure what this all meant, but realizing it had something to do with wine, she called Lakeport and told Mattingly she needed to contact the Beverage Institute about the contest entry. Mattingly groaned. Had she botched the entry? Did the wine arrive too late? She took a deep breath and called the institute back and learned there had been no problem with the entry—just the opposite. Vintner's Reserve had killed it, receiving the first-ever Platinum Award for an American Chardonnay. The judging had been at a massive restaurant industry event where more than 3,000 restaurant owners and managers—the men and women who decided what wines to stock, pour, and push—saw Kendall-Jackson's upstart superblend with the unfashionably broad California appellation beat out an array of better-known, more traditional wines. Jackson made her repeat the news three times when she reached him at the law office. He was jubilant.

The wine won top honors in the next contest Mattingly entered, too, the 1983 Los Angeles County Fair. Orders began to spike as the awards were reported in trade publications and mainstream newspapers. And the trickle of tasting-room visitors became a steady stream. Kendall-Jackson was on the map.

The publicity and accolades triggered a second and far more pivotal event. A Sacramento wine seller who for years had been advising presidential administrations on good wines to pour during celebrations and affairs of state sent one of his periodic samplers of California wines to First Lady Nancy Reagan. Included in the mix were a couple of bottles of a new Chardonnay he specifically and enthusiastically recommended for the White House cellar: Kendall-Jackson Vintner's Reserve. The former California governor occupying the White House at the time insisted on serving California wines, and his wife liked the taste of Kendall-Jackson. She decided to feature it at an upcoming state dinner. When the White House staff called the winery to make arrangements for a large shipment, Jed Steele picked up the phone. When the caller identified himself, the burly winemaker laughed out loud, said something to the effect of "Good one," and hung up. It took a second call before Steele realized it was for real. Jackson was at the law office and was ecstatic when he heard, but he was worried about getting the ten cases shipped to the White House in time. He ordered Mattingly to get it done, and she ended up loading her car with the wine and driving it herself to San Francisco International Airport three hours away.

In itself, this might not have created much buzz for Kendall-Jackson if not for the fact that the *San Francisco Chronicle*'s Pulitzer Prize–winning columnist and city icon, Herb Caen, caught wind of the story and wrote that the First Family's new favorite wine was Kendall-Jackson. The columnist referred to the Vintner's Reserve Chardonnay as "Nancy's Wine."

No amount of marketing or advertising could have generated the rush of business and interest this column sparked. The crazy blend of grapes from up and down the coast spiked by a stuck fermentation and conceived by a San Francisco lawyer had produced Nancy's Wine. The Kendall-Jackson brand caught fire. Within six months of Jess's first sale at the Oyster Bar, all 16,000 cases of "VR" had sold out and Jess was preparing twice as much Vintner's Reserve for the next year's vintage, along with a more upscale "Proprietor's Reserve" made with the most select grapes—and priced at about twice as much as Vintner's Reserve. A Cabernet Sauvignon and other varietals were also in the works as Jackson quickly churned revenues back into vineyards and contracts for more premium grapes.

Wine Country tourists started showing up in Lakeport in greater numbers looking for the Kendall-Jackson tasting room, and the modest pouring area in a barn with barrels for counters had to be fixed up quickly. Steele had a friend with some large redwood slabs—highly polished but with the rough bark still on the edges—that he said would make a beautiful wine bar. Everyone working at the winery was too busy to go fetch the heavy pieces of wood stored in Napa, and paying to have them shipped was out of the question. There was no money for that—everything was put back into the next year's wine. So Mattingly borrowed a dump truck from someone Jess knew—a vehicle she had neither the experience nor the heavy-equipment license to drive, though she realized she was breaking the law only much later. She practiced navigating the big rig in the parking lot for a bit, got the hang of it, and headed off to Napa to pick up the redwood slabs. It was a can-do operation back then, Mattingly recalled, and whatever job needed to be done, the least idle hands took it on. After that Kendall-Jackson had a proper tasting room, even if the only heat at the chilly Lake County location consisted of whatever blaze Mattingly could get going in the fireplace.

Suddenly the winery was fashionable—rustic but fashionable. And the name Kendall-Jackson would no longer draw blank stares during sales calls. It was the White House favorite. It had cachet. And at $5.95 a bottle, it was a steal.

DESPITE A SHAKY, debt-ridden, catastrophe-burdened launch, Kendall-Jackson used its sudden visibility to close out 1983 with a startling success and a sellout of its 1982 vintage Chardonnay. As release of the following year's vintage approached, the company remained as fragile as ever, channeling its revenues back into grapes and vines, borrowing against future harvests in order to fund expansion, and still dependent upon subsidies from Jackson's legal practice. The winery could do so because the 1982 vintage sales and back orders suggested plenty of room for growth. This was the gamble and trap, the farmer's dilemma: always planning, planting, and paying for the next year's harvest knowing the earnings from those efforts would be at least two years off and, for new vines, four or five years in the future.

Jackson thought he could handle that part of the vintner's juggling act. He had a wine that almost overnight had become one of the most popular Chardonnays in America. But there was a new problem. Now that the still-fledgling winery had at least some brand recognition, Jackson worried about safeguarding and growing brand loyalty. He wanted to build Vintner's Reserve's reputation as the first consumer-friendly California Chardonnay and then use that as the cornerstone of a whole family of wines with similar pricing and qualities: whites, reds, blends, and single-estate bottlings.

The more immediate challenge he foresaw, however, revolved around one wine: He had to replicate that first Chardonnay faithfully. But re-creating the original fortuitous blend built from glut-driven bargain grapes and a stuck fermentation would not be a simple matter. Could that happy accident and necessity-driven invention even be re-created? Could Jed Steele and Jess Jackson figure out how to produce a consistent wine across seasons, vintages, and the vagaries of nature, and do it all on purpose rather than partly by chance? And could they secure the same wondrous grapes year after year required to do the job—with next to no capital or credit?

It would be up to Jed to work the blending magic, to re-create the formula from harvest to harvest and vintage to vintage, and to find a way to bottle the same slight sweetness and buttery flavor without the stuck fermentation. If the flavor profiles evolved over time into something different, richer, better, that would be fine—in fact, it would be critical—so long as it happened very gradually and so long as, year to year, a customer, reviewer, or taster would be able to recognize the essential qualities of that first Vintner's Reserve, evoked rather than slavishly copied.

At the same time it would be Jess's job to make sure Kendall-Jackson obtained the grapes the winemaker needed to accomplish that goal and to devise ways to market the result on a shoestring. And while wheeling and dealing and calling in favors could get the right fruit for the time being, Jackson realized that gluts eventually ended and bargains vanished, with short supplies and untenably high prices eventually taking their place. And then there would be no more Vintner's Reserve. There was only one way to be sure his creation could continue and grow. He couldn't just buy the grapes from somebody else's vineyards. He had to own them. Nothing else would do in the long term. That, more than any one blend or wine, slogan or ploy, would form the basis of success, Jackson decided. It had to be the land.

Kendall-Jackson would have to stop being a wine company at its core and start being the thing Jackson understood best: It would become a land company that happened to produce wine, run by a lawyer and investor who knew real estate better than almost anyone else. Wine would be the product, but real estate would be the real value, the golden asset. The key to success would be the land, the thing Jess loved above all else, good, rich, fertile land, where the finest wineries once dwelled before Prohibition and forgetfulness and snobbery had conspired to end them. All the better, Jackson figured. He would sniff those vineyards out and snap them up. All he needed was a few good years, a few good harvests, and he would have the capital to make his move.

By the end of 1983, with only a single successful vintage behind him, Jackson had already begun laying plans to dominate California Wine Country's most hallowed ground. He shared this plan with no one at the time, understanding that the sheer audacity and hubris of it would, at that point, seem ludicrous. He had just been forced, after all, to sell his house out from under his wife to keep his winery afloat. He could barely pay his bills and sometimes didn't pay them at all. Yet he had scratched out the plan with his beloved Ticonderoga number two pencil on his omnipresent yellow legal pad, giving his vision force and life. It would take a few years before he could create beachheads beyond Lakeport, before he could abandon his law practice and become a full-time wine baron, but he knew that would happen some day, had to happen. This, he felt sure, was why fate had put him on that plane a decade earlier with Hank Bartolucci: so that he could build a portfolio of the best wine-growing properties in the world and use them to launch a business that could last centuries.

But there was another hurdle to get past. Jackson wanted out of more than just his law practice. There was the problem of Jane.

The success sparked by Nancy Reagan and Herb Caen felt like vindication to Jackson. He had been as excited as a child at his combination law firm/wine office when the news came in. Corks had been pulled, toasts made. Then he had raced up to Lakeport, where he and Jed had exchanged bear hugs and toasted their good fortune as they sat plotting the future. Jackson felt energized in a way that he hadn't been since his first years out of law school.

But the accolades had not brought him closer to his wife. Though she worked at keeping the books for the wine business, and she attended events and tastings and proselytized the brand to the media just as Jess asked her, she remained upset about the sale of their home of nearly twenty years. Her daughters recalled that Jane felt she had been disregarded and disrespected, forced to take a path she feared was too risky. And now that the Jacksons' solvency had survived—barely—all her husband could talk about was taking even greater risks with their future and their security.

Jess felt no less bitter toward Jane. She had not even been mollified when he chose to include her name on the winery, he complained. Instead, she had doubted him when he had asked for her support. That was the betrayal he saw in their conflict: the refusal to trust his vision. And he had been right, hadn't he? To him, the breakout success of Vintner's Reserve showed just how far apart they were—and how wrong she had been to doubt him and to continue to doubt his vision for the future.

If he was to transition fully from law to wine—and he wanted to accomplish that now more than ever—it would be a high-wire act of constant gambling and risk, of betting everything for years to come before the company could be truly secure, if any company could ever be secure that depended for its well-being on the soil, the rain, and the fickleness of markets and consumers. "The vagaries of farming, the cyclical nature of seasons and harvests, the mystery of what makes some vintages great and others disappointing would mean the risk of financial setbacks, even ruin, would always be there," Jackson later said. "That's the nature of the beast."

He had no problem welcoming such risk as a permanent house guest rather than an occasional visitor. But could he convince Jane to do the same? He feared not, though he wasn't sure what to do about it. And so he said nothing and withdrew into work and silence.

5

Joe Goodguy
of the Berkeley PD

AT BERKELEY, WHERE JACK AND JANE FIRST MET AND
their friends dubbed them the ideal couple, a pairing built
to last, Jackson's fraternity brothers had a slightly different take
on their friend: they nicknamed him the Ghost—the man who was
never there. Whenever there was a beer bust, a dance, or a frat-house
bull session, he would be there one minute, then gone the next. His
friends would turn to where he had been sitting, only to find he had
slipped off to work or to cram for a test or to catch a few extra hours
of sleep or to report for ROTC training. He was the Ghost. Pleasant,
everyone thought, fun even, when he could be nailed down. But
mostly Jack Jackson just wasn't there. Overloaded, overworked, and
overtired, he focused always on the next thing.

He hadn't planned it that way, hadn't arrived at the University
of California at Berkeley intending to be too busy to enjoy the experience. His need to work may have forced him to miss out on so
many of the extras that high school had to offer, but he did not want
to repeat that pattern at Berkeley. He had it all worked out: college

would be underwritten by a partial academic scholarship, a second scholarship to play freshman football, additional support from joining the Reserve Officer Training Corps, and his own nest egg accumulated from seven months of steady full-time employment before his first college semester started. San Francisco's Lincoln High School had staggered graduations in those days, so Jackson got his diploma in February 1948, leaving him more than half a year to work and save up before he had to report to Berkeley in the fall. College recruiters set him up with a truck-driving job delivering plumbing supplies and dry goods that earned Teamsters union pay scale—less than 2 bucks an hour then, but still more than double the 1948 minimum wage of 86¢. Today such assistance from recruiters would be a scandalous violation of college athletic rules, but back then, long before collegiate sports had mutated into multibillion-dollar media monsters, this was simply a way to help a poor kid make ends meet. Jack felt that, between his scholarships and his savings, he should be able to avoid having to hold down a job during the school year. He could concentrate on classes, on university life, on *having* a life.

It was a good plan. But it lasted barely a semester, brought down by rush week, a cranky French teacher, and a wayward log.

First came the log. As summer began, Jack and an old high school football buddy, Bill Perdew, heard about a logging camp up in Northern California where they could work as lumberjacks for wages even better than the Teamster rate Jack was getting as a truck driver—with free room and board thrown in. "A last adventure before we move on," Jackson enthused, and Perdew, who had hitchhiked up to Northern California with Jackson a few years earlier for a fishing getaway, readily agreed. Only later did Perdew remember how that previous adventure had worked out: Jack, either out of kindness, chivalry, or a desire to impress, had given their paltry pocket money to some girls he ran into who needed cash to get home. He had exercised this act of joint generosity without consulting his friend. Jackson had just decided it and later offered no apology or sheepish grins, explaining merely, "They needed it more than we did." Then Perdew had been stuck working all day on a hops farm, where ten hours of backbreaking labor earned him $3.86 and the small satisfaction that his work product would one day make a fine bottle of beer.

"The logging camp turned out to be quite an adventure, too," Perdew would recall many years later. "If by adventure you mean disaster."

The two young men soon learned that slogging out to a logging camp in remote Northern California, deep in the wilds up near the Oregon border, was less an adventuresome trek and more akin to being marooned in the outback. Once there they were stuck in a company "town"—a rather generous term for a small shanty settlement set up for the loggers, where the company owned everything and charged for everything. The boys had to have proper boots, proper gloves, proper headgear, all of which the company store happily provided and happily deducted from their paychecks. Then there were the cramped and airless rooms they were given to sleep in. The desultory company man who assigned their bunks warned, "Sleep with the lights on, boys. It discourages the bedbugs." In the morning the company fed them watery oatmeal for breakfast (Perdew found a used Band-Aid floating in his that first day), then herded them onto a temporary train line set up to haul logs out from the forest. The tracks would be moved periodically to each new area to be logged. The crews would be given bagged lunches to eat out in the forest, but the fare was worse than the oatmeal. "Jack," Perdew complained one day as he eyed his sandwich, "my baloney's green. I don't think baloney is supposed to be green." Jackson looked at the stuff between his slices of white bread, grimaced, and they both tossed their bags aside.

The work was even more dangerous that the food. Perdew spent his days knocking knots off fresh-cut logs with a big ax, which could be hazardous as well as exhausting. Jackson, though, had the riskier job: he was given hooker duty, assigned the task of setting large hooks in the ends of logs. The hooks were attached to chains, which were lifted by a crane so that the huge, heavy logs could be placed on a railcar. Two hookers worked together, each tackling an end of a felled tree. The hookers worked under time pressure as the task required the hooks to be set and the workers to scramble clear as the massive raw wood was lifted away. Then the men moved on to the next log as quickly as possible.

Toward the end of the boys' second week in the forest, one end of a log tore free from its hook. With only one hook set, the log pivoted in a long arc, like a massive baseball bat in full swing, aimed right at Jackson, who never saw it coming. The log barely grazed his head, yet the force of the blow sent him flying. This was a stroke of impressive luck, the old-timers later told him. A direct hit from such a heavy, huge mass of wood would have pulped his brain and killed him instantly. As it was, the graze knocked him cold. He was brought back to town, where the company doctor looked him over and sent him to bed, pronouncing the injury nothing to worry about, though Jackson later could barely recall the next twenty-four hours as he slipped in and out of consciousness in his bedbuggy quarters. The next day he and Perdew agreed they had had enough of the lumberjack life and hitchhiked home, Jackson's swollen head pounding painfully.

The head injury left Jackson plagued by frequent headaches through his entire freshman year. The injury also limited his football play, and he was cut, never advancing beyond the freshman team. He turned to rugby for the next two years and he excelled, but there was a problem: unlike football, rugby offered no scholarship money.

His financial situation grew worse still when he lost his partial academic scholarship. The conditions attached to that money were exacting: he was expected to earn straight As on all his academic subjects during an intense semester in which his chosen course load tallied twenty-one units. A normal load was fifteen, but he felt the need to pile on. He made the required grades in every subject but one: French. He had got a B on one test—the one he took during "hell week," the traditional rush to join fraternities that kept freshmen up with long nights of initiations and parties. Jackson begged his French instructor to weigh that last test with all his other weekly exam grades, every one of them an A, which meant his average for the class merited an A grade. But the teacher—a part-time instructor deeply resentful over being denied a permanent faculty position—shook his head. "I hope your fraternity membership was worth the cost," the professor smirked, and Jackson, perceiving him as a pompous little man delighting in this small measure of power to make someone else miserable, had to rush from the room to suppress the urge to strike him. Sixty-two years later Jackson's voice was uncharacteristically venomous in describing the incident. He had never forgiven the man for stripping him of his scholarship—or himself for being foolish enough to put himself at the mercy of such a mean-spirited functionary.

And so with his scholarship money gone and his football career over before it had started, Jackson returned to the lifestyle he had known through high school, one marked by study, multiple jobs, and constant sleep deprivation. After that one inaugural semester of normalcy, he became the Ghost.

The first thing he did was cut a deal with his new fraternity, Phi Gamma Delta, usually referred to by its nickname, FIJI, as members were supposed to hold the formal Greek letters too sacred to utter aloud. In exchange for deeply discounted room and board at the frat house, he and another new pledge, Don Pringle, who would go on to a long career in the US Navy and retire an admiral, agreed to wash dishes and assume cleaning duties for the rest of the house. Then Jackson took a longshoreman's job at a waterfront warehouse loading and unloading cargo not far from San Francisco's landmark Ferry Building. Sometimes he'd work the swing shift, which allowed him to knock off at eleven or midnight, race home, study for a few hours, then get a couple hours of sleep. On other days he drew graveyard shift duty, which meant he'd have to go right from work to morning classes.

The hectic demands on his time forced Jackson to develop a method of studying while on the job. He'd speed-read ahead in his course texts before his shift, then bring his notes with him to work, scanning them during breaks or while walking across the dock. During the long hours of physical labor of handling cargo, he'd try to recall every detail in those notes and his reading, reciting them back in his head to cement them in his memory. He convinced himself that the monotony of warehouse work freed his mind to learn, just as he had tried to turn his labor into a game in high school. This study method was far from ideal, he'd tell his friends, but this "warehouse cram" he devised allowed him to maintain at least a B in his classes for the next two years.

"I found a way to make it work," Jackson would later recall. "It was a less than optimum way to learn. I suppose you could say it was a sacrifice. But it was necessary. It may not have been what I imagined the experience of college education should be. I did feel I was missing out on many things I could never get back. It wasn't all that much fun being the Ghost. But I was determined to make it work, and I discovered early on that I had a capacity to work very hard and for very long hours, more than most, I suppose. I grew accustomed to it, and I've never really stopped. What choice did I have?"

Uncertain about choosing a specific major, and with no particular profession calling to him, Jackson decided to pursue a general studies program. He called it "the everything major": a little physics, a little law, philosophy courses, business classes, some Russian history. He wanted as big a cross-section of study as he could muster, guessing this might point him toward his great, as-yet-undiscovered passion. He ruled out only two areas: poetry, for which he felt no affinity, and agriculture, which he loved but which, ironically enough, he had rejected as a career path.

The next two years passed in a blur of study and work. Then he met Jane. Her effect on the Ghost was immediately apparent to all his friends and fraternity brothers: Jackson never disappeared when Jane was around.

Their initial meeting left little impression on Jane when the two first crossed paths at a fraternity dinner party. Jane had come as the date of one of Jackson's frat brothers. Although Jack made a point of introducing himself to the vivacious young woman, then vied with a flock of other fraternity brothers to strike up a conversation with her, Jane had no memory of meeting him that night. He even lingered at the party far longer than normal, hoping to make an impression, but all he got for his effort was a reprimand for showing up late for his shift on the loading dock. He, however, remembered her very well, seeing Jane as a bright and charming presence who stood out from the party crowd as if in a spotlight. He had to keep reminding himself not to stare. Many years later he would recall that it was her laugh that first drew his attention—what he quickly discerned as the expression of a sparkling sense of humor. Her laugh made her even more attractive, Jackson thought. He was not alone in this opinion, as Jane had just been voted campus Daffodil Queen, an annual ritual at the time that capped the Berkeley campus's springtime Daffodil Festival. Jackson, who had devoted next to no time and energy to dating since arriving at Berkeley, began scheming for ways to meet Jane or at least get her to notice him.

Jackson did not do the obvious thing at that point: simply ask her out. It was not clear, least of all to Jackson, why this was so. Perhaps he was reluctant to pursue a fellow fraternity member's date. Perhaps he feared rejection if he was too forward. Or it could have been innate shyness. He really could never explain why he chose a more covert course of action in pursuing Jane, setting out to contrive circumstances that would throw the two of them together as if by chance. First he snooped around to find out what courses she was taking so that he could attend one of them himself. Jane was a psych major, intent on a career as a social worker after graduation, so Jackson chose one of her psychology classes. Because he didn't want to drop any of his current courses, and there was no way he could do the work for yet another class, he signed up for Jane's class under a false name. "Joe Goodguy" finagled a seat in the lecture hall next to Jane. He came to several lectures and actually handed in a paper—he got an A, the same as Jane—but he never worked up the nerve to strike up a conversation with her, much less ask her out on a date. Eventually, he had to ditch the psych class before his gambit was found out, his mission to get the girl a complete failure. Joe Goodguy, meanwhile, flunked the course owing to excessive absences and failure to complete the work.

A mutual friend finally took pity on Jackson and introduced the two, and they hit it off. Jane turned out to be easy to talk to and be with. Jackson felt ridiculous about his lame ruse—and thankful he had never introduced himself under the alias. He did not mention his brief stint as Joe Goodguy to Jane while they dated but finally admitted it once she agreed to marry him. Many years later his eldest daughter, Jenny, by then married and with kids of her own, heard the story from her mom and suggested such a ploy would be viewed in the twenty-first century less as lovesick sweetness and more as creepy stalker tactics. Jackson, gruffly and somewhat conveniently, professed not to recall the episode at all. Jane betrayed no qualms with it at the time, however. Once he confessed, she told Jackson she thought his ploy was cute.

DURING HIS SENIOR year Jackson left the longshoreman work behind and took a new job as a Berkeley city cop. He started out as a "patrolman clerk," a position that gave him a badge and a gun but that put him primarily in the station house filing reports, monitoring the police radio, and manning the front desk. The gun and badge were not exactly department issue; he had to buy them himself. The job required him to provide his own uniform and car, too. A family member provided the car—an old, barely running jalopy that otherwise would have been consigned to the junkyard. Jackson borrowed the money from a friend's father for the police equipment. This embarrassed Jackson, but his benefactor kept the loan between the two of them; not even the friend knew about it. Other than supplying his own equipment, a Berkeley policeman at the time encountered little in the way of requirements and training. No police academy or college law enforcement course was needed, just some on-the-job, learn-as-you-go training and a basic psychological test. This held true even though the job was not completely clerical. On busy nights Jackson would be summoned to street duty as a backup patrolman.

Police work, like longshoreman duty, is a twenty-four-hour-a-day enterprise, and as usual Jackson worked the swing and graveyard shifts, student by day, cop by night, and young man courting Jane whenever he could find time in between. When he was working the police desk, he had time to study. But as the months went by and he became a known quantity in the small department, he started drawing more street duty. Some nights he'd drive the city ambulance. After transporting a heart attack victim from home to the hospital one night, he learned the next day that he had been carrying the mayor of Berkeley. Sometimes he'd be sent to accident scenes to take reports or statements. Other evenings he'd have to help canvas a neighborhood for crime witnesses.

Then there was the night he was called to a disturbance on Piedmont Circle, a very familiar street to Jackson: it was the location of the FIJI frat house. The call came on the night before a big football game against local rival Stanford University, and Jackson, dreading what he'd find at the other end of the call, was not surprised to find his old fraternity brothers at the center of some pep rally mayhem gone wild. The frat boys had decided to mark the occasion of the big game by drinking heavily, then building a bonfire in the street, which, unfortunately, had spread to some of the lovely old oak trees lining Piedmont. When the fire truck arrived to extinguish the flames, the partiers thought it would be fun to turn the truck over. The police were called, and Jackson was faced with the prospect of having to arrest his fraternity brothers. Instead, he suggested to his partner that they should put the frat boys to work instead of putting them in jail. He ordered the miscreants to roll the fire truck back onto its tires, then help put out the fire. Sheepish at being chastised by one of their own, they did as they were told. The trees, most of them anyway, were saved from serious injury.

Jackson liked police work and he was good at it, particularly when it came to diffusing tense situations. Not every cop could turn a street full of tipsy arson suspects into a firefighting crew. He could see himself some day as a police detective or district attorney investigator, solving crimes, protecting people. Or better yet, as a prosecuting attorney, a step up in the law enforcement food chain. Such work could be personally rewarding as well as a public service, he figured. For someone who had experienced the uncertainty and economic distress of the Depression, the allure of a secure civil service job with a steady paycheck was immense.

His favorite professor, blind lawyer and scholar Jacobus tenBroek, also prompted Jackson's move in this direction. A legendary figure at Berkeley, tenBroek's courses and lectures in the university's Speech Department bridged law, philosophy, literature, science, civil rights, politics, and world history—what his eulogist would refer to years later as "a liberal arts college in microcosm." Dr. tenBroek could almost always identify a student by the sound of his or her footsteps. Jackson, rushing in from work, would often be the last to arrive, so class more than once commenced with the professor cocking his ear, then gently chiding, "Mr. Jackson, thank you for joining us." Jackson didn't mind; he reveled in tenBroek's Socratic method of teaching through questioning, debates, and logical arguments, forcing his students to cast aside old assumptions and lazy thinking. Everything came under scrutiny in the tenBroek classroom, from the implications for democracy of the World War II internment of Japanese American citizens, to the meaning of de Tocqueville's warning that a society in which equality is enshrined so single-mindedly may end up threatening individual liberty.

The professor's influence went far beyond the classroom: he founded the National Federation of the Blind, and his civil rights advocacy provided the basis for modern legal protections for the disabled. His breakthrough scholarship on the antislavery origins of the Thirteenth and Fourteenth Amendments to the Constitution would form the basis for subsequent US Supreme Court decisions on racial discrimination, beginning with the landmark school desegregation case, *Brown v. Board of Education*. TenBroek's passion for the Constitution and the determination that allowed him to overcome poverty and blindness deeply influenced Jackson's personal and professional ambitions, pushing him toward law school after Berkeley. "I learned more in his classes than in all my other college courses combined," Jackson would recall. "He didn't just make me think. He taught us *how* to think, how to question."

As Jack prepared to graduate in the top third of his class, he applied to Boalt Hall, the respected law school at UC Berkeley. This way, he wouldn't have to move, he wouldn't have to give up his police job, and he could stay close to his aging and ailing parents and help support them. He also could stay close to Jane and her family. Boalt would be perfect.

Shortly before graduation, his law school acceptance letter in hand, he proposed to Jane. He looked at her expectantly, a little shyly, and then gave her one of his quirky, enormous smiles. He had a rugged, handsome face, Jane thought, but that grin of his was so endearingly big and loopy that it made him look like a boy again, or a cartoon of a boy. She said yes, their engagement sealed, and both would recall that moment as one of their happiest in life, a time full of uncertainty and promise.

But life-changing decisions didn't mean Jackson's life would change all that much, at least in the near term. To the surprise of no one who knew the Ghost well, Jess Jackson missed his own graduation ceremony. He had to take a shift at the Berkeley PD instead.

"Work was more important," he recalled with a shrug. "I got my diploma, though. It came in the mail."

JACKSON BEGAN HIS three years of law school in the fall of 1952. Jane, meanwhile, still living with her parents, took a job as a social worker at Kaiser Hospital in Oakland. She also worked occasional fashion model gigs for San Francisco studios and department stores, something she had done off and on since her teen years. She and Jack were saving money feverishly for their upcoming wedding and life together. When Jane's parents, Tom and Lillian Wadlow, learned Jackson was sending much of what he made with the Berkeley PD to his own parents, they suggested the financially strapped law student move in and stay in their basement. Jackson gratefully accepted the offer. He had immediately hit it off with his future father-in-law. Lillian, however, was another story. Their quirky, sometimes thorny relationship is best summed up by the half-affectionate, half-pointed nickname Jackson gave her shortly after taking lodging on a cot in their dank cellar: Beady Eyes.

Jane's family story was nothing at all like Jackson's. Both her parents were southern progressives from families with a rich heritage of living and thinking outside the box. Thomas Wesley Wadlow was descended from a prominent newspaper family in New Orleans. His great aunt, Julia Kendall, was part of the founding family of the New Orleans *Picayune* newspaper (which later became the *Times-Picayune*), and she worked as the society editor there in the late nineteenth century. Her last name, Kendall, became a traditional middle name for women in the family, honoring the accomplishments of a strong woman in an era when opportunities for women to succeed professionally were all too scant.

Unlike her husband, Lillian White was not born to privilege. Her father died shortly after her birth, and her young mother, neither emotionally nor financially able to deal with an infant, turned her over to the nuns of a convent in Birmingham. She left the nuns in her late teens and moved to New Orleans, where she worked as a musician and singer. When she and Tom met, fell in love, and married, a minor southern society scandal ensued, and the couple responded by moving north to Detroit, where Tom took a banking job and Lillian became a newspaper columnist and, later, a radio show host. After Jane was born, Tom took an international banking job with Bank of America, traveling the world on the bank's business, and the family relocated first to Los Angeles, then to San Francisco. Jane attended Hollywood High School and lived in those years in a house in the Hollywood Hills within walking distance of the famous Hollywood sign. To Jack, it seemed his fiancée had led a charmed, even magical life—the girl who went home to dinner beneath Hollywood's most famous landmark, where, he was quite sure, no one ever tried to serve up a beloved pet as the main course for dinner.

Tom Wadlow was a soft-spoken and gentle man, welcoming and quietly generous to Jack. He was a voracious reader and news junkie who loved to engage his daughter's fiancé in political debates. To Jackson, he was everything a father should be, and Jack ended up enjoying a much closer relationship with his father-in-law than he had ever had with his own father. Lillian, in contrast, loved to give her future son-in-law a hard time, delighting in staring him down with her "beady eyes" whenever he said something with which she disagreed, which was often. Eventually, they found something they both loved and loved doing together: the horse races, where Beady Eyes gave Jackson lessons in in how to interpret a racing form and expertly handicap horses. On his rare days off from work and school, they would sometimes spend afternoons at the track together, scrutinizing the horses and their own notes in companionable silence.

Jackson's juggling of law school and police work came to an abrupt end following a brutal night shift in which the dispatcher sent him to the scene of an attempted suicide—a young man who had slit both wrists and partially cut his own throat. Jack had no idea what awaited him until he saw the blood everywhere. He had no medical equipment, just his pistol and nightstick, and so clamped the man's veins shut with his bare hands while waiting for the ambulance, then rode with his patient in the back as they raced to the hospital, his fingers cramping as he tried to keep the man from bleeding out.

They won that race to the hospital. The man lived. But the race to campus was another story. Jack had just enough time to get back to his eight o'clock class in real property law. He had hastily replaced his bloody work shirt with a clean one he had with him, but there was nothing he could do about his bloodied khakis. So he just smoothed his hair and strode into class as unobtrusively as possible, hoping the professor wouldn't notice his stained pants. But he noticed. The whole class gasped: Jackson looked as if he had just murdered someone. The professor stopped speaking in midsentence and demanded an explanation.

"I was coming to the aid of a man who attempted to commit suicide," Jackson said. And when the professor continued to stare, clearly waiting for more, Jackson reluctantly added, "I was working for the Berkeley Police Department. I didn't have time to change."

A few minutes later Jackson and his blood-soaked pants were standing in the dean's office. At that time law students were supposed to be law students—full-time, all the time, not working as cops. But the dean did nothing more than order Jackson to never come to school looking like that again. Instead of ordering him to quit his job or worse, the dean accepted that Jackson needed to work his way through school, allowing him to continue a few more months of police work. Then Jackson was expected to leave the force in order to prepare for law school finals, with plans to return to campus next fall with the one job deemed acceptable by the law school: working as a teaching assistant and part-time instructor for undergrads at Berkeley.

Jane felt relieved. She had worried about his police work constantly, and the new and more reasonable work hours allowed the couple to spend more time together. A year later, in August 1953, Jack and Jane married, and they moved into a small apartment in Oakland, their lives dominated by school, work, study, and tight budgets, even as they imagined a more prosperous future once Jackson had his law degree. Jane's social work and modeling provided their main financial support in those days, supplemented by Jack's part-time teaching while he finished his last year of law school.

The question weighing on Jackson was what to do next. He had a military obligation from ROTC that had been deferred while

he was in law school, but he would have to serve once his education concluded. He could do two years of active duty as an officer
and military lawyer with the Judge Advocate General, which
sounded terrific to Jackson. He had been advised that he had a
strong chance of getting an assignment overseas, most likely in
Heidelberg, Germany. He had never been abroad, and the prospect
excited him and Jane as well. But no, he decided. There were too
many obligations tying him to home. He worried about his mother
and felt he had to support his parents, regardless of his feelings
about his father. And in early 1955 during Jackson's final semester
of law school, the couple learned that Jane was pregnant. Her due
date was in November. That ended any thought of a two-year so-
journ to Germany.

Jackson had another option. Instead of military duty, he could
take a job in public service for two and a half years and his military
obligation would be deemed satisfied. He decided this was his only
realistic choice. He'd graduate in May and have six months before
he and Jane were parents and he'd be the sole breadwinner for the
family. He had to be set in a job long before then.

A friend he knew from pickup games of basketball—a young
Democratic Party activist by the name of George Moscone, who
would go on to be California Senate Majority Leader and mayor
of San Francisco—gave him some inside information about some
job opportunities. The state attorney general and one of the local
district attorneys needed new lawyers, and either job would satisfy
Jackson's ROTC public service obligation. So Jackson applied to
work in the Alameda County District Attorney's Office in Oakland
as an investigator, assisting prosecutors with criminal cases while
he awaited the results of his California bar exam. If he passed,
as it seemed likely he would, then he could become a prosecuting
attorney himself in the very office where former governor and then
newly appointed Supreme Court justice Earl Warren had got his
start. Jackson also applied for a spot in the State Attorney General's Office in San Francisco, where, if he got the job, he would be

assigned to the state's Department of Public Works. He decided to take whatever offer came first.

He felt slightly disappointed with that first call from the attorney general rather than the district attorney, but he took the job without hesitation. He had a baby coming and a crib and diapers to pay for, and he needed that modest civil servant paycheck as soon as he could get it. Jackson would later say that his life would have taken a very different course had the first call come from the DA. That fork in the road, had it gone the other way, could easily have been just as satisfying and challenging, he reflected, with prosecuting criminals perhaps leading to a judgeship or political office. He guessed he would have been successful and happy in the alternate universe. But that path almost certainly would have skirted the series of events that led to the founding of Kendall-Jackson and entering the Preakness Stakes and taking a place on the list of the world's richest men. "It's good to remember what lies behind our supposedly great accomplishments and triumphs," Jackson observed toward the end of his life. "There almost always is a turn of events, some bit of good timing or luck outside of our control, that makes all the difference. Remembering that keeps us humble. And it reminds us to seize the opportunities that fate presents."

His starting take-home pay working for the attorney general was all of $100 a month, matched—"Thank God," he often thought—by Jane's county social worker pay. He was not without ambitions—he felt certain that law, his knack for finding some new or unorthodox approach, and his ability to work very long hours would pave his way to success and some measure of financial security. But did he imagine a future life as a globe-trotting tycoon? He not only didn't daydream about such a life, he recalled much later, he probably would have disdained it. As an attorney, he might no longer be getting warehouse grime or crime scene blood on his clothes, but he worked for a living.

The young couple had given up their Oakland apartment and moved back in with the Wadlows as Jane's due date approached.

Jennifer Lee Jackson was born on November 30, 1955, without com-
plications or worry. It was a bright, crisp Wednesday; all was well
at the hospital and mother and child were both sound asleep by
noon. Beady Eyes and Jess stood in the hospital room staring, with
nothing left to say after pronouncing the baby beautiful and the
day a remarkable joy. Jackson started to grow uncomfortable. He
had hated hospitals ever since those awful visits during his mother's
illness. He had the whole day off, but the idea of staying there left
him uneasy. Then Beady Eyes spoke up.

"Let's go to the track," she suggested. An hour later they were
at the horse races, poring over the racing form and looking for
a likely bet to mark Jenny's birth. (Three years later when her
sister, Laura, was born, Jess continued the tradition by going to the
baseball park to see the Giants play their very first game in San
Francisco. It was, Jackson would later say, only a bit defensively, a
very special occasion.)

A month after Jenny's birth, the Jacksons moved into a rental
duplex in San Francisco. Jess had passed the bar exam a month
before the birth and was able to move up from his initial job doing
investigations and research for Highway Department legal cases to a
trial attorney position. He worked within the Highway Department
but was an employee of the state attorney general, who served as the
legal representative for all state agencies. Jackson took on a series
of property cases involving securing rights-of-way for freeway projects, highway ramps, and other major public works. The goal was
very simple: to secure at the lowest possible cost the land the state
needed to grow. The state had the power of eminent domain—to
compel the granting of rights-of-way or the sale of private property
for the public good—but it had to pay a fair market price to the
owner. Figuring out that price was the tricky part, the source of
endless disputes—the arena where Jess learned that good lawyering
could make all the difference in the world.

Soon he found himself going up against some of the top lawyers
in the state and doing well, acknowledged as a rising star in the

office. It was an exciting time in California. Cities were booming, the aerospace industry had taken off, and the need to construct roads, bridges, university campuses, parks, and other grand public works for the influx of people, cars, and prosperity became a constant. Jess grew so skilled at representing the state's interest in getting the land it needed to build the infrastructure that would sustain California for the next fifty years that the attorney general tapped him to write the office manual on eminent domain.

But over time Jackson found the cases were not always leaving the sort of legacy he would have liked. When US Highway 101 entrance and exit ramps were planned for the North Coast town of Santa Rosa, local business interests rejected the highway engineer's first choice of a bypass to avoid the downtown area. Instead, in the belief that the traffic would bring in valuable customers and trade, they insisted that the right-of-way run through the middle of downtown. Ironically, as the region grew, the ramp placement became an impediment to business and parking, a source of constant congestion that hindered, rather than helped, commerce.

In 1958, shortly after the birth of their second daughter, Laura, Jackson decided to try his hand at private practice. This is the time Jack became Jess: Jess Jackson, attorney at law. He figured his true name looked and sounded more imposing on a law office door or legal brief.

Jackson had met a lawyer in the Bay Area town of San Mateo who had a successful practice specializing in representing various small towns, water districts, and other municipal entities, acting as their attorney and handling exactly the sort of land-use cases Jess knew so well. The lawyer hired Jackson as his associate, then made him a partner, and eventually turned over the entire practice to the young attorney, who suddenly found he had a stable of fifteen government entities as clients. This required him to become a kind of circuit rider, driving from town to town, council meeting to council meeting, dispensing legal advice and preparing documents. He was very busy, though not particularly well paid: the little towns and regulatory districts couldn't afford to pay top dollar legal fees for the same reason they had no budget for a full-time city attorney. Jackson spent much of his time keeping these clients out of trouble, convincing town councils and administrators that paying a fair price for someone's land or right-of-way would avoid delays and litigation costs and was ultimately more cost effective than trying to lowball everyone. Sometimes he had to deal with stubborn and avaricious property owners who tried to game the system, but philosophically he felt increasing sympathy for the families, businesses, and neighborhoods that just wanted to be left alone. Over time his practice expanded to include representing the interests of private property owners, and he developed an expertise in the specialized area of inverse condemnations, a type of case in which property owners whose land values were affected by regulations or zoning changes were able to demand compensation under the theory that the regulation was a kind of unconstitutional taking of private property. This was an emerging area of the law that few attorneys had mastered: complex, esoteric, and filled with opportunity for a smart, hardworking litigator to seize as his own because in some cases there were millions of dollars at stake.

The sixties began an era of rapid expansion of parks and preserves established to slow the breakneck development of coastal California that was threatening to pave over the state's most valuable scenic and recreation areas: its beaches. And while Jackson was a nature lover and sympathetic to that goal, he had no trouble at all arguing that private property owners had a right to be justly compensated and to have their constitutional rights safeguarded. The difference in value between private beachfront property that could be developed as a resort or an upscale housing development or a country club and the same private property suddenly designated a no-development zone by regulators was exactly the sort of question inverse condemnation law was created to address, with enormous potential payoffs for landowners who hired the right lawyer. Jackson hired junior attorneys to take over the routine city attorney duties and the rest of his general civic practice, and he concentrated on the big and lucrative property cases. (In later years he would shed those other portions of his practice and concentrate solely on inverse condemnation and related property cases.)

And if the resulting legal fees helped the Jackson family become homeowners instead of renters, that would be all right, too. Before little Laura Jackson was out of her crib, Jess and Jane used some of his first big contingency fee to buy their first house, a three-bedroom, one-bath postwar tract home on Sunset Terrace in San Mateo. It was a cookie-cutter house, identical to every other one on the block, right down to the one young sycamore tree centered in the small front yard. In 1959 the 1,200-square-foot house set them back $25,000, financed with a thirty-year mortgage—a sum and commitment that gave Jess and Jane the sweats. But Jess was so proud and excited about this accomplishment, he didn't just walk as he carried in the boxes and furniture during the move. He ran.

Jenny and Laura's earliest memories began with this house: of their dad trundling home with a briefcase packed with yellow pads and legal papers, of him propped up in bed on pillows, writing arguments longhand, jotting notes from law books, crumbling up papers and starting over. They loved to look at his papers, at the geometric symbols—triangles, squares, circles—he used to code different sections and passages, in his meticulous, small scrawl. He would spend hours working on his legal papers every day, even weekends and vacations, a lifelong habit. The girls, though allowed to watch, were told never to interrupt his work. They had to get in their playtime with him before he settled in with his papers, so every day when he came home, they would hide—always in the same three places, in the linen closet, under the table, or behind the couch. Every day he would pretend that he was mystified by their cunning concealment, that he couldn't hear Laura's giggles or Jenny's exasperated whisper.

One day he surprised them. He appeared from work not just carrying his briefcase and work clothes, but wearing a cape as if he were Superman. Jenny noticed the cape looked suspiciously like their for-company-only tablecloth, but she didn't say anything to Laura, who peered from their hiding place wide-eyed, entranced. Jackson raced in the house, looked around, pretending he couldn't see the girls, and, satisfied that he was alone, struck a superhero pose, arms akimbo. He strode to the window at the back of their small dining area, which overlooked a grassy slope behind their house. Then he slid open the door, raced out to the terrace, leaped as if launching himself into the air, and, for all the astonished girls could see, flew out of sight over the San Francisco Bay.

They ran out onto the deck. But he was gone. The girls, unsure whether to laugh, cry, or shout for help, stood in awe. Could it really be true? Their dad, who was so big and so strong, seemed to know something about everything, whether it was explaining why the sky was blue or showing them how to plant a seed and make a flower. They were little enough to believe that just maybe he knew how to fly, too.

Jackson, who created the illusion of flying by diving down the hillside and quickly hiding himself (along with his less-than-super torn pants and scraped knees), wasn't about to set them straight. For years after that he kept hinting that he really had superpowers, that he could fly off with a leap and a bound whenever he wished. Even when the girls grew too old to believe such things literally, the idea that they had a father who could do almost anything stayed with them for many years—right up until the winery tore apart their family.

6

Bending and Blending

BEFORE THE BREAKTHROUGH SUCCESS OF THE FIRST Vintner's Reserve in 1983, in the desperate time of winery construction and stuck fermentation, Jackson had telephoned his daughter with bad news: he could no longer cover her law school expenses. She would have to line up some student loans for her second year at Santa Clara University.

"What's wrong, Dad?" Jenny asked, his clipped tone priming her for a fight. They had barely spoken for a year. She hadn't even come home for the holidays, staying instead with her boyfriend and his family. After initially supporting her ambitions to follow in his footsteps by pursuing a law degree, Jess had reversed himself and angrily opposed her choice. They had a terrible falling out when she refused to abide by his new demand that she study for a business degree rather than the law. Now she waited, already fuming, expecting him to renew the old argument and use money as his cudgel. But he surprised her.

"It's the winery," he said flatly.

After a long silence Jenny responded, "What winery?"

Her communication with home had grown so poor in the previous year that she knew nothing about the winery construction project, the spin-up of Kendall-Jackson wines, the loans, or the tension these events had provoked between her parents. Everything was tied up in this new business venture, Jackson explained to his stunned daughter. He had been working toward this for a long time, he said, seeking to transition from the law to wine, from a business in which the opportunities were shrinking to one in which the sky would be the limit. Laura, in her second year at the University of California at Santa Barbara, already had agreed to take a break from school and become a full-time employee of Kendall-Jackson Wine, he told Jenny. Her office was in the basement of the Hillsborough house. Jackson said he wanted Jenny's help, too.

At last, her father's baffling opposition to her going to law school made sense. Initially he had encouraged her to apply, urging Jenny on with the refrain she had heard from him all her life: that she could accomplish anything with sufficient determination and hard work. She had taken off a year after earning her undergraduate degree and worked at her dad's law office as he had requested. Then she decided on law school, with both of them talking about how she could return with a law degree and work for him at the firm. But then Jackson abruptly suggested that law school was not the right choice for Jenny, and when she refused to change course, his suggestions became increasingly urgent. When she did poorly in her first go at the infamous LSAT—Law School Admission Test—and had to retake it, he opined that she would never get into law school. When she improved her score dramatically the second time around, he predicted that she would never graduate. Go get an MBA instead, he urged.

He had wounded Jenny, but she set out to do exactly as he would have done in her place: prove him wrong. Only years later would she realize her father had a hidden agenda all along: he really did want Jenny to follow in his footsteps and come work for him. He really did think she could succeed at anything she chose to pursue wholeheartedly. But he wanted her to join him in the wine business, not the law practice. He just hadn't been ready to reveal his intentions at that point, and his frustration spilled over into anger and seeming disapproval.

When Jenny made clear she intended to go to law school against his wishes, Jess had treated her as if she were abandoning him. On the day Jenny was to leave, when her mother was out of town visiting a sick relative and Jackson was supposed to help her move, she came home at the agreed-upon time to find the basement door of the Hillsborough house locked. Typically, this door was left open; someone was always forgetting the key in the busy Jackson household. But she had her key, and when she pushed it into the lock, the door suddenly flew open, and there stood the imposing figure of her dad, glowering and holding out his hand in a gesture of demand.

"Give me your key," he said through tight lips.

"What?" Jenny asked. "Why?"

"Just give me your key," Jackson repeated.

"Why, Dad?" Jenny wasn't sure what the problem was. Had he lost his own key?

"Because you're no longer welcome in this house without an invitation."

Jenny just stood there open-mouthed. Then she slowly dropped the key in her dad's large hand and watched him turn and walk away. She ended up calling Laura and her boyfriend, who helped her pack and then took her on the half-hour drive south to Santa Clara.

"So I started law school with a broken heart," she recalled. "And I didn't really understand why. Not then. But I was determined to do it, to make it through law school. I had no idea, until much later, why my dad was acting that way. Apparently I had broken his heart, too, but I had no way of knowing that. He never told me. He wanted my help, but he couldn't admit it and never asked."

Now, a year later, he was on the phone asking. She guessed why: the enormous changes in the Jackson business and fortunes, and the sacrifices required from everyone in the family, made a thaw in

Jess's frosty attitude inevitable. They both had hated the rift, but neither would make the first move to bridge it. In the end Jess decided to pretend it had never happened.

"You'll come home and help over the summer?" Jackson asked. Gruffness mostly, but not entirely, concealed the note of pleading in his voice that she heard over the phone line. Jenny realized this admission from her father that he needed her would be the closest thing to an apology she'd ever get. After a long silence she sighed and said, "Of course, Dad."

IN THOSE EARLY days of Kendall-Jackson, the business was truly a family enterprise. Everyone pitched in. It had been that way since the Jacksons bought the farm. That first summer of 1974, Jane, Jenny, and Laura all worked together to plant the first fields of grapevines, spending the summer alongside Jess. The teens chafed at being marooned in distant Lakeport, far from their friends, in a place with no television reception or cable, no place to hang out—just day after day of hot, difficult fieldwork. Jenny was nineteen that year, her first year at the University of Oregon in Eugene behind her, and Laura had just turned fifteen and had completed her sophomore year in high school only to learn she and her sister would be their dad's farmhands all summer. The highlight of the week in Lakeport was going to the local drive-in movie theater with their parents. "We called it our summer of slave labor," Jenny recalled. "Our dad works very hard, whatever he choses to do. And he expected us to keep up."

They grumbled and felt put upon, but they also learned about planting and caring for grapevines and, over the course of the next two years, how to succor them, painstakingly trimming off extraneous shoots and branches, then training the fruit-bearing vines onto trellises. Jess and Jane, meanwhile, took some extension courses on viticulture and wine appreciation at the University of California at Davis, renowned for its wine education program. Jess found, to his mild surprise, that he enjoyed wine tasting and learning to perceive the nuances of flavors, the florals, fruits, and other metaphors for describing wine. He set about educating his palate and his wife and kids with him. All the while, Jess would commute back to the Bay Area for a few days of legal work, then return and squint suspiciously at the planting progress in his absence, guessing (correctly) that Jane hadn't been quite the taskmaster he tended to be.

That same year the Jacksons also took a family vacation to Europe, where Jess bought what would become his favorite vehicle ever, a 1974 Volkswagen bus with pop-up camper top. They drove all over France and Germany, checking out vineyards, sometimes jogging through them, other times stopping in driveways and engaging the locals in conversation. In France the four were repeatedly mistaken for German tourists because of the bus, which led Laura to start calling her dad "Attila the Hun," to which Jess responded, "That makes you girls my Hunnies." It was a fun trip, not least because it provided a long respite from vineyard duty. As they prepared to leave, Jess arranged to have his VW shipped home.

By the fall of 1976 the fields of Chardonnay, Sauvignon Blanc, and Cabernet Sauvignon had yielded a very small harvest of grapes—far too few to sell but enough for Jess to try his hand at making wine on his own. He took one more course at UC Davis, read voraciously on the subject of winemaking and its history, and found a shop in Berkeley that sold him a home winemaking kit that included a small, hand-turned wine press for crushing the fruit. Then he set to work with the Cabernet grapes. He remembered from his childhood the Italian American family in his neighborhood who made red wine every year and so knew it was possible—conveniently forgetting how awful he had judged that homemade wine. And so Jess Jackson's first vintage came into the world.

"Let's just say I learned something in the process," Jackson would later say. "I learned that I know good wine. As far as making good wine, well, I learned the value of hiring a great winemaker."

Jackson had only the most primitive equipment for that first foray into winemaking: no wooden barrels, no stainless steel casks, no monitoring equipment to determine the acidity and sugar content during fermentation, no additives to control and slow the fermentation process. He had his crush, he had yeast, and he had some eight-gallon glass containers called "carboys," a term that has nothing to do with cars or male children but is derived from the Persian world *qarabah*—"big jug." He started the fermentation in Lakeport, and then he and the girls loaded the big carboys into his Volkswagen bus and drove them down the winding mountain passes to Hillsborough, where they could keep an eye on his project. Laura remembered coming home from her first year in college and wondering about that strange smell and cloud of tiny flying insects—fruit flies and gnats—in the garage. Then she realized the rank aroma emanated from the row of jugs with their cloudy red contents. The bugs weren't just circling, she saw. They were inside the jugs, too. "That's nothing," Jess harrumphed. "Those little flies are always drawn to fermenting wine. Every winery has to contend with that. It'll be fine." He'd periodically sample the brew as the months went by and report that it was coming along but wasn't quite there yet. It seemed to the rest of the family that he was trying to convince himself as much as his wife and children.

While hosting a family gathering for Easter, Jess announced that it was time to sample his first Lakeport wine. The girls had come home from college: Laura had just started at UC Santa Barbara, and Jenny was in her last year at Eugene. All four grandparents were there for Easter dinner, too, and Jess decided it would be the perfect special occasion to pour his first bottle of wine. He proudly filled the glasses.

Everyone who sipped it fell silent, not sure what to say. The word "terrible" could only begin to describe the foul flavor, bitter and harsh. Finally, Jess laughed and broke the silence. "That wine is so bad only the gnats will drink it. And I'm not even sure about that." From then on the family's first vintage would be forever known as the Gnat Wine.

"He never expected to produce an awarding-winning wine that way—just a drinkable one," Jenny recalled. "But this taught him an important lesson: he was not a winemaker. He had an excellent palate, he knew better than most winemakers what would appeal to the average American consumer, and he was a great businessman and a farmer. But making wine is a blend of art and science. It's alchemy, and he never forgot that after the adventure of the Gnat Wine. So when the time came to make wine for real, he knew he needed professional help. He needed a real winemaker."

The following year, 1977, brought a major milestone: the first full harvest. That fall Jackson would have enough grapes to sell on the bulk market. It was time to find a winemaker he could do business with.

That meant another drive through Wine Country with Jane and their daughters. Before he met Hank Bartolucci and settled on the Lakeport property, Jess had been searching for years for the right piece of land. He had launched a series of arduous family day trips and weekend outings all over Northern California in search of the perfect agricultural Shangri-La. He would hook up a camper to the Yellow Banana and take the family on a big, winding loop north of San Francisco, through Marin, Sonoma, Mendocino, Lake, and Napa Counties, scouting out and pricing land for sale. One day it would be horse property, the next cattle; then it would be orchards and vineyards, dairy and goats. Everything looked good, Jenny recalled, but nothing was just right. She wasn't sure if her dad was being picky or if he was unwilling to commit to any choice because buying a retirement property would mean actually doing something no one in the family, least of all Jess, could actually imagine him doing: retiring. Sometimes Jess would deny that retirement was even a goal. "Buying a farm doesn't have to be a career ender," he'd say. "It could be my career extender. If I find a place to get away from the stress and find some serenity, I can keep practicing law longer." This ambiguity continued even after he had found and bought the Lakeport property.

With the new harvest fast approaching, Jess once again packed up the family for an extended Wine Country drive, this time ending in the Mendocino County town of Ukiah and in the driveway of

Barney Fetzer, the patriarch of what was then an up-and-coming family winery. Fetzer's growing sales required more grapes than the family farm could produce on its own—quite a bit more.

"Dad," a mortified Jenny exclaimed as the car crunched to halt on the gravel of the ranch drive. "You can't just show up here!"

"I called first. Stop worrying," Jackson said, waving her off and clambering out of the VW bus.

Laura leaned over and whispered into her sister's ear, "Well, that's a first."

Barney Fetzer and Jess Jackson hit it off immediately. They had remarkably similar backgrounds. Fetzer was ten years older, a World War II merchant marine who came home to work in the lumber business, then bought a ranch and launched a second career in 1968 as grape grower and self-taught winemaker. His original wines were atrocious—not as bad as the Gnat Wine because he managed to sell some—but his brand took off in 1975 when he hired a professional winemaker. Another worshipper at the altar of the work ethic, Fetzer was tireless in his labors and expected the same from his eleven children, all of whom had to work the fields and learn "the three Ps" from the elder Fetzer: picking, planning, and pruning. "See, they run a winery with their kids as the workers," Jess said triumphantly.

"Yes, Dad," Jenny shot back, "but there's only two of us and eleven of them."

Fetzer and Jackson ending up haggling and cutting a deal over a glass of wine. Fetzer would buy all Jackson's grapes that year. Jess was so delighted and excited that he immediately laid plans to plant more vines. He also bartered some legal work for Fetzer and helped him structure a loan to purchase barrels for his winery.

The following year Fetzer and Jackson met again, had a long conversation about life and wine, drank on the porch beneath a full moon, and Fetzer agreed, once again, to buy the Lakeport grapes. Jackson planted even more and the following year sold to Fetzer and two other prominent California wine families, Parducci and

Bensinger. Jackson was getting $500 to $600 per ton for his Chardonnay grapes—a particularly fine fruit, though Chardonnay as a wine was little known and seldom drunk in California at that time and the grapes were used in other blends. That was of no concern to Jackson, though. What he and Jane cared about was that the vineyard had started to move out of the red ink and into the black. The farm that was supposed to have been Jackson's relaxing getaway had been turning into a source of stress and financial pressure: the vineyard trap.

Then came the glut, forcing Jackson to turn a vineyard into a winery. In the first year of the glut, he actually started out small, as Jane wished, by resorting to a "custom crush" of his unsold grapes. This fell short of building a winery; Jackson instead relied on contract facilities to make his grapes into wine, then bottle it for him. Several wines were produced that way, including a commemorative bottling for Stanford University and the California Historical Society. But Jess also produced his first commercial Lakeport wine under the label "Chateau du Lac." The idea was to trade off the popularity of French wines with a French-sounding name. But the Sauvignon Blanc, Chardonnay, Cabernet, and Napa Gamay produced under that label did not do well. Only a few hundred cases were produced, priced to move as low as $3.99 a bottle, but few consumers knew where or what Lake County was, why a wine from there would bear a fake French name, or why it sported a stodgy pin-striped label that looked as if it had been inspired by a banker's three-piece suit. Sales were poor, and the expense of having someone else make and bottle the wine for the vineyard ate up any hope of profit.

Jess and Jane had bought the Lakeport farm in complete agreement: it was to be their retirement property and investment, the culmination of years of hard work and partnership. The agreement began to splinter with the glut and the failure of Chateau du Lac. Yes, both saw that that there were only two ways to salvage the situation: close down, possibly sell the vineyard, or build a winery of their own. Unwilling to concede defeat, they agreed on the winery: the only way to thrive in the business was to control the whole process, from vine to bottle. The only point they disagreed on—but it was a critical point—was the amount of risk they should take in this new venture.

Jane wanted a slow and conservative approach, a small winery that would allow them to develop capital and then expand as needed over time without putting their other real estate investments and savings at risk. Jane saw this as the only sensible approach.

Jess wanted to forge ahead and commit all their resources to creating a massive winery that could produce a bumper crop of wine that would catapult them forward. Jane's hesitance rankled Jess. He felt her unwillingness to share his vision was an expression of her lack of confidence in him.

Jackson felt strongly it was time to set aside such reservations and go big. He felt certain that a timid, risk-averse approach would not get them out of the hole and might just end up sucking them dry, leaving nothing. He believed an immediate large investment, risky but calculated, would create a winery that could produce a great wine in sufficient volume to capture a sizable slice of a wide-open California market. He would seize and fill the vacuum between the lower-shelf industrial wines and the boutique and foreign wines perceived by consumers as superior. If he failed to seize this opportunity to define a new category of premium yet affordable wines, someone else would—he felt sure of it. Where Jackson's confidence that he could produce such a wine came from—given that his track record to that point consisted of the failed Chateau du Lac and the undrinkable Gnat Wine—is one of the great mysteries of the California wine business. Not even Jane understood it. But Jackson's confidence—fueled by a private desperation that he felt left him no choice but to succeed—remained unshakable.

DESPITE JANE'S RESERVATIONS, Jackson still insisted that Kendall-Jackson be a family enterprise, which was why, he said, he wanted the company to bear names derived from both sides of the family. He hoped this would bolster Jane's enthusiasm, he would later say, but he also had a thing for names with "K" sounds in them, which he believed were deeply appealing to consumers. He also wanted buy-in from the kids, insisting they, too, learn the three Ps. Everyone had to contribute, with full participation all around as Jess struggled to balance the law practice that paid the bills with the wine business that fueled his passion, if not his profits. So Jane hosted tastings and Bay Area events. Laura ran the business office and made deliveries. And Jenny, her fight with her father papered over if not forgotten, worked projects to drum up media coverage and public attention for the new company.

The first of these events was a series of gatherings Jackson called "blending seminars." They were not a typical wine industry event. They played off the early criticism of the Vintner's Reserve superblend, which, despite its popularity with consumers and the White House, had been knocked by wine critics for its central conceit: the blending of grapes from multiple California regions. The vast majority of these critics preferred the traditional approach of bottling from a single vineyard or, at the very least, using grapes from within the same regional appellation. Jackson had broken the unwritten rules; he had "cheated," as the traditionalists saw it, and they disdained the results as evidence that Kendall-Jackson's wine lacked skill and finesse.

The seminars, by contrast, were designed to celebrate the idea of blending as an homage to the best of California grapes. The events also sought to demonstrate that making a really good blend of this type required *greater* winemaking skills. Jackson's goal was to take the aspect of his wine that the critics attacked as a negative and turn it into the wine's signature quality, its greatest asset. It was, Jenny thought, a big gamble—brilliant but high risk because in the end he was calling attention to the one great weakness conventional wisdom perceived in his product.

The kickoff blending seminar took place on familiar, friendly turf: San Francisco's opulent St. Francis Hotel at Union Square—Nancy and Ronald Reagan's favorite place to stay when in the Bay Area.

Jackson invited wine critics and writers, as well as top distributors and restaurateurs to attend. They walked into the hotel ballroom to find an array of Chardonnays from ten different vineyards from the same set of regions that Jackson had used to construct Vintner's Reserve. Some of these wines had been barrel aged longer than others, some had been matured in American oak barrels, others had reached maturity in French oak, and a few had no oak flavor at all. There were sweet and dry choices, fruity and vegetal—the gamut of potential tastes. The guests were challenged to taste them all, then construct what they thought would be the best Chardonnay blend and the closest to Jess's Vintner's Reserve.

Then Jackson explained his wild vision behind the superblend— wild, at least, to the assembled writers and critics. As wine writer Richard Paul Hinkle later wrote of Jackson's "revolutionary thought," the lawyer-turned-winemaker told the seminar attendees that he felt the virtues of California's best red wines—"the backbone of Cabernet, the fleshiness of Merlot, the aromatics of Cabernet Franc, the color of Petit Verdot, the powerful fruit tannins of Malbec—could be brought to Chardonnay through the artful blending of vineyards the full length of California's fog-cooled coastline." It was all about blending the right fruit from the right place at the right time, Jackson told them. It was all about the land, the soil, the *terroir*—that almost mystical blend of geography, climate, soil, and sun that imbued grapes with distinct character just waiting to be captured in crush and barrel and bottle. Jenny, who had grown up watching her father mesmerize juries with his logic and passion, was blown away once again by his ability to transport an audience and marveled that this was the same tongue-tied and inarticulate father figure who fumbled for words when it came to asking his daughter for help or apologizing for banishing her from home. When he finished, father and daughter circulated through the hall, helping their guests with wine selections and collecting each "formula" for their personal blends when they finished.

A sumptuous meal paid for by Kendall-Jackson followed, capped afterward by a tasting and judging—a bit more raucous than the usual staid wine competitions—in which Jess and Jed Steele rated each blend and declared a winner. The event proved wildly popular, generating numerous articles by the journalist guests and a slew of wine orders from the others. Jackson re-created similar events in New York, Los Angeles, and Chicago, and at the end of the year the best blender of all, the one judged to be closest to matching the Vintner's Reserve, became the guest of honor at a lavish party hosted by Kendall-Jackson. And every participant received a case of his or her own custom blend no matter how bad or good it had been judged. Most were pretty terrible; blending was, it turned out, pretty hard to do well.

"After that," recalled Jenny Jackson, "blending seemed much cooler. People loved those seminars."

The next vintage of Vintner's Reserve showed dramatic growth, from the original run of 16,000 cases sold in 1983 to 36,000 in 1984. By 1986 sales would reach 98,000 cases. Jackson and Steele also came out with smaller bottlings of meritage wine—a blend of Cabernet Sauvignon and Merlot aged in oak—as well as Riesling, Zinfandel, and the upscale $22 version of VR aged longer and made from their choicest grapes: Jackson's "Proprietor's Reserve." All sold well, and all won gold medals at various competitions, but the original Vintner's Reserve became, in essence, the company franchise, the big-volume moneymaker that powered everything else. The rise of Vintner's Reserve helped define a new movement in California winemaking, which came to be known as the era of the "fighting varietals." This period was marked by a battle for supremacy between the old-school generic jug wines, led by Ernest and Julio Gallo, and inexpensive but higher-quality varietal wines—Cabernet Sauvignon, Johannesburg Riesling, Zinfandel—that American consumers were just beginning to discover and prefer over jugs and screw tops. Jackson brought Chardonnay into this mix in a big way, with Vintner's Reserve emerging as one of the biggest winners among the fighting varietals. Wine writer Richard Paul Hinkle concluded that Jackson had essentially saved Chardonnay from bottom-shelf oblivion. "You see, Chardonnay was very near the drowning point, about to be dismissed forever as a boring white wine," he wrote in a 1998 retrospective on Jackson's legacy. "Vintner's Reserve saved this noble white varietal from a fate—dare I say without risk of hyperbolic excess—worse than death."

Jenny credited VR's explosive grown to Jackson's ability to satisfy wine consumer tastes rather than focus on critics and wine aficionados, coupled with his clever salesmanship, marked by his ability to turn the perception of blending from curse to virtue. "It was brilliant marketing by Dad. He was so competitive himself, so he knew how excited people would get trying to outblend the experts. . . . No amount of advertising could have achieved the excitement those events generated."

At the same time, Jenny would later say, the success of the wine enterprise and the lessening financial stress it represented did not bring the family back together. If anything, she recalled, tensions grew worse, and her parents couldn't or wouldn't fix the problem.

THERE WAS A time when Jenny felt her dad could fix anything, with or without a hero's cape. She vividly recalled so dreading going to school in third grade that she woke up with a stomachache every weekday. A group of bullying kids in the neighborhood had been tormenting her as she left the cul de sac where the Jacksons lived. It had started with teasing, then nasty chalk scrawls on the sidewalk. Then one day they had chased her and smashed garden snails in her hair. Jenny had kept the torment to herself. Little Laura knew, but Jenny had sworn her to silence. Jess finally found out when he stumbled on a scrawled note, laced with profanity, stuffed in the mailbox. Mom and Dad—social worker and lawyer—sat Jenny down for a thorough interrogation, and the nine-year-old burst into tears, finally spilling her secret.

Jane was bewildered by her daughter's silence—this had been going on for more than a year—but Jess understood. She was like him. But now he was livid. Jess got the names of the boys out of Jenny, then marched to each house, banging on doors and telling the fathers that if their sons got near Jenny again or looked at her or came within twenty feet of her, he would sue them all into the poorhouse. He was a tall, imposing man, a lawyer throwing around legal-sounding terms, and his voice shook with anger. Most of the parents hauled the boys out and scolded them on the spot, red-faced apologies forced out of them, eyes never meeting Jackson's stony glare. One mother dragged her son onto the sidewalk, pulled his pants down, and publicly spanked him—an old-school humiliation that horrified Jenny, who had never been spanked in her life. She wasn't sure if she felt relieved or guilty at this turn of events. The family never spoke of it again, she recalled, but the next day when she got up for school, her stomachache failed to appear for the first time in a very long time. And the snail smashers kept their distance.

As the girls grew older, Jess's early playfulness with them took on a more educational bent. He would lecture his daughters, as well as their friends, about the Constitution and the Bill of Rights. When Jenny was ten, he had her memorize amortization tables before she could go out and ride bikes with the other kids. Jenny and Laura both remember Jackson as a voracious reader and history buff, always eager to share what he learned with his children, no matter how widely divorced it might be from Winnie the Pooh or comic books. Jenny was the only kid she knew who could recite a working definition of inverse condemnation. Jess proudly versed the girls in the story of early American colonist Roger Williams, a Jackson ancestor, according to family legend. Williams had crafted legislation that eventually inspired the First Amendment—principles, Jackson said, that lay at the root of his own legal work. And all those complex legal principles, he explained, were rooted in much simpler but no less vital ideals: family values and a strong work ethic. The girls heard some variation on this lecture weekly.

"That's why the American ideal is about farmers," he told them. "In Europe back then, you didn't get a chance to own the land. Most of it was the king's or some royal humpty dump somewhere. So that's what the attraction to America was—the freedom to own your land, to think the way you want, to be free of oppression. The Bill of Rights expresses all those human characteristics that other people throughout the world want and that we sometimes ignore. So my life as a lawyer is dedicated to civil rights. The right to own property. One of our ancestors championed those rights, way back. I was taught all that, and now I'm passing that on to you. And when I go to court, I'm helping people avoid having their land and wealth confiscated. That's our family tradition, our family business." Both girls recalled not fully understanding all this, but they were fascinated to think that their long-ago relative helped "invent America," as Jess put it, and that two centuries later their dad was like some courtroom knight defending those same important ideals.

In the summers of Jenny's and Laura's grade school years, the family usually drove to Tahoe for vacations, where they rented a rustic cabin on the lake and Jess taught the girls to water ski and fish. They would go on nature hikes, and Jess, who had read about the local history and geology, would recite Native American lore about the area or point out the types of trees and rock formations around the lake. Sometimes the four of them would take shorter vacations in Lakeport, where an attorney friend of Jess's had a summer home on Clear Lake and where, fifteen years later, Jess and Jane would buy their own farm and build a vineyard.

In the early sixties Jess represented a series of clients who owned land on the California coast that the National Park Service wanted for the Golden State National Recreation Area. There were a dairy farm, a duck club, and several other large properties with huge development potential, worth many millions, that would be profoundly affected by the park expansion. Jess won large amounts of money for these families, and also made sure that they would be able to continue to use their properties as they always had. They couldn't build or develop the land, but they could maintain their existing homes and businesses there. These lawsuits were time consuming and initially represented nothing but a cost and financial burden for Jess. Some of the clients paid him not with cash but with cars—a little red Porsche, which didn't stay long, and the big dandelion-colored Cadillac, which Jess loved and kept for years as the family car. He had never bought a new car to that point—budgets were still too tight—and the cars in lieu of fees were a welcome way to upgrade the family transportation. Jess bolted a trailer hitch on the hulking Coupe de Ville, hooked a camper on the back, and drove the Yellow Banana everywhere for family road trips.

In 1965, when some of the big contingency fees started coming in, Jess suggested he and Jane start hunting for a bigger, better house than their crowded little Sunset Terrace place. He wanted a home with a proper office work space, a real dining room, and some room for trees and a garden—a home that would also be a good investment, appreciating in value in a way that their humble Sunset cracker box never would. "There's a place I saw that you might like," Jess told Jane, and he drove her to the neighboring town of Hillsborough, just two miles but a world of affluence away from what the Jacksons were used to in San Mateo. Hillsborough was exclusive, a San Francisco bastion of old money and one of the wealthiest communities in America. William Randolph Hearst had built his home in Hillsborough. So had the Crocker family, heirs to rail and banking fortunes, owners of Hillsborough's lavish Sky Farm estate. Nearby lived the heirs of the Pullman railcar family. Entertainer Bing Crosby lived in Hillsborough with his family, and Jess said he had often spotted the famous performer strolling beneath the oak trees that arched across the wide suburban streets. Hillsborough was then and remains a who's who of the rich and famous, a town of mansions and leafy roads with no sidewalks and high walls.

"What are we doing here, Jack?" Jane asked her husband. "This isn't us."

"I just want you to see this one place," he replied, as the Yellow Banana crunched to a stop in front of a beautiful, sprawling white house with a terrace, a broad front lawn, and a huge stand of towering oak trees surrounding it in cool shade. It looked like nearly an acre of land and 5,000 square feet of house, Jane thought. "It's beautiful," Jane said, shaking her head, "but it's too big."

Jackson just smiled. "Oh well, too late. It's ours." He had already made the winning offer on the place—$99,000. He had bought the house without ever showing it to his wife or discussing the purchase. It was just too good a deal to pass up, he explained. He expected Jane to be delighted and was mystified when she objected to being left out of the loop on such a momentous and costly decision. "I don't believe you, Jack," she had sputtered.

After walking through the spacious, elegant house and hearing the breeze rattle the leaves in those majestic oaks, Jane admitted, somewhat grudgingly, that she loved the place. The kids would go nuts for it as well, she predicted correctly. They would have their own bedrooms instead of sharing, endless trees to climb, and room to play and have pets. The neighborhood was amazing. But there could be no denying that this marked an evolution in the marriage, a transformation Jane didn't care for. Theirs had been a complete partnership since they had started out after law school, both working to support the family, making decisions large and small together. Jane had been working every day for at least a few hours in the law office, keeping the books, dealing with supplies, serving as office administrator, which saved them money and helped Jess immensely, and yet he had never let on that he was angling to buy a new home. Jess had even undercut a good friend who was trying to buy the house himself, ending the friendship.

Jess seemed unable to comprehend Jane's anger. Buying the Hillsborough house had been the right decision. It was an amazing deal and a rare opportunity to buy into a fine house and neighborhood, and nothing could have dissuaded him. He expected his wife and family to support him. But why, Jane wondered, hadn't he just come to her and made his case? She might have agreed wholeheartedly. Or she might have had valid reasons to hold back, to avoid risking so much of their financial future. If he was so sure he was right, why did he feel compelled to go behind her back? If she balked,

Jess would be hurt and angry—for such a tough and accomplished courtroom combatant, his family knew him to be remarkably sensitive to criticism and easily wounded by those close to him. If she accepted the house, Jane guessed this would not be the last time she would have her hands tied and her mind made up for her because Jess decided he knew best. A new custom and practice would be established. Ever the lawyer, Jess would see it as a precedent.

But beyond scolding him over being so secretive, she voiced none of these doubts and did not challenge him beyond a token squabble. She really did love the house, and the purchase price, though frighteningly large for a family that had lived so frugally for so long, represented a real bargain for this prestigious community. She was as smart about real estate as he was, and she realized this house represented a valuable investment that could easily secure their financial future. So she acquiesced. "I don't like the way you went about it," she finally said, "but I do love the house."

It would be Jenny, many years later, who thought she had an explanation for her father's behavior with the home purchase and for his apparent inability to see any harm in what he had done. Jenny knew it was not because he held some sexist view that such decisions ought be left to men. That wasn't him. Rather, she realized it had to do with his most beloved and respected role model, his uncle, Doc Ballenger.

Jackson would have had a very different childhood, and had been a very different man, if not for the summers he spent at the various family farms, learning farming and animal care from a succession of "alter-fathers" and "alter-mothers," as he called them. "Those summers saved me," he often said.

First there was his paternal grandfather, Jess Alexander Jackson, who was raised as a sharecropper in Tennessee, though he had a farm in Colorado by the time young Jack came to visit. The man who had such a violent, troubled relationship with Jess Sr. showed an entirely different side as a grandfather, patient and nurturing. He taught Jack to hoe and harvest corn at age six, which was hard work for the boy. But he always dangled a reward for his grandson's best efforts. Do a good job, he'd say, and tomorrow we'll go fishing. Jack was required to learn the skills of a farmer, but there was always an incentive to go with it, and so the boy adored his grandfather. Two summers later Jackson was on a Texas ranch with his maternal grandmother, Ethel May Brock, who taught young Jack how to shoot, how to ride a horse, how to milk a cow, and how to hunt. It was, Jackson would recall many years later, the best summer of his life, with a walking legend, his teetotaling grandma, who during Prohibition had cleared a saloon with a loaded six-gun and the power of her righteous glare. She single-handedly sent a crowd of heavy-drinking men home to their wives. He learned more about nature, farming, and living off the land from that matriarch in those few months than all his years at home and in school in San Francisco had taught him, he'd later say, and it had been joyous and fun rather than filled with drudgery.

Then there were the summers with the relative who most influenced Jackson in his youth—his uncle in New Mexico. Irby Baxter Ballenger had grown up barefoot and poor in Arkansas but proved to be a brilliant student, eventually earning scholarships to college and medical school. He returned home with his medical degree to pioneer surgical treatments for tuberculosis. He ended up contracting the disease himself and moved to the dry climate of New Mexico to recover. He settled there with his wife, Jackson's favorite aunt on his father's side, Mary Lou, who had become family matriarch, and whose home became the vacation pilgrimage for the rest of the clan. Doc Ballenger settled in to raise his family and combine a rural general practice with public medicine, providing indigent medical care to the Navajo.

Jackson spent several summers with Doc Ballenger, riding with him across the dirt roads outside Albuquerque on moonless nights, bouncing in his old sedan across arroyos so that Doc could deliver a Navajo baby or administer care to a desperately ill child. Jack served as his assistant on these house calls. Ballenger also raised horses and raced thoroughbreds and gave young Jack his first lessons on horse racing. Jack idolized Ballenger and consciously modeled himself on the man. "He shaped my male attitudes, my self-realization, my male identity," Jacksons would recall. "That's why I called him my alter-father."

Jackson learned more than horses and altruism from Ballenger. During one pivotal visit Ballenger grew concerned about Jack's persistent cough and bouts of sore throat, which had lingered for many months. Ballenger had suggested a visit to dry New Mexico would resolve that cough, and so his parents had sent Jackson there to stay for an extended visit without them. But when the cough failed to go away, Ballenger felt he must act more decisively. One morning he walked into Jack's room and told him to get dressed. He would be coming to the hospital with his uncle that day. Jack obeyed, no questions asked, and when they arrived, Ballenger booked his nephew for surgery to have his tonsils and adenoids removed. Doc did the surgery himself—without telling his wife (who was the actual blood relative) or Jess Sr. or Gertrude back in San Francisco. There was no parental consent.

The surgery cured Jack's cough and chronic sore throat, but his parents were understandably upset by Doc's high-handed decision to operate without so much as a phone call until it was over and done. Jackson's take on it—then as a teenager, as well as later as an adult—was quite different. Like Ballenger himself, Jack disagreed with his parents' outrage and saw them, not Doc, as unreasonable. He admired Ballenger for acting decisively and correctly and in what he knew to be his nephew's best interest. "He knew what had to be done, he diagnosed the problem, and he cured it then and there," Jackson said. "He knew it was the right thing to do, and it was."

This certitude and resoluteness of Ballenger's, his willingness to make decisions without seeking permission or buy-in from those directly affected, would exert a powerful influence over Jackson. This was one way he would follow in his alter-father's footsteps, and, like Doc, he would be mystified by the reactions he'd provoke with what his daughters nicknamed "Dad's I-know-best-ism." It wasn't that he didn't understand how people would object to being excluded. It's just that he expected that once he explained his reasoning, they'd see that he had been right and done right. Like his grandmother clearing the saloon, or his uncle curing his nephew, decisions were made not for selfish reasons or personal gain, but for the greater good, for family, for the best. That was how Jackson wanted to conduct himself, and so he had acted to buy their new house. In Jess's view, he had done what Doc Ballenger had done: the right thing in urgent circumstances. He had to move fast or risk losing the house, and had he taken the days or weeks needed to convince Jane, they would have missed out, and the family would have suffered. When Jane expressed only token opposition after the fact, he wasn't relieved as much as confirmed in feeling his wisdom had been ratified and his way of going about buying the house endorsed. And lawyers love precedents.

The move to Hillsborough represented a big step up for the Jacksons. They had more empty space that fall inside that sprawling house; the Sunset Terrace furniture couldn't begin to fill all the new rooms and expanse. Jess had put aside $25,000 in contingency fee money for a decorating and furniture budget, and he and Jane gradually furnished the big house. They could not afford a housekeeper, as almost everyone else in Hillsborough seemed to do. Jane did all the cooking, cleaning, and chores, with the girls' help, and Jackson did the lawn care and leaf raking. The aging Yellow Banana remained the family car.

Moving to Hillsborough also meant new friends for the family and for the kids, and into this vacuum stepped an extraordinary nine-year-old girl named Linny Brewer, who became Laura's best friend. Linny's older sister also babysat both girls, and through those links the two families grew close. But Linny was the catalyst and the star, outgoing where Laura was shy and quiet, the sort of kid who engaged everyone around her, children, teenagers, and adults alike. She always had a plan. One day they'd be telling stories. The next they'd be reenacting her favorite scene from *The Wizard of Oz*, with Linny casting the characters and coaching them how to deliver their lines. And if that meant Jess had to be a rather enormous Munchkin rather than the Tin Man role he coveted, well, for Linny he'd do it with a smile. She had her own adoring parents and was in no way deprived of care or love, but Jess and Jane came to view Linny as a third daughter and a part of the Jackson family, too. Jess was so warm and doting with her that Laura and Jenny felt occasional pangs of jealousy at his attentiveness. "Is Linny coming over to-day?" Jess would ask hopefully. "Why don't you give her a call?"

On Thanksgiving Day 1966, while Linny and her family were driving to dinner at her grandmother's house, a drunken driver went the wrong way on a highway exit and plowed into the Brewer family car. Linny made it to the hospital, conscious and seemingly okay, but she later died of a ruptured spleen before doctors could diagnose the cause of her internal bleeding.

Linny's death hit the entire Jackson family very hard. Laura couldn't stop crying. Jenny became morose and silent again. And Jess and Jane, who had not lost anyone close to them—their parents, uncles, aunts, and Jane's siblings all were alive then—felt devastated and at a loss when it came to comforting their children and themselves. Jess retreated to the lovely rosewood paneled office he had created for himself in the new house and buried himself in work. Jane's depression lingered, and she grew newly fearful and protective of her own daughters. Instead of pulling them together for mutual comfort and support, Linny's death drove Jess and Jane even further apart. Years later Jenny would be convinced that this tragedy, as much as the purchase of the house or any disagreement that followed, set her parents' marriage on a slow downward spiral. They didn't talk about their grief or share their despair, it seemed to Jenny, and so the distance between them solidified. "In the absence of solace," Jenny said, "they let silence take over."

"Dad hated not being able to fix something," Jenny recalled. "In an emergency, when swift action was needed, Jess was the best to have around. We'll go right to the hospital, he'd say. We'll do this, I'll take care of that: he was the guy to have, who kept a cool head and always knew what to do. When I had a burst appendix in law school and didn't know it, it was Dad who showed up and literally carried me out to the car and got me to the emergency room, Superman saving the day.

"But he couldn't fix this. Linny was gone, and he couldn't remedy his broken heart or our broken hearts. And it devastated him. So he shut down emotionally and ran off to work. He wasn't there for us like he used to be."

NOBODY THREW HIMSELF into work like Jess Jackson, his daughters would say years later. The combination of his inward-turned grief over Linny's sudden death and a prodigious work ethic honed from his college-cop-warehouse days of constant hustling might not have made life in the Jackson family home idyllic. But it certainly made that life prosperous. One of Jess's ways of filling the void and coping with grief, of making sure he did not become his father (aside from never spanking or raising a hand to his children), was to provide. If nothing else, he would be the über-provider for his family. If that meant he was a little less fun, a little less available, it was a small price to pay. Once he and his family were financially secure, maybe in ten or fifteen years, he figured he could relax and enjoy himself and his loved ones. Whenever Jane would question his latest plot or plan, or the girls would beg for more of his time, he would say he had to work hard now to provide for all their futures. There'd be plenty of time to play later.

Years later Jess would be shocked when his daughters recalled him being emotionally distant and overly strict with them. He would not accept their assessment. He had to learn his way as a new parent, he recalled, and no doubt made his share of mistakes, but he had one advantage: he figured he had a very precise model of what *not* to be as a parent from his life with Jess Sr. He recalled a father who was uninterested in his son's activities and aspirations, who had little ambition of his own, and who often resorted to violence. By contrast, spanking and physical abuse were verboten in the Jackson household, and Jess felt he went out of his way to both demonstrate and preach the value of hard work. He felt he was intensely interested in his children's academic accomplishment and needs and showed both girls he was ambitious not only for himself, but also for them. He told them both on a weekly basis that they could accomplish anything in life with hard work and determination. "That was our mantra. I led by example and by encouragement—things I did not have from my own father."

He went so far as to shield his daughters from his own father's negative influence. They would dutifully go to Gertrude and Jess Senior's house for Sunday dinners, but whenever an argument would flare up between the elder Jacksons, who would rail and even strike each other if not restrained, Jess would spring up, pick up the girls, one under each arm like footballs, and say, "Jane, we're leaving." This was Jess imposing consequences on his parents for their misconduct, and it usually worked—they hated when Jess did this. Both of them were warm and loving with their grandchildren; to them, Jess's father was nothing like the man Jess had grown up with, as Jenny and Laura found their granddad warm and kindly. But Jackson tried to make sure they never were present to see the darker side of his father's personality.

With Jess working harder than ever, the law practice began to grow rapidly. He took on increasing numbers of cases and hired young lawyers to handle the load: first two, then five, eventually ten. Growing towns have growing legal needs, and Jackson's expertise, and the reputation he established early on with local judges, left him well positioned to get all the work he could handle. As the billables increased, he invested his profits in income property: the building that housed his law office, an antique mall, and a couple of other commercial buildings in San Mateo eventually rounded out a portfolio that Jane helped manage—purchases made, for the most part, by joint agreement rather than ducal fiat.

The extra work meant the piles of yellow legal pads Jackson always brought home grew substantially, as did his hours writing in them in his study, at the dining room table, and propped up in bed working. On weekends, unwilling to be abandoned while he worked away his Saturdays and Sundays, he sometimes told the girls to stay home and do chores, help with his files, or read and study instead of going off with their friends. When they complained or begged for release, he'd say no, they should be together as a family, especially on Sundays. He might be focused, he might demand silence and complain bitterly over childish interruptions, but Jenny and Laura had an insight about their father during these long and tedious Sundays: he hated to be alone. Even at work, hunkered over his desk at the law office, he liked Jane to bring the girls over, where they could have some hard candy and sit and watch him work or they could read a book.

"We learned at an early age to sit very quietly for hours at a time," Laura recalled.

Jess's long-standing desire for a piece of farmland became an active search in 1972 when he finally had the money to afford it after winning a $700,000 judgment for the owners of one hundred acres of land known as Drake's Beach in Marin County. Jackson's share of the verdict was more than $200,000, which was quite a payout in 1972 (with inflation, it would be worth more than $1.1 million in 2013 dollars). The land had been seized by the federal government to create the Point Reyes National Seashore, one of the most spectacular stretches of open coastline in Northern California. The owners turned to Jess when the federal government offered to pay only $171,000 for this iconic land. The whole Jackson family decamped to Marin County for a tense and intense month of trial preparation, and Jenny and Laura, still serving as his legal lackeys, sat through much of the long trial. It was the first time they had seen their father in action, and to them he became a different person in the courtroom, an actor on a stage. "We never realized how brilliant he was, how persuasive," Jenny would later recall. "We knew he was a bright and knowledgeable man, but watching him build his case, the inexorable logic he employed, how he communicated his palpable sense of injustice to the jurors, it was stunning. It's what inspired me to want to go to law school and follow in his footsteps."

Only on annual summer vacations would the playful, exuberant dad they remembered from the Sunset Terrace days resurface. Every trip became an adventure, thanks in large part to the two main rules of traveling with Jess: never admit you're lost, and don't hesitate to walk up someone's driveway and ask for a local tour or to see if someone might rent out or lend a truck or jeep for the day. His daughters would be mortified and embarrassed by Jess's penchant for descending on and engaging strangers, but somehow it always seemed to work out. Jess, with his big man's shambling stride and booming voice and hearty handshake, could make friends in a heartbeat. And the next thing they knew, they'd all be banging down some dirt road in the New Mexico hinterland or raising a cloud of dust in a part of Hawaii far off the tourist trail, checking out a lava field or a waterfall nobody else knew about but the locals, with Jess delivering a local history and mythology lesson with the aplomb of a tour guide.

These were the trips where Jenny learned to scuba dive and surf with her dad and Laura caught her first fish. She was so nervous when she finally hooked one that she forgot to crank the reel and just ran up the pier, the fish trailing and bumping behind her across the boards as Jess laughed and cheered. Later he took her river fishing and showed her the shady spots where fish like to congregate and how they would come if she was very quiet. Fifty years later she still remembered that day on the river, the sound of the water and the wind in the trees and her dad seeming to know something about everything. "Jackson of all trades," Jenny nicknamed him. She said it was exactly that quality of Jess's, his capacity to pick up new skills and knowledge and excel at so many disparate things, that kept his family from thinking him insane when he plunged into the wine business.

Jane, however, had been pushed to the periphery by the wine business as she held down things on the home front in Hillsborough, feeling increasingly disconnected from her husband and his new enterprise. As the first vintage sent him on many long drives to Lakeport to meet with his cabal of winemakers, Jess began loading his VW microbus with all sorts of household items he had cleared out of the basement. He wanted to put the stuff into storage in the barn next to the new winery. Ski equipment, tennis rackets, croquet sets, boxes of mothballed clothes, scuba gear—all the possessions of twenty-five years of marriage that had ended up stored in the basement at Hillsborough began appearing in Lakeport. Ostensibly, these shipments were to make room for the new winery's business office in the Hillsborough basement, but something about Jess's determined, almost manic piling of stuff into the van didn't seem quite right to Jane. It felt more like a division of community property than an efficacious move of unwanted items. He brought it all up north, careening around the hairpin turns with that overloaded Volkswagen van he loved like a favorite dog. Once there he stuffed everything in wine barrels and banged the wooden lids down on them to keep the contents dry and safe inside the unheated and marginally weatherproof barn at the Lakeport vineyard.

Jane drove up to the place herself to help out at the winery while Jess was gone on that first sales trip to New York. She hadn't been happy about the risky loan to build the giant winery, but she still wanted to be involved in the business. It was half hers, after all, and her name was on the bottle, top billing and everything. She wanted to do her part. There were interviews to give to the local press, releases to mail out, tastings to host for potential sellers and distributors.

During a break Jane found herself looking through the storage barrels to see what Jackson had thrown together in there, and she realized that the barn, in essence, was now filled with their history together, the detritus of vacations and barbecues and camping trips and adventures, all of it jumbled and thrown together in no apparent order. Only later would it become clear to the rest of the family that this was more than a simple storage issue. It was another of Jess's unilateral decisions for the greater good. He knew that they might have to sell the Hillsborough home to keep the new wine business afloat, and though he had not told anyone about this possibility yet, he wanted to be prepared for the move.

Jane opened up several of the barrels, curious about the contents. Then she found it, the thing that spoke volumes to her. Inside one barrel, beneath a jumble of ski boots and racquetball racquets, she found a crumpled dry cleaner bag. The bag held her wedding dress. It had been balled up and tossed in hastily, not maliciously, just thoughtlessly, another piece of unused stuff to be stored with no more or less care than a disused set of golf clubs. She put the lid back on the barrel, gathered her things, and then went to her car for the long drive home.

"That's when," she would tell her daughters many years later, "I knew for sure that the marriage was over."

7

The New King
of Wine Country
Meets His Match

E VEN AS JESS JACKSON'S MARRIAGE CANTED TOWARD disaster after more than a quarter century, his wine—the business he swore he never wanted, his inexorable, beautiful trap—seemingly could do no wrong. Two years after the first 16,000-case sellout, production fast approached the 100,000-case mark. Now Jackson experienced the opposite of the grape glut that had forced him into the wine business in the first place: he had more orders than he could fill, despite having US distribution deals in only half the states. This success meant—perversely, he complained—that he was constantly broke, forced to plow his revenue back into more vines and more grapes, and borrow even more money against the following year's harvest, just to keep up. Pausing to catch his breath was not an option.

At the same time, Kendall-Jackson had become an object of fascination within the industry, the Apple Computer of wine, though whether Jackson represented an emerging new power or a flash in the cellar remained a matter of debate. Either way representatives from distributors, the beverage industry, and retail chains made periodic pilgrimages in their Lear jets and Mercedes to visit the obscure place in Lakeport first settled by a band of Missourians on a wagon train led by Daniel Boone's brother—a story that Jackson the history buff loved to tell his guests. They came to meet with the makers of this new wine phenomenon and cut deals to extend Kendall-Jackson's reach even farther, driving production to a frantic pace.

A group of executives from Remy Martin, makers of the famous French cognac, arrived for one such visit to the vineyard, with its rustic tasting room decorated with slabs of redwood and an old wagon wheel. Jess conducted vineyard tours in his VW van. The Remy crew reciprocated with an invitation to a special tasting at their more glamorous San Francisco offices, attended by Jackson, his daughters, and head of sales Dennis Canning, who had been with Jackson since that first wild sales trip to New York and the Oyster Bar. The visitors tasted a series of rare cognacs brought out one at a time—first a snifter with twenty-five-year-old champagne cognac, then fifty-, then seventy-five-, and finally a century-old distillation, heady and aromatic, smooth delicious fire on the tongue. In a play on the old Paul Masson slogan, "We will sell no wine before it's time," the Remy Martin people joked that for them it was "Sell no wine until the winemaker's dead." Later Canning quipped on the ride home that Kendall-Jackson's turnaround from barrel to bottle to retail had become so short because of high demand that the winery might have to adopt the slogan "We'll sell no wine before it's bottled." The in-house joke was that the company had to rely on "freeway aging" of its wines as bottles were shipped.

"We grew beyond anyone's expectations," Jackson later recalled. "Except for my expectations. Our growth has been compared to the growth of Starbucks. We did in wine what they did in coffee. Over time, a long period of time, we elevated our price from $5 and change to $14. We were still the affordable luxury for our customers, but I could afford to stay in business—and grow the business. At that point I had no choice. I was dragged in kicking and screaming, but it worked out all right in the end."

If becoming a billionaire can be defined as working out "all right," this is a pretty good story. But Jackson always seemed to be suppressing a smile when he told his story this way. And the reason for that, said his son-in-law Don Hartford, who worked in Jackson's law firm, then became general counsel of the wine business, was that Jess had been much more calculating than the story of the reluctant winemaker suggests. Yes, said Hartford, the inability to sell grapes on the bulk market had forced a turning point for Jackson. But, according to Hartford, the fact is that Jackson could have simply decided to eat the loss of the unsellable harvest during that first grape glut. He could have pulled back on his vineyard until the next market swing. Walking away wouldn't have broken him. The glut hadn't so much forced Jackson to become a winemaker, as Hartford saw it. It was his *excuse*. It was a catalyst. After Barney Fetzer told him, "Sorry, Jess, I've already got more grapes than I know what to do with," Jackson had sat up nights with his beloved legal pad, ciphering and charting, considering the cost of growing his grapes, of packaging, of hiring a winemaker. Then he had factored in an American wine market awash with cheap jug wine at one end and expensive premium wine at the other, with nothing much in the middle. Jackson saw a chance to make a move, Hartford recalled. And to make millions.

"With or without the glut," Hartford said, "he would have gotten there eventually. He had caught the bug, the romance of winemaking, the connection with the land and with winemaking's deep history and culture. More than that, he was sure it would make him rich. There's an old joke: 'What's the fastest way to become a millionaire in the wine business? Answer: Start with $3 million.' That's what Jane feared—that Jess would turn their $4 million in assets into $1 million.

"But Jess's idea was different. I saw him handicap horses. He was good. He would do ten different calculations for every horse, all these factors, and skip betting every race but one. And on that one, he'd bet big. Not to show or place, just to win. And he almost always left the track with money, which isn't easy and certainly isn't common. He did the same thing at casinos. We were at the old Merv Griffin's Resorts International in the Bahamas one time, and he was playing blackjack, holding back, holding back, then making these huge bets. He walked out of there with $50,000, and I'm saying to myself, 'I'm gambling here with James Bond.' That's what it felt like. And that's what he did with wine. He went all in. Because that's what he did with everything, big risks with big payoffs. But he wasn't dragged in. He dove in, eyes open, with a plan."

Jackson preferred the myth of the reluctant winemaker, which made for a great tale, a humble image, a nice bit of marketing, and it cast him as the Everyman making the best of a bad hand dealt by fate. And he cultivated the myth for years as a form of business camouflage, too, until his competitors in the wine trade finally saw through it. Because his story, beyond its entertainment value, made his initial success with Kendall-Jackson Chardonnay seem to be a happy accident, a fluke, rather than a well-thought-out and calculated campaign. Competitors don't try to copy lucky breaks, Jackson knew. Strategies designed to capture a lucrative market everyone else had overlooked were another matter. Better to let them think he was a rube.

"Jess loved to be underestimated," Hartford recalled. "That, and being told that something he wanted to do couldn't be done. Nothing motivated him more than his natural desire to be a contrarian."

Yet he did not like to be contradicted on his home turf. His inability to see eye-to-eye with Jane over the business began to grow as rapidly as the business did. As he would recall it, Jane liked the romance and culture of the wine business and was enthusiastic when it had been a sideline and future retirement project. But now he was gambling everything, borrowing to expand rather than taking it slow. Jane had wanted him to wait until the next big legal verdict came in, a $1.3 million fee owed Jess in a big condemnation case he had won. The government had wanted to pay only $900,000 for the land; Jackson won a verdict in 1978 that brought the price tag up to $3.8 million, more than four times the government's offer. But his clients balked at paying the agreed-upon one-third fee, and the money had been tied up in lawsuits and appeals ever since. Jackson argued that waiting for the big legal fee would take too long and kill the wine business. He wanted to strike while Kendall-Jackson was hot. But Jess, Jane argued, we're comfortable now, we have plenty. Why risk it?

That simple, sensible question cinched it for Jackson. He realized he and his wife would never be on the same page again. How, he wondered, could this woman he'd been with all his adult life think that this grand project, this reinvention of their lives and futures, was just about dollars and cents? This was about building some-thing real, something beyond arguing somebody else's contract in court. This was going to be the family legacy.

It was then, as Jackson would recall, that their legacy became, in his mind, *his* legacy. "The last thing Jess wanted to do was drag her along unwilling on this meteor ride of decisionmaking and risk that it was going to take to build the wine business into what Jess envisioned it could be," Hartford recalled. "It had been a long time coming for Jess, although everyone, including Jane and the girls, were pretty surprised in the end."

The end came in 1984, on the day of Jess's fifty-fourth birthday. He told Jane he could no longer imagine doing what needed to be done with a reluctant, doubting partner always questioning his vi-sion and goals. He announced that he wanted a divorce. An hour later he had packed and moved out.

It was, he announced, not just his birthday. It was his Indepen-dence Day.

BY THE END of 1984 Jackson's law practice still consumed half his time, but he desperately wanted to shift more of his workday and energy to wine. Kendall-Jackson not only needed his constant attention. It also was where he wanted to be. Toward that end he had enticed Don Hartford, then his daughter Jenny's fiancé, to join his legal practice, persuading him to accept a large cut in pay in exchange for a lucrative future partnership that somehow never seemed to materialize. Jackson then lured another attorney to come work for him as well, hiring her away from a larger firm he had partnered with on several big cases. Barbara Banke was a real estate expert, and Jackson had mentored her in his specialty of inverse condemnations for several years. Now she agreed to assume some of his workload so that he could focus on Kendall-Jackson.

At thirty-one Banke was more than two decades younger than Jackson, but the youthful and charming winemaker and the intense, ambitious attorney found they enjoyed each other's company despite the age difference. With Jackson's divorce under way, albeit slowly, and his opposition to any reconciliation with Jane adamant, his relationship with Banke soon evolved into something more than collegial.

Barbara Banke grew up in the Los Angeles suburb of Rancho Palos Verdes. Her father, a test engineer for Rockwell, worked on the heat shields for the Apollo spacecraft and, later, the ablative ceramic tiles that covered the space shuttle. Given the vagaries of space program funding—budgets and enthusiasm quickly faded once walking on the moon started seeming commonplace—her father had suffered repeated layoffs throughout her childhood. The whole family had learned how to be very careful with money. Her parents had planned for the uncertain future of space exploration, however, by investing in some apartments that would generate rental income to keep the family going even during layoffs. This had been a risk that stretched the family finances quite thin for a while, but it ultimately paid off. The apartments became a family business, with Barbara, starting at age nine, becoming an apartment cleaner and painter. She always had a job after that—restaurants, fast food, babysitting—and she put herself through Hastings Law School, graduating in 1975. In certain respects—her childhood job experiences, her work ethic, her family's understanding of what it was like to struggle for money—Banke's background seemed remarkably similar to Jackson's. Whether they agreed on something or not, they easily understood what made the other tick.

They had from the start argued for sport, challenging each other's views on the law, on history, on books and art. They also talked at length about the wine business. Banke professed to know nothing about wine, but she found the idea of Jess transitioning from the law to the high-stakes world of winemaking exhilarating. Yes, it was risky, she said, but that just meant the rewards would be all the greater if he succeeded. She was excited by an insight he had shared with her: that many, if not most, wineries in that era in California were either hobbies for owners who felt no need to make them profitable businesses, or they were controlled by conglomerates with distant headquarters and too many other lines of business to pay attention to anything beyond profits and losses. There were exceptions to this rule, but the general pattern held true enough to represent a significant opportunity.

Banke understood at once how Jackson's business model could ameliorate the risk of trying to create Kendall-Jackson. If he could run a winery with the kind of drive, focus, and attention that melded high quality with high volume and consumer-friendly tastes, he would surge ahead of the gentleman farmers who came up from the big city on the weekends to smell the fresh air, walk through the vineyard, and then shovel another boatload of cash from their real jobs down the hatch to keep the thing afloat. These wineries might make a good wine now and then, but they weren't sound businesses. The giant corporate wineries, on the other hand, were satisfied by volume and efficiency, with quality far less a concern. They were formidable competitors for the cheap, jug wine trade, but Jackson had no interest in going after that space. Banke immediately saw the same hole in the market Jackson saw and the largely untapped opportunity it represented. Her main complaint was that as Jess transitioned to more wine and less law while she shouldered more responsibility for the legal business, "you're going to have all the fun."

There was probably no better or more alluring thing she could have said to Jackson, the exact opposite of how Jane had reacted. Banke got it, he realized; she shared his vision. Later he would recall that, more than her youth, her good looks, and her mental toughness, this compatibility of visions, this ability to see opportunities others had missed, entranced him.

After leaving Jane, Jess had moved into a condo in downtown San Francisco close to work, perfectly convenient: just him, his books, his beloved Volkswagen van, and his surfboard. He told most people he reveled in the bachelor's life, but in truth he felt terribly lonely. After the initial shock of their father's departure, Jenny and Laura tried to stay on good terms with both parents. But they had busy lives and fiancés of their own, and Jess suspected his daughters blamed him (unfairly, in his view) more than Jane for the divorce. He missed them but was too proud to say so. The thought had never occurred to him until he sat alone in that condo one night, staring at the sandwich he had made for dinner, that he had never lived alone in his life, not even in college. He had gone from his parents' house to the fraternity house at Berkeley to his in-laws' basement to his home with Jane. He did not know how to be alone, and he hated it. Banke, who was going through her own divorce after a brief and disastrously mismatched marriage, had sensed this about Jess. One evening she offered to come over to the condo and cook dinner for the two of them while he was at work. It was to be a simple meal, a simple date, but it turned out to be anything but.

With her chicken piccata simmering on the stove, Banke left the kitchen for a few moments, then returned to find the room filling with smoke, the main course in flames. Mortified, she phoned Jess to tell him there had been a small fire and he'd better come home. When she hung up, she realized it hadn't been so small after all and had spread, so she called the fire department and awaited Jackson's arrival with dread. But his first comment was wry, not angry: "Well, I guess we're going out to dinner."

When the firemen were through and the smoke had cleared, Jess and Barbara saw the damage wasn't so bad—nothing a kitchen remodel and thorough airing couldn't fix. They strolled to a local café to eat and Jess was so solicitous and kind that the first-date fiasco ended up bringing them together rather than cutting things short. "We were fairly inseparable after that," Barbara recalls. "It seemed to both of us that we belonged together."

Within a few months Barbara, her dog, and her cat had moved into the condo, and Jess's new life, his second act as winemaker and new husband redux, had begun in earnest. They hiked, surfed, and golfed together. Jess started running every day, too, working up to as many as fifteen miles a day before heading off to work. He was lean and in the best shape he'd been since his rugby days. By 1985 Barbara was pregnant, and in January 1986 their first child, Katie, was born. Energized by his new family, Jess would leap out of bed when the baby cried in the night, driving the restless infant in the car to rock her to sleep or putting her car seat on the clothes dryer to soothe her into snores. He had been through all this a quarter century before and knew the ropes.

In May 1986 Jenny Jackson and Don Hartford, who by then were living together in the Lakeport vineyard house, married. The two had met on the day of law school registration, and they had been together ever since. Hartford was a few years older, having taught high school Spanish in his native Massachusetts for three years (and spent another year in Spain teaching English as a second language) before attending Santa Clara University Law School. He had been working for a labor law firm in San Francisco for a year before Jess lured him away to work in the downsized law office in San Francisco in 1982. Hartford had been promoted at his first job and was making $80,000 a year—quite high for a new lawyer at that time—yet Jackson somehow persuaded him to come work for a third of that salary, with promises of riches down the line. "You know Will Rogers always said he never met a man he didn't like," Hartford recalled. "Jess was kind of the same: he never met anyone he couldn't hire."

Jackson had needed a reliable legal associate to hold down the office while he was splitting his time between the law practice and his wine, and Hartford seemed the perfect choice because it also allowed Jess to suck Jenny back into his orbit. As soon as she was out of law school, Jenny also ended up working for Jess: in wine sales and marketing, not law, but working out of the law office. After a while several additional employees of the winery, including Laura and Jane, also were stationed at the law office. The divorce was under way, but the company was still legally Jane's property, too, even if it had become Jess's in practice, and she continued to contribute. Hartford, meanwhile, decided to leave Jackson's firm and start his own law practice in Lakeport, and the vineyard would now be the setting for his and Jenny's wedding.

Three hundred guests attended the outdoor ceremony. The Jacksons' divorce was still in the works then, and property settlement negotiations had gone from cordial to grueling to outright combative. Yet few of the relatives and friends who trekked up to Lakeport knew that Jane and Jess were divorcing. Banke and five-month-old Katie did not come. Jenny wouldn't have minded, but she and Laura felt seeing Barbara and little Katie there would have been too much for their mother. As it was, the receiving line proved difficult, filled with old friends, colleagues, and Jane's and Jess's former classmates, who, one after another, mixed their congratulations for the newlyweds with astonishment at learning that the Jacksons were ending their marriage. "They were always the perfect couple," one old friend from the Berkeley fraternity days couldn't stop himself from blurting.

Jess was in great spirits despite this gloomy backdrop and the absences of Barbara and their new baby. Undaunted by the heat—it was an uncharacteristic mideighties in Lakeport that spring day—Jackson wore a sleek black tuxedo as he gave away the bride. After the toast and the traditional first dance with his daughter, Jackson retreated to the house, hung his tux in the closet, put on his old vineyard work clothes and his broken-down work boots, and started driving people around on vineyard tours. He made extra seats out of old milk crates inside his VW van for the visitors, filled all their glasses with Vintner's Reserve Chardonnay, and showed everyone the vines and the land.

Two months later, as Jackson made it clear to Jane that he wanted a wedding of his own, she told her lawyers to allow the divorce to become final. Jane had previously wanted to settle property and money issues first, then dissolve the marriage, but she relented so that Jackson and Banke could marry. The financial settlement would take another year to hash out, and Jane would come to regret her generosity and the leverage she had surrendered to accommodate Jess.

Jess and Barbara went to Hawaii, where they were married on the beach, a casual affair, no family or guests. They called and told everyone the news once they got back home.

They were back to Hawaii within the year—it would become the vacation retreat for the new Jackson-Banke family—though this time it was for Jess's last big case: an appeal of an adverse ruling against a large resort developer. The client's property had lost most of its commercial value when the city of Honolulu redesignated the area, known as Queens Beach, for preservation. Jackson had started and fought the multimillion-dollar case for years, but in this final argument before the Ninth Circuit Court of Appeal, his new priorities became clear: he sat out in the corridor playing with little Katie while Banke made the oral arguments before a court second only to the U.S. Supreme Court in the judicial pecking order.

When she emerged, Barbara told him the argument they had perfected together and that seemed so strong to them did not seem to sway the court. This might once have set his blood boiling—Jackson felt strongly that the city had behaved with criminal disregard for property rights and the law—but he found it hard to muster the old outrage this time. The passion wasn't there anymore, and he realized something he had been feeling for some time: this would be his last case. He told his wife the law practice was all hers. "I'm just going to make wine from now on," he announced, bouncing Katie on his knee.

By then their second child, Julia, was on the way, to be followed two years later by Jess's fifth child and only son, Christopher, born just a few months before Jess's sixtieth birthday. Banke nodded and repeated what she had said two years earlier: "You just want to have all the fun."

THAT PERIOD MARKED more than the start of a second family for Jess Jackson. It would also mark the time that his vision of Kendall-Jackson expanding to vineyards beyond Lakeport finally moved from his yellow legal tablets to the real world.

Jess long had his eye on the luscious fruit of Tepusquet vineyard in the Santa Maria Valley near Santa Barbara in California's Central Coast region. This rolling property ringed with majestic California oaks had been the source of the fine Chardonnay grapes, with the tropical, almost pineapple flavor, that had been a critical component of the first Vintner's Reserve and of every one that followed. These grapes formed the backbone of Jackson's signature wine, and he wanted control of that vineyard before a competitor could acquire it and take away fruit he absolutely needed.

The possibility of losing access to the Tepusquet grapes posed a very real threat because the vineyard owners, like many wine growers in those years, faced mounting financial pressures that made selling to one of the big wine conglomerates an attractive solution to the problem of being land rich but cash poor. However, Jackson knew one of the investor-owners, who had been his neighbor in Hillsborough, and he used that entrée to engineer a way of ensuring he'd have a fighting chance to keep control of those grapes no matter what. The property had not yet gone on the market, and even if it had, Jackson lacked the cash or credit at that point to buy it. Instead, Jackson talked the controlling partner, Louis Lucas, into selling him an option on the Tepusquet vineyard—a first right of refusal in exchange for $500,000. Lucas promised to continue selling Kendall-Jackson the grapes the winemaker needed for Vintner's Reserve, and Jess didn't have to do anything but pay for the fruit. But if Lucas put the property on the market and it sold, Jackson had bought the right to match the price and take the property out from under any other buyer if he could come up with the cash. The Tepusquet owners also agreed, at Jackson's insistence, to keep the option deal secret or forfeit the $500,000. Jackson feared that if the agreement were disclosed, a potential buyer with deep pockets might jack up an offer just to make sure Jackson couldn't match it.

The original planting of the Tepusquet grapes in 1970 had marked an important milestone in California wine history, as the property became one of the first commercial vineyards in the Santa Barbara region. This Central Coastal area of the state had long been thought to be poor for wine grapes, but Tepusquet proved otherwise, leading to recognition of the region as a California gem, with its Santa Maria and Santa Ynez Valleys in particular producing world-class wines. Before buying the Tepusquet land in Santa Maria Valley, Lucas had grown grapes in the broad, flat, warm Central Valley—easy for industrial farming compared to the hills and stony soil of coast regions but not known for its high-quality fruit. That was the trade-off of fine wine, Jackson had learned early on: often the most difficult terrain and trying conditions made the best wine grapes. "That's why we sometimes refer to the grapes from the Central Valley as the 'inferior interior,'" he liked to say. "The coastal areas are where the finest wines in California are made. Or rather nature creates those special grapes that make the finest wines possible." Most California wine grapes were then (and are now) grown in the inferior interior because it was cheap and easy. Jackson always said he had no interest in going that route, and he avoided those grapes no matter how desperate he was at times for fruit to fill demand for his product.

Prior to creating Tepusquet, Lucas asked the wine chemist at Mont La Salle monastery—best known for its storied winery, Christian Brothers—to help find the right place for a Santa Barbara County vineyard. Brother Timothy, whose beatific image was a familiar fixture in national advertisements for Christian Brothers in the decades after the repeal of Prohibition, visited the land that would become Tepusquet, told Lucas it contained a great deal of limestone, and pronounced it ideal for Chardonnay. Timothy found the soil profiles very much like those of Burgundy in France, blessed with a coastal climate and the right amounts of cool fog to be ideal for growing fine grapes. Brother Timothy knew his stuff: Jackson and his first winemaker, Jed Steele, felt that some of the finest Chardonnay grapes in the world were being produced on that favored land. The same conditions also proved excellent for growing Pinot Noir grapes.

The large property was divided into two mesas with a valley separating them. The west mesa had been planted with Chardonnay and Pinot; that was the area Jackson wanted. The east mesa had been planted with mostly Cabernet Sauvignon grapes. The growing conditions for that fruit were not particularly good, and Jackson felt the wine from those east mesa grapes tended to have a disagreeable vegetal, bell pepper taste. Lucas planted them because several companies, including the massive Beringer Wines, had asked for them and the grower had been happy to plant whatever grapes the big wineries wanted to buy. And despite the odd flavor, Beringer bought these grapes harvest after harvest to use in various blends.

In 1986, with Tepusquet on the verge of bankruptcy, Lucas put the property on the market, and Beringer, by then a subsidiary of the global Nestlé conglomerate, made a firm offer for both mesas at a price the owners liked: $11.5 million. Jackson's option to buy at the same price then kicked in. There was a problem, though. He still had no ready cash and little credit, certainly nothing close to eight figures. He had maxed out his existing line of credit to buy several thousand imported French oak barrels. At $500 each that had been a costly purchase—essential, as Jackson and his winemaker saw it, but expensive. The cheap shortcuts big wineries sometimes made—using less desirable American oak barrels or simply soaking oak chips in stainless steel tanks of wine—did not produce the mellow, deep, toasty flavors that Kendall-Jackson customers had come to expect. This was one of the differentiators for Vintner's Reserve, and it was a major marketing point to be able to assert this traditional, handcrafted winemaking method as the old-world legacy of each amber vintage.

Then again all the barrels in the world wouldn't make up for losing the single most important element of the VR blend: those Santa Barbara grapes. Beringer had been a respected family-owned winery since the 1930s, and back then the Beringer family had played a major role in turning Napa Valley into a travel destination; the family gave away clever promotional maps of the area extolling the joys of wine tourism and including the slogan "All roads lead to Beringer." The winery had recruited Hollywood stars of the day to make well-publicized visits, among them Clark Gable and Carole Lombard, and suddenly California Wine Country was cool. Although the Beringer family had sold the business to a global conglomerate in 1970, the brand remained popular, and Jackson had no doubt that the conglomerate would keep the Tepusquet grapes for its own products rather than sell to competitors.

So Jackson recruited Banke to put her real estate expertise to work in structuring a deal to allow Kendall-Jackson to acquire critical land it couldn't actually afford. "If Beringer bought that vineyard, we knew it would be catastrophic," Banke later recalled. "We would lose grapes that had become the backbone of our most important wine. It was unthinkable."

In the end Banke and Jackson decided the only way to corral Tepusquet and keep Beringer from taking over those coveted vineyards would be to use the secret option agreement to attract a partner with deep pockets who wanted the east mesa and its Cabernet grapes, yet would be willing to cede to Kendall-Jackson the west mesa with its Chardonnay and Pinot. The two of them would just have to hope this as-yet-nonexistent partner wouldn't realize that the west mesa was the real treasure in the deal. Such a partnership could split the cost and subdivide the parcel, and Kendall-Jackson would need to borrow only half as much to get the share it wanted. That was still a tall order, but perhaps not impossible.

Jess called the CEO of the prosperous and ever-expanding Mondavi Winery in Napa and proposed that the two wineries purchase Tepusquet together. Mondavi agreed, eager to get a foothold in

Santa Barbara and at the same time foil Beringer—then a far more dangerous rival than little Kendall-Jackson. Best of all, Jackson told Banke, the Mondavi people had made it clear they couldn't care less about those treasured Chardonnay grapes on the western side of the property. The company wanted the east mesa Cabernet grapes that Jackson and Banke thought tasted like rancid bell peppers. It was a perfect marriage of convenience. Mondavi even agreed to provide temporary financing for the entire Tepusquet property obtained through Jackson's option agreement. This would complete the purchase, cutting Beringer out while also allowing the buyers to file the legal papers with the county needed to split the land in half, creating two separately owned and financed parcels. Then Kendall-Jackson could (Banke and Jackson hoped) secure a loan big enough to reimburse Mondavi for covering the purchase of the western half of the Tepusquet property. It was an elegant, seemingly flawless solution in which everybody would get what he or she wanted—except, of course, for Beringer. Executives there became furious when they learned of the secret option deal, decrying Jackson's lawyerly maneuvering that pulled the rug out from under the company whose offer to buy Tepusquet had set these machinations in motion.

Banke brought in a loan officer from the Equitable, a large Chicago-based insurance company that maintained a division in California specializing in real estate loans to the wine industry. (The company has since been bought out by the French conglomerate AXA and is known now as AXA Equitable Life Insurance.) The Equitable representative came to Jackson's San Francisco office to prepare the loan application and asked for some basic background information, starting with the company's standard annual financial statements. Banke and Jackson asked for the files and were mortified to learn that no financial statements had been prepared for the previous two years. All the records were in disarray.

By then Kendall-Jackson had a small staff spread between the law office in San Francisco and the winery in Lakeport. There were the winemaker, his assistant, and production staff at the vineyard.

There was a small sales and marketing force at the law office. And Kendall-Jackson had a chief financial officer charged with handling the books, the accounts, purchasing, and collections. Juggling all that at the frequently cash-starved business, with a leader who changed course, marching order, and direction on a weekly basis, had been extremely stressful for the CFO. When Laura Jackson handled some of those duties in the cellar of the family home, they frequently drove her to tears. Things weren't much better in 1986, and the fellow occupying the job at the time had been forced to take time off, as other staffers warned Jackson that they feared he might be on the verge of a nervous breakdown. Even so, no one at the busy, seat-of-the-pants company had noticed the absence of annual financial statements until they were needed for a loan application. The CFO simply hadn't had the time to create them.

Banke had to return to the conference room where the Equitable representative waited and tell him all they could find were a year's worth of bills, receipts, and accounts receivable tossed in a box. The loan officer, Harold Kelly, surprised her with his reaction to this embarrassing revelation. He did not do the reasonable thing, which would have been to gather up his papers and leave, as Banke later said she might have done had their positions been reversed. Kelly, it turned out, was passionate about preserving the character and natural beauty of California Wine Country from overdevelopment and environmental degradation. He had come up with the idea of Equitable establishing a vineyard and winery lending program for new and upcoming wineries. Kelly would go on to become a Napa city councilman and the president of the Napa Land Trust. He was not, Banke recalled, a typical loan officer. He took the box of receipts from her and said, "Let's see what you've got. It may not be as bad as you think."

Kelly's willingness to find a way to help the fledgling company with a crucial acquisition would prove to be one of those key events in the company's history: a make-or-break moment. When Banke carted in the enormous box of papers, Kelly waved off her apology and spent the next three days going through those records. When he returned, he handed Jackson the financial statement he had written up himself for Kendall-Jackson and gave the carton of records back, too. Then Kelly told Jess, "You're in great shape. We'll lend you the money."

With that hurdle cleared, Jackson called the Mondavi executive assigned to spearhead the deal to tell him everything was set to conclude the Tepusquet purchase and their brief partnership. Jess just needed Mondavi to sign the paper requesting county officials to split the vineyard into two parcels, east and west mesas, Chardonnay and Cabernet, each with separate ownership. Then Kendal-Jackson could complete its loan application with Equitable and reimburse Mondavi, and the two wine companies could go their separate ways.

But Jackson could not reach the executive. When no one returned his call, he phoned again. And again. He logged ten calls in all over the course of a week, never getting past a secretary. Then Jackson learned he wasn't the only one who could play hardball. Mondavi filed a foreclosure notice against Kendall-Jackson for failing to pay its $5.7 million share of the Tepusquet purchase. Never mind that the failure to pay was caused by Mondavi's refusal to sign off on the parcel split as promised, thereby preventing Kendall-Jackson from closing its loan. The foreclosure would allow Mondavi to take ownership of the entire vineyard—a property the company never would have sought or even known about had Jackson not offered a piece of his option agreement with Louis Lucas. Beringer, meanwhile, already feeling betrayed by Tepusquet's secret option deal with Jackson, was in a position to make legal trouble because its original offer to purchase had been waylaid by Jackson's option to buy, yet Kendall-Jackson wasn't even taking ownership.

Jackson and Banke knew they had to force Mondavi's hand. While Jackson started calling Mondavi's attorneys, thundering about unethical practice and breach of contract, Banke decided she would confront in person the executive handling the deal. He was the company official refusing to sign the parcel split papers, which should have been nothing more than a rubber-stamped formality, so that's where Banke decided she needed to be. "He can dodge our calls, but let him try to get past me," she told Jackson.

Banke arrived at Mondavi's Napa Valley headquarters shortly after the office opened the next morning. She introduced herself to the secretary, explained why she had come, then sat and waited. After the first hour she figured her executive might just be swamped. After two hours she thought he was just trying to put the upstart winemakers in their place but would eventually come out and do her the favor of signing the document Mondavi had promised to sign and was, by contract, obligated to sign.

After three hours Banke realized the Mondavi front man had no intention of seeing or acknowledging her. Instead, he simply did not leave his office. He even had his lunch delivered so that he didn't have to emerge and face Banke waving the critical document at him. It was as if he were trying to dodge being served with court papers. When Banke was forced to leave at closing time, he had still not shown himself.

Banke returned the next day, this time packing a lunch and a book to help pass the time. By the third day a deadline to file the property documents loomed, but she had bonded with the secretary, who expressed an embarrassed sympathy over the bizarre standoff. The executive finally emerged at noon that day for lunch, having been told by the secretary that Banke was not in sight. But Banke had just walked away for a moment, saw her target emerge, and pounced. The Mondavi company's behavior was appalling, she told him, the very definition of bad faith. The two companies had an agreement. Mondavi could not now evade that agreement in order to enable a foreclosure on property it could never have obtained without Kendall-Jackson opening the door and inviting Mondavi's participation in the first place. Banke promised him a lawsuit, promised Kendall-Jackson would win both in the courtroom and in the court of public opinion, and noted that Kendall-Jackson's lawyers also ran the company—they'd work the lawsuit for free, as long as it took, she said.

She had caught the executive in the open. Avoidance was one thing: it might be rude and cowardly, but it was also legally ambiguous, not quite a refusal or a broken promise. Face-to-face notification and rejection, though, constituted something else; there was nothing ambiguous about that. There were witnesses. Whatever the reason—threat of lawsuits, a concession to the inevitable, a decision to finally do the right thing, or simple deer-in-the-headlights embarrassment—the Mondavi official signed the papers and Banke rushed out. Kendall-Jackson had until the end of the business day to get all the necessary papers filed, the loan approved, and the foreclosure proceedings halted. Filings had to be made in two courthouses 440 miles apart, one in Santa Barbara and the other in Lake County. The messengers she and Jess dispatched made it with fifteen minutes to spare. The deal had been saved.

Kendall-Jackson had a new vineyard, a beachhead in Santa Barbara County long before it was recognized by the California wine industry as a premier growing region. Jackson renamed his side of the old Tepusquet property Cambria. It cost him $5.7 million, but it would soon be worth three times as much. And a core ingredient of his signature Vintner's Reserve could never be taken away.

8

Birth of a **Terroi***rist*

A FTER WINNING THE BATTLE OVER THOSE PRECIOUS
Santa Barbara Chardonnay grapes, Jess Jackson made obtaining more coastal and mountainous vineyards his priority. More
than that, it became his obsession: he wanted a piece, in some cases
a big piece, of each of California's finest vineyard regions, and not
just for Chardonnay. He wanted to grow other varieties of grapes
as well for wines that would traverse all price ranges, from $5 a
bottle to $500. His original idea still held: Kendall-Jackson would
be, underneath the barrels and vats and harvesting machines and
tasting rooms, a real estate company that made wine.

So whenever Kendall-Jackson's expanding market share produced enough cash, or at least credit, Jackson immediately sought
to buy, plant, or rehabilitate more vineyards. He knew there were
still some bargains to be had in those early years of the modern
California wine business, viticultural gems forgotten or disused that
he could bring back to life. All those drives through Wine Country in
the Yellow Banana, all the research, all his reading, all the driveway
conversations with Barney Fetzer and Hank Bartolucci and anyone

else he could pigeonhole, were about to serve Jackson well as he embarked on a ten-year Wine Country buying spree unlike any other before or since.

Jackson's next big purchase after Santa Barbara came in 1988 when he bought out the struggling Edmeades vineyards in chilly northern Mendocino County. Edmeades owned sixty-five prime acres and a small winery in the brisk coastal range of Anderson Valley, with only about a dozen miles of hilly country buffering it from the Pacific. The valley, resplendent with winding rustic roads and a climate seemingly best suited to oak trees and apple orchards, had hosted one failed wine project after another since the end of Prohibition. The most spectacular of these failures was the two-hundred-acre land purchase and planting in the 1940s by the once dominant Italian Swiss Colony Wine Company. That incarnation of the vineyard featured a hundred acres of acidic Ugni Blanc and Colombard grapes (the two are often blended), with smaller plantings of Semillon, Carignane, and Palomino fruit. For the most part these were the wrong grapes for the area; these varieties crave warmer weather than the rocky, mountainous Edmeades property offered, and so they never ripened sufficiently to make decent wines. Swiss Colony finally gave up the project in the fifties.

A few years later a Pasadena cardiologist, Dr. Donald Edmeades, bought a piece of the land as an investment and a retreat. In 1964 he decided to plant twenty-four acres of grapes, despite repeated warnings from locals who told him he would likely meet the same fate as Swiss Colony's winemakers and others before them. Edmeades apparently had a vision, or at least a streak of stubbornness, rejecting the advice but acknowledging it with humor, posting a sign in the driveway of his vineyard near the small town of Philo that read "Edmeades' Folly." He has been credited over time with the first successful Anderson Valley vineyard since pioneer days, but that's more legend than fact, as his main plantings—Colombard and Cabernet grapes—did no better than Italian Swiss Colony's. It wasn't until Edmeades died and his son Deron took over that things turned around. The younger Edmeades hired a brash young winemaker named Jedediah Tecumseh Steele, who arrived with a newly minted masters degree in enology in hand; he soon established a reputation for good Anderson Valley wines, including a cult favorite labeled "Rain Wine" made from de-acidified Colombard grape juice from Edmeades's original plantings. But mostly Jed Steele made well-regarded Cabernets and Zinfandels from grapes he bought from other growers, while the Edmeades fruit went to the bulk market. This was what he was doing in 1983 when Jackson hired him away to make Vintner's Reserve.

Five years later, with the search for new properties picking up steam at Kendall-Jackson, Steele pointed Jackson toward Edmeades and told him the hilly terrain and soil there were fantastic, just not for the grape varieties that had been planted there. The two men drove up together, and Jackson saw what he believed was the perfect hilly, cool, coastal property for the Chardonnay grapes he needed, as well as for the Pinot Noir he wanted to develop into his next big thing. The two often do well in the same vineyards; unlike Swiss Colony's choices, these grapes like the cold. Edmeades, Jackson believed, possessed the precise conditions that had caused the modern wine grape to evolve in the first place. And he wanted the vineyard badly.

In choosing Edmeades, as well as vineyards that would follow, Jackson embraced a French concept about land and growing called *terroir*, which he tied to the history of the wine grape as he understood it and which held for him the power of myth, archetype, and scripture rolled into one. This was a tale he never tired of telling or discussing, and he imbued it with an aura of magic, of how that first modern wine grape originated in the harsh terrain of the Caucasus Mountains in what is now the Eurasian Republic of Georgia near the Black Sea. This region figures in such ancient epics as *The Odyssey* and *The Epic of Gilgamesh*; it's where the mythic Jason sought his Golden Fleece and where real archaeologists unearthed what are believed to be the world's first true vineyards and winery, dating back 6,000 years.

"This is where the wine grape we use today—the same vines, the same DNA—originated, the *vitis vinifera*, high in the Caucasus Mountains," Jackson would say. "The soil there is thin and rocky, and the roots have to reach down deep for water and nourishment. When the dry season comes, all the energy and effort of the vines goes into the seeds and the fruit, into producing the vine's children, its babies. The vine is taught: 'It's time to ripen my fruit.' It's time to make sure the next generation survives; nothing else matters. And this is where the most amazing flavors come from, rooted in that original *vinifera* DNA, waiting to be teased out, and you can only get it from those mountains, those rocky hillsides, that cool coastal climate. And that is why I decided to buy land on hillsides and mountains and benches [narrow, level, plantable benchlike strips of land on slopes]. Anyone can grow ten tons of grapes in the Great Central Valley; that's where 85 percent of California wine comes from, the flat inferior interior. But that's not where world-class wines are grown."

Those extraordinary vines cultivated in the Caucasus found their way through the slow, sure flow of trade into Persia and Egypt and then to the ancient seafaring Greeks, who spread *vinifera* across the Mediterranean and beyond. The vines soon were planted and cultivated throughout the ancient world. Other types of grapes—and other fruit for that matter—can be fermented into wine. But *vinifera* became the most prized and has maintained its most favored status throughout the long march of civilization.

In trying to re-create the conditions that powered the evolution of those original wine grapes and forced them to produce the fruit best suited for great wine, Jackson had embraced an ancient concept: that wine is best understood as a uniquely local phenomenon rather than a product identified more broadly by a particular type of grape, a mix of soil, climate, water, temperature, and overall environment that combine to make the taste of a vineyard unique. The French use the word *terroir* to make this physical and philosophical distinction, a word that has no direct English equivalent but that

Jackson came to live and breathe as he considered new vineyards to buy and plant. This idea captivated Jackson. He loved to read about it, expound on it, and, ultimately, he built his empire around the idea of *terroir*.

The concept is nearly as old as wine and civilization themselves, and Jackson relished this tale, too: when the ancient Greek trade ships were plying the Mediterranean thousands of years ago, the wine import-export merchants made a habit of stamping each amphora (the industrial-strength ceramic containers that contained up to thirty-nine liters of wine each) with the seal of the place where the wine was made. From ancient times on the perceived quality and uniqueness of a wine were judged by the place, climate, and culture in which it originated; the variety of grape had little or no importance, and most consumers couldn't have said one way or the other. What they knew was that Chian wine, one of the first reds, was among the most prized in the ancient world. It came from the wineries of the ancient Greek island of Chios, where a moderate climate and coastal coolness produced legendary vintages. Imported Chian wine was the most expensive vintage served in ancient Rome, reserved only for the most lavish meals and sometimes doled out as medicine in minute quantities because of its supposed curative powers. Chian's only rival came from the vineyards of the Greek island of Lesbos, which produced wines celebrated by the poet Homer. The Greeks pioneered techniques still used today in vineyards: succoring, training and tying vines, and using cuttings, rather than seedlings, to propagate strong vines with desirable genetic traits. And it seems the Greeks also developed the earliest version of appellations that defined a wine's regional identity. They developed at least eleven appellations known for their outstanding quality, and there were others that served as the ancient equivalent of plonk. The ancient Egyptians were similarly fixated on associating wine with place: near King Tut's tomb rows of wine jars sat ready for the afterlife, each bearing an inventory reporting the wine's origin date, place, and vintage. Wine, like politics, was seen first and foremost as local.

The Grecian winemaking techniques were handed down across generations and spread to other cultures and countries through trade and conquest. The French adopted and advanced these ideas with particular passion, tracking the regional origins of their wines for the last thousand years. A hundred years before Columbus set sail for the New World, monks tending vineyards in Burgundy established the first appellations that identified the growing places for specific varietal wines, beginning with Pinot Noir. The modern idea of *terroir* started there, evolving over time to include, along with geographic location, soil, weather, terrain, and growing culture, all of which contribute to taste. The concept of *terroir* elevates this broad place identity, emphasizing it as far more important to a wine's taste and character than any specific brand, winery, or winemaker. According to wine writer Hugh Johnson, in a foreward to James Wilson's book *Terroir*, "It means the whole ecology of a vineyard: every aspect of its surroundings from bedrock to late frosts and autumn mists, not excluding the way a vineyard is tended, nor even the soul of the *vigneron*."

The French may have accepted the concept as a given, but this was not the case in American winemaking circles when Jackson bought his first vineyard in Lakeport. Back then, US wine companies were primarily interested in mixing grapes from various locations in order to provide a consistent taste for a generic chablis, Burgundy, or rosé regardless of the *terroir*. And while the French considered soil type and the taste it conferred on grapes as the single most critical ingredient of *terroir*, Americans were far more obsessed with climate. Soil was soil, but the weather was king for the New World vintners. A handful of winemakers concerned with elevating the reputation of California wines began trying to change that, and Jackson counted himself among those pioneers. The *terroir* that interested him the most lay in the vineyards that most faithfully captured the lush yet harsh mountainous conditions that were the hallmark of those first *vinifera* grapes harvested in the Caucasus. That's what he wanted: coastal, cooling morning mists and fogs; thin mountain soils; and hot California days. "That's what makes great wine—the vineyard, not the winemaker," he once observed. "Forget all the egos in the winemaking. Mostly, we're just wine *watchers*."

When Jackson started his vineyard search, Edmeades, for all its potential and its compelling *terroir*, had not been doing well as a business concern, like all those that came before to this Anderson Valley locale. As with many small wineries at the time, financial failure seemed imminent despite the label's good reputation. Jackson was able to pick up the distressed winery, the Edmeades brand, and its vineyards for $750,000. A common practice in the California wine trade at that point would have been a kind of cannibalization, Jackson observed. A bigger company swooped in, gobbled up a prestigious but money-losing brand, cut costs, lowered quality, then sold as much so-so wine with a high-end label (and price tag) as possible until consumers caught on and the brand died in both sales and reputation. This happened time and again when big chains bought up little wineries. The emphasis was on short-term gain.

Jackson, however, always the contrarian, envisioned a reverse trend: rehabilitation rather than cannibalization, an investment that took the long view that great wine properties would be exponentially more valuable in a then-unlikely future in which California wines were revered rather than dismissed. He immediately began ripping out most of the old vines and replanting with Chardonnay and Pinot, with the harvests going to Kendall-Jackson wines rather than being bottled as Edmeades vintages. He put the Edmeades Winery operation and label into mothballs for the next few years, though eventually Jackson would plant Zinfandel grapes there and in 1994 begin producing wine again at the site. Bottled under the Edmeades brand, those Anderson Valley Zinfandels would earn numerous awards and maintain and improve the reputation of the brand. In the meantime another vital link in the Vintner's Reserve blend came under Jackson's direct control: he owned fine Mendocino Chardonnay grapes for his secret formula.

Jackson would explain years later that his vineyard acquisitions were never just a land grab for the sake of expanding company-owned grape tonnage, nor were they merely a means of assuring a guaranteed supply of blend ingredients for his most critical product, the Vintner's Reserve. Certainly, Jackson told everyone at the time that these were among his goals, an absolute business necessity given that Kendall-Jackson had laid plains for doubling production to 200,000 cases by 1988. But such business concerns were not all that drove Jackson's vineyard real estate hunt. If arable land and burgeoning crop yields were all he was after, Jackson could have found and planted more convenient, easier-to-tend, and cheaper-to-operate vineyards than the coveted coastal properties he ended up buying. He could have just cashed in on Vintner's Reserve and kept churning it out without trying to improve it or expand into other varieties and price ranges. That, some advisers told him, would make for a sensible and proven course. Add a couple of inexpensive reds under the Vintner's Reserve brand with grapes once again plentiful on the bulk market, and he could just rake in the cash without investing large amounts of capital in pricey land purchases.

That's what Fred Franzia, Ernesto Gallo's nephew, did when he founded California's Bronco Winery in the 1990s, making immense quantities of $2 Charles Shaw wines sold at the Trader Joe's grocery chain: cheap, popular, not-very-tasty varietal wines nicknamed "Two Buck Chuck." Franzia would make a fortune with a Napa Valley address from which he sold inland Central Valley wines, content to be a vineyard bottom feeder. Jackson, however, dreamed of dominating the high end as well as the inexpensive supermarket shelf wines, which was why he focused on buying coastal and mountain vineyards rather than the inland valleys that made Franzia, not to mention the Gallo family, rich.

"That's the difference between the two," wine writer Steve Heimoff would later observe. "Jess had ambition, yes, but he had taste. He wanted to leave his mark on California not just at the fighting varietal level but at the highest level and every level in between."

Less than a year after the Edmeades purchase, Jackson set his sights on a more valuable piece of vineyard property in Sonoma County's lush Alexander Valley. He had been scouting out land all over Sonoma for some time, but he had settled on Alexander Valley as the place he most wanted to farm.

Alexander Valley is bisected by the broad banks of the Russian River, a waterway long recognized as a marker for prime vineyard territory up and down its length. Alexander Valley offers a climate conducive to growing virtually anything, from heirloom tomatoes to fields of corn to vineyards of just about any variety, white or red. The weather is so gentle that, even at the upper end, where the city of Cloverdale stands, the valley encompasses the farthest point north in coastal California in which orange groves can still flourish and fully ripen. This would be a fitting center for a new wine empire, Jackson knew. He longed to make Sonoma County his mainstay—then still largely unexploited but right next door to the more developed and well-known Napa, dominated by Mondavi, Fetzer, and a host of other big wineries. Sonoma could be the next Napa, Jackson knew. After all, in the not-so-distant past it had been an earlier empire's headquarters, too. That history drew him as much as the *terroir*.

Alexander Valley was named for a fur trapper from Pennsylvania, Cyrus Alexander, who came west to find gold in the 1830s. Failing to support himself with either pelts or precious metals, he moved from job to job until he ended up in the thriving port town of San Diego, then part of the Mexican territory of Alta California. There he finally landed a job that suited him: working for Captain Henry Delano Fitch, an early California merchant and trader blessed with money and political connections in both Mexico and Washington. Alexander's mission was to make the long ride north to Napa, then explore the surrounding region, looking for unclaimed land to settle and farm. In 1840 he found a verdant but sparsely populated valley along the Russian River, a gentle landscape leading into the foothills of the Mayacamas Mountains. Alexander wrote Fitch a letter that left no room for uncertainty about how he felt about his new valley: he had stumbled upon "the brightest and best spot in the world." Fitch immediately sought and received a 48,800-acre land grant to establish Rancho Sotoyome, which Alexander managed with a thousand horses and equally large herds of cattle and sheep, the first major foothold in this part of what would become modern Sonoma County. Russian traders at nearby Fort Ross are said to have provided cuttings for the first grape vines in the valley.

The area's suitability for wine grapes was soon noticed by Italian and German immigrants who trickled into the valley after Alexander and planted small vineyards. But the full potential for viticulture on a massive scale did not become clear until 1881 when Antonio Sbarboro founded a new community in Alexander Valley dedicated to winemaking that he dubbed "Asti," after the northern Italian town by the same name famous for producing the cheap champagne alternative Asti Spumante. Asti would be the headquarters for California's leading winery of the era, Italian Swiss Colony. The sprawling operation eventually covered more than 6,000 acres and created some of America's most popular wines before and immediately after World War II, while laying the groundwork for all future commercial winemaking in Sonoma County.

Italian Swiss Colony established rail and shipping infrastructure for wine businesses and trained a generation of winemakers and production staff by offering newly arrived immigrants a decent wage and even an employee stock-purchasing plan (a $5 deduction from the $35 monthly paycheck), one of the first such programs of its kind. The company dominated the nation's wine sales for decades. Swiss Colony's campy TV commercials later became an early television-age staple, featuring an elderly, elfin fellow in lederhosen and suspenders uttering the company's slogan: "Made by the little old winemaker—me!" In the late fifties and earlier sixties, Asti and its landmark winery and cellars, with immense, vat-sized barrels and 500,000-gallon wine cistern, had become the number two tourist stop in California, behind only Disneyland.

By today's standards (and European standards of the day), Italian Swiss Colony wines were very cheap and tasted like it. The vineyards were planted for the most part as "field blends," in which a mixture of varietal grapes were planted and harvested together, rather than the contemporary practice of segregating varieties in their own plantings and doing the blending, if any, after the grapes become wine. The main advantage of field blends was to provide insurance against adverse weather. Conditions that harm some varieties—too much cold, warmth, rain, or drought—will ruin some grape varieties but may favor others in the same field, which means there will always be a usable harvest every year. The downside is that such field blends can make for highly variable wines year to year depending on the weather, and, like mixing too many colors in a painter's palette, field blends can produce muddy, rather than miraculous, flavors. It was upstart California winemakers in the seventies and eighties, including Kendall-Jackson, who rebelled against such wine, championing instead specific grape varieties that came to be known as "the fighting varietals."

In its day Italian Swiss Colony produced prodigious amounts of generic jug wine and screw top, along with fortified wines (which have added distilled alcohol) and flavored wines available by the pint. Some high-end products, such as vermouth, sherry, and Madeira, are fortified wines, but it was Swiss Colony's success in the downscale fortified wine market, sometimes known by the derogatory term "bum wine," that led its then-smaller competitor—Gallo—in the late 1950s to create one of the most notorious products in that category. It was a cheap, lemon-flavored fortified wine called Thunderbird, which quickly became Gallo's top seller at 60¢ a quart and helped propel the company from third place behind Swiss Colony to the number one wine company in California and, later, in the nation.

Swiss Colony had begun a rapid fade by then, with its old-fashioned image, generic wines, and brand names gone stale ("Mello-Red," "Early Colonist," and "Vin Rose" had been top offerings). Consumers had begun to associate good bottles of wine with actual corks, and the marketing connection was never quite clear between California wine and a Swiss guy in alpine clothes that conjured images of snowy, vineyard-unfriendly landscapes. The Italian Swiss Colony wines were relegated from coveted eye-level store display to retailers' dusty bottom shelves—the place wines go to die. By the 1970s, after a succession of ownership changes and dispirited sales, the once mighty Italian Swiss Colony went out of business in all but name only.

The decline of this Sonoma winemaking powerhouse did not occur because of some fault of Alexander Valley's climate, geography, or soil. The winemaker died from a failure to evolve as the market changed. It didn't help that the wrong grapes had been planted with the wrong techniques—wrong, that is, if consistently good-tasting wines were the goal. The company's bulk industrial techniques neutralized Sonoma County's coastal advantages in taste and quality, producing wine indistinguishable from the inferior interior's. Italian Swiss Colony winemakers cared nothing for *terroir*. They liked Alexander Valley because it was fertile, had easy-to-plant flatlands stretched between its mountains and ridges, and so could easily and efficiently yield many tons of hearty but mediocre grapes. But Jackson saw other possibilities in this green slice of Wine Country, as did a small cadre of other knowledgeable growers and winemakers who settled in the area in the sixties, seventies, and eighties, led by Robert Young, who tore out his prune orchard in 1963 and started growing fine Alexander Valley Cabernet.

When Jackson learned that the sixty-five-acre Stephen Zellerbach Vineyards in a prime Alexander Valley location might be available, he jumped at the chance to establish a beachhead in Sonoma County. Zellerbach would be the perfect location for the red varietals he wanted to produce under the Vintner's Reserve brand, the neat rows of vines already planted with military precision under Cabernet Sauvignon and Merlot. The vineyard had been founded by the nephew of J. D. Zellerbach, a paper company magnate, former US ambassador, and founder of Sonoma's legendary Hanzell Winery, where so many of the winemaking techniques Jackson later embraced and popularized had been pioneered decades before anyone else in the United States was willing to try them. Nephew Stephen clearly knew how to pick and plant a vineyard, too. His winery lay in the foothills of the Mayacamas at a kind of appellation crossroads, where three separate American Viticultural Areas—the all-important AVAs that anchor a wine to a particular place—came together: Alexander Valley, Chalk Hill, and Knights Valley.

There were more than forty different types of soil in the immediate area, each offering unique qualities and flavor potentials for varietal grapes so that within a single vineyard entirely different growing environments could be achieved. Depending on elevation and position relative to sun, fog, and prevailing winds, that same vineyard could be planted to take advantage of a series of varied microclimates as well, contrasting conditions from one block of vines to the next. Jackson envisioned such a property as having many small vineyards in one, and this special place in Alexander Valley would be his first chance to test out and exploit a concept he hoped to build into every other vineyard he acquired. Jackson had to have the Zellerbach land, his living laboratory for wine. He wanted to name it for his great-grandfather and his own unusual middle name: Stonestreet Winery. He even liked the experienced winemaker who had just come on board a year earlier, Stephen Test, and wanted to keep him on.

There was a problem, however: the vineyard was embroiled in a tangle of lawsuits and disagreements among the owner, the person who had leased the vineyard, and the people who had subleased the property and actually occupied it. The conflict over rights, ownership of the crop, and the future of the vineyard had grown so ugly that during one confrontation on the property guns had been drawn. Most potential buyers would take one look at that explosive situation, and at the small legion of lawyers amassed to sort it out with years of court hearings and mounds of legal papers ahead of them, and stay as far away as possible.

"But it was a very good property," Banke recalled, "and Jess wanted it. It was where we needed to be. So we got creative. . . . We don't mind lawyers. That's our comfort zone."

As she had with the Mondavi impasse in Santa Barbara, Banke came up with a creative solution for Kendall-Jackson's problem. This time she persuaded the lawyers for the three Zellerbach factions to meet together in one room, where she made them an offer: $3.4 million in exchange for the property, free and clear of all their competing claims. Kendall-Jackson had just come off another good year of sales growth, and Jackson had renegotiated a new bank line of credit with vineyard purchases specifically in mind. For once he actually had the money for more real estate—no more Mondavi foreclosure madness in order to make a deal work. For the Zellerbach lawyers, the money offered a neat and profitable way out: instead of a three-way fight over the property, the owner and leaseholders could fight over the money, which would sit in the bank awaiting settlement. It would be a lot easier to divide that way, Banke suggested, and the existence of an actual pile of money might make the warring parties more amenable to putting the dispute to rest. It would also enable them to give clear title to the property without actually having to kiss and make up or go to trial; Kendall-Jackson could then get its Alexander Valley foothold sooner rather than later. The Zellerbach attorneys agreed, the sale went through, and Jackson had his first, but certainly not his last, Sonoma winery. The signs renaming it Stonestreet went up just in time for harvest.

As Kendall-Jackson's holdings expanded, the new sources of premium grapes fueled increases in wine production, which generated more sales revenues and in turn allowed Jackson to continue funding an insatiable desire for yet more land. Land, grapes, revenue, land: Jackson had closed the loop, creating his own personal wine boom. But that boom touched only one segment of the wine market: the premium wine category, in which he was, for the moment at least, the only maker of large quantities of affordable premium wine (with "premium" defined by the industry rather liberally as in the

$7 range; superpremium and ultrapremium were above that). Other winemakers couldn't help but notice this positioning, along with the fact that it was making Jackson rich. Gallo began snapping up properties and planting vines in Alexander Valley, too, preparing to launch a premium wine brand of its own—a move that would spark a feud between the Gallos and Jackson that would continue for years.

Meanwhile, Jackson's success—this feedback loop of premium sales fueling more land buys, which in turn upped the volume of premium grapes—brought some challenges that the original, scrappy, cash-poor incarnation of Kendall-Jackson never had to face. The quirky start-up, featuring a CEO who pounded the bricks door-to-door in Manhattan and a dump-truck-driving tasting-room manager in the Lakeport hinterland, had come of age and had to start acting as the big business it was rapidly becoming.

First there were issues of distance: field to factory, for one. Jackson's main winery lay far north in Lake County, which had made sense when his vineyards consisted of eighty-four acres wrapped around the winemaking facility like a cape. That was the ideal setup—virtually no distances to travel from vine to crush to barrel to bottle, which meant minimal transport costs and minimal damage to the fruit from packing, bumping, and roadway temperature extremes. But as the eighties drew to a close, Kendall-Jackson had expanded to grow in Sonoma and Santa Barbara, while still buying grapes up and down the coast to fill the secret Vintner's Reserve recipe. The arduous and costly transporting of grapes to Lakeport began weighing the company down and no longer made much sense. The haul between the original winery and the new showpiece vineyards in Santa Barbara, where the quality of the grapes was an order of magnitude greater than most of the Lakeport fruit, exceeded four hundred miles. It took eight to ten hours to get those prized grapes from Santa Barbara to Lakeport, and the clusters would get bruised and smashed in their bins on the way north, causing the juices to oxidize, a wine flavor killer. This was particularly damaging for the

Chardonnay and Pinot grapes that were at the heart of the company's leading products, robbing them of their delicate flavors.

So in 1988 Jackson commissioned plans to build new wineries in Santa Barbara and Sonoma, with the first one to be built on his Cambria vineyards in the Santa Maria Valley of Santa Barbara County. It would take years to get the permits and environmental reviews completed before even one shovelful of dirt could be turned for those wineries, but Kendall-Jackson was able to exploit a quirk in the law that allowed for the immediate construction of open-air crush pads at the Santa Barbara vineyard. Because there was no enclosed building or structure, just crushing equipment and stainless steel tanks to hold the juice, the permitting process was simple and quick, and the vineyard crews had everything they needed to crush the juice from harvested grapes on the site. Jackson and Banke, who held the title of president at Cambria Winery by then, could then ship juice instead of fruit to Lakeport, ensconced in refrigerated tanker trucks, avoiding the bruising and oxidation problems. Similar temporary fixes were used to get Sonoma and Anderson Valley grapes to the winery, too. These weren't cheap or optimum solutions, Banke and Jackson knew, but they were the best that could be done until new wineries could be brought on line.

The other distance issue had to do with the company headquarters. Kendall-Jackson staff had been scattered from the beginning, with some working out of the law office in San Francisco and several employees stationed up in Lakeport. After Vintner's Reserve took off, Jackson had stationed more employees in rented office space in Sausalito, a couple of miles north of the Golden Gate Bridge. Now there was the Zellerbach Winery, which came with a house converted to offices, and Jackson made that building, as part of the new Stonestreet Winery, the first true headquarters for Kendall-Jackson in Sonoma County. About a dozen employees worked there for about a year. They called the building "the meat locker" because it had no heating. Employees had to wear coats while at work during winter. Larger (and heated) offices eventually were rented, but only temporarily, while Jackson built a permanent office space—"the campus," as he called it—in a commercial park near the Sonoma County Airport in Santa Rosa, the county seat. After that Kendall-Jackson stopped being the little wine curiosity in far-off Lakeport, the scrappy outlier with much to prove, and instead assumed the image of an upscale Sonoma winemaker headquartered in the heart of California Wine Country. From that point on Kendall-Jackson would be known as Sonoma's leading winemaker and, eventually, its largest employer.

Along with a shift in locations came a revamping of the Kendall-Jackson organization from its original, unstructured start-up mode to a more conventional business—not corporate, exactly, because its leader still set the tone with an open-door policy for all levels of employees, a penchant for "keeping things fresh" by periodically (and unexpectedly) reassigning people to new jobs, and a love for lengthy Socratic dialogue. The company continued to be a creature of Jackson's distinctive vision; he was still an inveterate micromanager, as if his business were just one big court case to research, distill, and dominate. And he still worked fourteen hours day; his nighttime reading simply shifted from legal briefs to spreadsheets and cost projections. Still, the size of the operation had reached a point where he had to set clear lines of leadership and responsibility and delegate significant parts of the business to other managers. Most in need of attention and reform as the eighties drew to a close were sales, the company's engine of growth, and distribution, its primary bottleneck to growth.

At the beginning there had been Dennis Canning, the company's first national sales director. He never had much staff; there was no money for much of a sales force in those days, and he, Jackson, and Jenny often traveled together on sales trips and met as a group with distributors. Canning worked hard and presided over several years of rapid growth in sales. But he and Jackson quarreled over sales projections, with Jess often setting expectations Canning felt would require a sales staff three times the size he had. Canning, in turn, pushed for lower retail prices in order to drive more orders and expand Kendall-Jackson's market share. Jackson adamantly opposed knocking down the price, insisting that the company should never try to compete at the bottom of the market. Jackson felt Kendall-Jackson should gently and regularly nudge prices *higher* in order to keep his corner of the premium wine category distinct and to protect Kendall-Jackson's margins. This drove Canning (as it would his successors) crazy because those price nudges never deterred Jess from insisting on wildly ambitious sales projections even though every extra nickel on a wine bottle's price made the sales manager's job that much harder. But there Jess would be, heading up the annual sales meeting in the old trailer in Lakeport where the first Vintner's Reserve had been concocted, waving a yellow legal pad filled with charts and numbers and his equations labeled "COGS" (cost of goods and services), explaining his vision of pricing, marketing, and expansion.

During one memorably hot and frustrating midwestern summer sales tour, Canning grew particularly exasperated with the old argument about pricing. It had been a bad trip, ending with an unsuccessful meeting with a Cleveland beer distributor who dragged out the discussion, then told them "no deal." The meeting had been at a grimy dive of a bar that smelled of stale beer and that deposited mustard and ketchup stains on their sleeves from tables that had seen many customers but few bar towels. The trio left Cleveland without a distributor anywhere in Ohio willing to carry the still new Kendall-Jackson brand, the familiar complaint ringing in Jackson's ears: *We can't move the California wines we already carry—why should we add yours?* At the airport Jackson and Canning argued yet again, and the sales director, short but powerfully built, slammed down his suitcase as hard as he could, banging it on the hard, thinly carpeted air terminal floor, purposely coming as close as he could to Jess's foot without actually hitting his boss. Except, he aimed poorly and really did hit Jackson's foot a crushing blow. Jenny had to suppress a laugh at the way her father hopped around the terminal, until she saw his face and the real pain reflected there. Canning was horrified and couldn't stop apologizing. Jackson limped for the rest of the trip and, though he waved the incident off, accepting that it had been an accident, that trip marked the end of Canning's tenure. He left a short time later—on good terms with Jackson but gone nevertheless.

For several years after that Jackson contracted with an outside agency to be his sales force, which spared him from having to hire a full-blown sales team with all the expenses associated with fully vested employees who had benefits, medical coverage, and pensions. It also spared him having to explain his pricing schemes; the contractor accepted them without question. The downside, however, was not being able to fully control things, which was anathema to Jackson, who eventually decided that his growing company needed a proper in-house sales and distribution division after all. He created a subsidiary he dubbed "Majestic Sales" and recruited for its leader a veteran beverage industry executive who had worked for Safeway, Liquor Barn, Seagram's, and Coca-Cola. Michael Haarstad was charged with creating a new kind of sales force for the company, with specific targets, goals, and products to emphasize (rather than letting each salesperson decide strategy on his or her own). Haarstad's disciplined approach would be credited by Jackson himself as a main factor in the rapid sales growth of Kendall-Jackson wines that followed.

Haarstad also created another subsidiary, Regal Wines, which became Kendall-Jackson's in-house distributor. The distribution of alcoholic beverages has long been a bane to bottlers, brewers, and, especially, winemakers because of the three-tier system created with the repeal of Prohibition in 1933. This tripod-shaped system of producer, distributor, and retailer enshrines a middleman—the distributor—between winemaker and wine seller. Because this setup confers licenses and territories to the distributors, they have enormous power to boost or impede the sales of a particular brand or product. Large and powerful brands—the market incumbents—end up getting most favorable treatment by distributors, while small upstarts tend to get lost in the shuffle. Haarstad spent a great deal of time and energy courting and cajoling distributors around the country, but it was the creation of Regal that excited him most. Initially, the new subsidiary handled only direct sales of wine to customers: bottles sold at the tasting rooms and the wine-by-the-glass program Kendall-Jackson marketed to restaurants as a means of introducing the brand to consumers. But in the years to come, Regal would become a vital part of Kendall-Jackson's growth as a full-blown distributor selling directly to retailers throughout the immense California market.

In the meantime the restaurant pours drew customers to Vintner's Reserve in droves. The combination of price incentives to restaurateurs and high quality compared to other wines in the price range made VR the most frequently served wine in American restaurants by the end of the 1980s. Data suggested that the program brought to the brand every year several thousand consumers who had tried Vintner's Reserve with a restaurant meal, then bought a bottle next time they were looking for wine to serve at home.

Haarstad and Jackson renewed the old battle over the value of price cuts versus price increases, and staffers got used to the sight of Haarstad shouting across the conference table at his boss, veins in his neck bulging, proclaiming that he had to "save Jess from himself." Jess would roar back at him as newer staffers looked on, horrified, while everyone else busied themselves with their papers and files, averting their eyes. This is how the two of them worked things out, it seemed; five minutes later they'd be laughing together, strolling through the office practically arm in arm. Jackson needed people who could push back against him, who provided some balance, who could tell him no. Banke was one person who could get Jackson to reconsider a decision or rethink a strategy; Haarstad was another. But Jess usually won his arguments, running meetings with the same Socratic method his favorite law professors had employed back at Berkeley, discussing everything, hearing all the arguments, weighing them all—and then doing exactly what he had wanted to do all along.

Jess stuck with the strategy he had outlined in Kendall-Jackson's first year, refusing to compete with lowest-common-denominator wines, arguing that he could never "out-Gallo Gallo" and would never want to try. He wanted to define a nascent premium wine market as his domain and build it up from scratch, inching up prices each year instead of cutting. His strategy went against conventional wisdom, but he insisted the point of premium wines was that they were better, of higher quality, and that consumers would be willing to pay a premium price and would be suspicious if there wasn't one—up to a point. The challenge would be to have the quality of the wines always exceed that of other similarly priced competitors, which led to Jackson's cardinal rule for the company. It would affect everything from technology modernization and farming techniques to pricing and marketing: he proclaimed that if Kendall-Jackson sold a $5 bottle of wine, it had to be better than everyone else's $10 bottle. A $10 bottle of KJ had to beat out $20 vintages in wine competitions and with consumers. And if customers paid $20 for his wine, Jackson said, they should feel they got a bargain because it would beat anybody else's $40 or $50 wine. This was the value equation that, for one thing, kept restaurant sommeliers coming back for more: they could make high profits selling KJ by the glass without totally gouging customers.

Still, in an industry so long divided between the expensive boutique wineries and the commodity merchants who sold bulk for cheap, Jackson pushed a disruptive model for the times. Kendall-Jackson stood alone, at least at first, and if its philosophy on pricing succeeded, this would not be because KJ won on market share but because it won on profitability. Haarstad did not disagree with the approach, just on how far and how fast the company should push prices upward. The arguments were simply about striking the right balance, and for that Jackson needed Haarstad there to push back.

More than a decade later another California company with a visionary and contrarian leader would adopt this same model of selling premium products that were priced higher than competing products but that were perceived as the superior value nonetheless, dominating and leading an industry with huge profitability rather than huge market share: Apple Computer. Jackson got there first, and he transformed the California wine industry as a result.

THE NEXT TASK Jackson set for the company was to make his pricing and quality model sustainable. Part one of this task would be straightforward, he announced to his staff: Kendall-Jackson had to grow big enough—and develop a supply chain deep enough—to churn out those boutique-quality premium wines in much larger quantities than any winemaker had ever attempted. So the nineties started with an explosion of construction plans at Kendall-Jackson, beginning with an announcement of an $18-million, 500,000-case, state-of-the art winery and warehouse complex that would include the world's largest oak barrel fermentation project—barrel aging on a scale never before seen anywhere in the world. He wanted to have the new winery up and running in Sonoma County in time for the 1992 harvest. That would be one goal that eluded and frustrated Jackson for years.

Part two of the drive to bolster Kendall-Jackson's prospects took place on a very different front: the convoluted politics and regulation of wine in California and nationwide. Jackson strove to become the voice of the beleaguered family wine business, tilting against a system he said was biased in favor of faceless corporations and big money.

This campaign fit firmly in Jackson's personal wheelhouse; even when he represented big-time developers in court, he positioned himself as the champion of property owners, of individual liberty, always seeing himself as the Everyman and the righteous underdog. No matter how big Kendall-Jackson grew, Jackson would not, and perhaps could not, change that perception of himself. And in this instance it was totally appropriate. Small and family wineries in California had complained for years of an uneven playing field in which regulation, taxation, and trade policies were stacked against them.

Jackson first joined a group of fellow winemakers suing an obscure but powerful state agency, the California Wine Commission. Then he and Kendall-Jackson quit the main industry trade group in California, the Wine Institute. Jackson and his fellow family winemakers asserted that this pair of organizations shamelessly favored policies that benefited a few huge wine companies, which had been granted controlling votes in the trade group based on market share and which were generous political donors as well.

Next Jackson became a founding member of a rival trade group, the Family Winemakers of California, created to promote the interests of small and family-owned wineries that he believed the Wine Institute had long disregarded. Among the new group's top priorities was to foster changes in the law that would let winemakers sell wine directly, by mail, phone, and, later, online, across state lines without having to battle fifty different state bureaucracies and archaic distribution regulations. The battles over the regulatory landscape for wine in California and the rest of the country that began with this vintner's equivalent of secession would continue for decades.

Part three of Jackson's plan to cement Kendall-Jackson's future revolved around bringing in some industry star power as the company expanded its varieties and price ranges of wines. Jackson hired away a number of key people from other wineries, most notably John Hawley, the respected head winemaker at the family-owned Clos du Bois in Alexander Valley. The enraged founder of the winery said he would never forgive Jackson for cherry-picking his best wine man, in violation of some gentleman farmer's code that Jackson never subscribed to. But Clos du Bois had joined the ranks of celebrated California premium wineries gobbled up by a conglomerate, so it wasn't clear to Jackson whether the owner was truly offended by his head-hunting or by the fact that his inability to include Hawley in the sale might have brought the price down. Jackson offered a pithy response to the ill will over his deal-making, real estate maneuvering, raiding of other wineries' employees, and willingness to sue opponents in the genteel ranks of winemakers: "We built this company against the odds. So I can't be a pussycat." His longtime consultant, winemaker Ric Foreman, part of the Vintner's Reserve original skunk works, put the matter even more bluntly: "He's outrageous. He thrives on the game. It's not the money for him; it's the game. There's always five deals on his plate."

Jackson finished out 1990 by again thumbing his nose at his adversaries, and a few friends, too, among California's major wine-makers by staging a blind tasting. He sought to test the virtues of a new Chardonnay produced by his Cambria Winery in Santa Bar-bara. Well aged for a Chardonnay from the 1986 vintage, Jackson's new wine beat out comparable vintages from Mondavi, Chateau St. Jean, Clos du Bois, and nine other winemakers, big and small. The Cambria wine came in second place in the blind tasting, exceeded, according to the impartial panel of judges, by only one other Char-donnay: Kendall-Jackson's Proprietor's Reserve, Jess's souped-up version of the Vintner's Reserve. This blind tasting had posed a seeming risk: both of Jackson's wines could have flopped with the critics, and he would have ended up paying for a marketing tri-umph his competitors could use against him. Instead, Jackson would still be chortling about the outcome years later, echoing Forman's comments: "I love making high quality wine—it's all about quality grapes and land. But I also love the game." Then he added, "I should say, I love *winning* the game."

9

VRU and
the Hard "C"

W ITH A NEW HEADQUARTERS IN SONOMA, A NEW SALES
and distribution force in place, a reform campaign roiling
the rest of the wine industry, and plans to build a state-of-the-art
winery in the heart of Wine Country, Jackson followed his blind-taste
triumph with a shopping spree of winery acquisitions. These land
grabs catapulted his once little Lake County operation into the big
time before the rest of the California wine industry realized what he
was doing or guessed what his endgame might be.

While the big wine powers were distracted by the success of the
Vintner's Reserve Chardonnay and were figuring out how to either
imitate it or undercut it with cheaper offerings, Jackson was talking
about the lessons of hockey great Wayne Gretzky: he needed to
skate to where the puck was going, not to where it had been. Jess
wanted to find his next big thing while everyone else sought to catch
up with his last.

The conventional wisdom in the trade, now that Jackson had his
VR cash cow, was that he would consolidate his business around

it. The idea never occurred to his competitors that he might try to use those revenues—and a pile of loans on top of them—to lock up California's most fabulous estate vineyards, the treasure troves of coastal grape production that had long been used to make some of the best wines in the state and that he had scouted out on countless trips, banging down country roads with Jenny and Laura in the old Yellow Banana. But that was his under-the-radar mission: to buy up the best vineyards he could find and to go a long way toward accomplishing that goal before anyone in the business took notice. He wanted the myth he had woven around himself to persist as long as possible, the story of that crazy lawyer up in the Lake County hinterland who had been dragged kicking and screaming into winemaking and whose spoiled fermentation accidentally created the desirable sweetness and unexpected success of Vintner's Reserve. Fearing that bigger wine companies with bigger bank accounts might be tipped off by a string of vineyard purchases, and that they might then try to interfere by going after the same properties, Jackson formed a dummy company to act as his bagman. This company, which he dubbed VRU, would deal with real estate agents, obtain loans, and otherwise appear on the public records, keeping the Kendall-Jackson name out of these transactions, at least for a while. Jackson's old fifth-grade pal, physician and cancer researcher Carl Mondon, sometimes lent his name to the deals and was named a principal of VRU.

"We have to sneak up on them," Jackson told Mondon. "They have the money, but we have the desire."

It was clear to Mondon that, beyond such practical considerations, Jackson enjoyed these cloak-and-dagger tactics and loved the consternation this mysterious VRU was causing in the industry. The wine world inner circle was abuzz about this faceless buyer. Several asked Jackson if he had any idea who this VRU might be. And by the time Jackson's rivals learned that this mysterious VRU was an acronym for Vineyards "R" Us, and that it was, in essence, Jess Jackson's alter ego, it would be too late to do anything about the empire he had assembled.

"They came out of nowhere," Douglas Walker, president of the Chateau St. Jean Winery, griped in 1995 in the journal *Wine Spectator*. And Michael Mondavi, then CEO and president of Robert Mondavi Winery, paid Jackson grudging respect in the same article: "He's been creative when the rest of the industry's been lethargic."

Jackson kicked off his buying spree in 1991 with a major acquisition to the south of Sonoma in Monterey County that other potential buyers had written off as a lost cause. Banke's old friend at Equitable Insurance's real estate division, who had penned Kendall-Jackson's early financial statements just in time to avoid disaster, had acquired several distressed vineyards near the town of Gonzales, in one of Monterey's most prized locales for growing wine grapes and another contributor to the Vintner's Reserve blend. The properties, known as Hacienda, Puente del Monte, and Rincon, had been bought years earlier by an investment group led by a well-known wine-growing family in the area, but the vineyards had been in decline for years, producing poor-quality fruit, mostly Cabernet grapes that were poorly suited to the cool local conditions. The vineyards finally reverted to Equitable, which had financed the purchase and planting. When Jackson came along, the vineyards had been untended for years and the vines lay in the grip of the parasite phylloxera (*Daktulosphaira vitifoliae*), marking Jackson's first encounter with the dreaded grape wine plague that had altered—and nearly ended—the world wine industry. Other potential buyers had run in the other direction as soon as they realized the grape-wasting disease was sweeping through those gorgeous, rolling vineyards.

Jackson, however, saw another opportunity—but only if he was willing to plan a decade in advance rather than look for returns by the next harvest or two (or in the case of more corporate wineries, the next fiscal quarter or two). There were risks to this approach, as long-range investing often left Jackson asset rich and cash poor, but he was used to that. If such investing meant he was worth $1 billion on paper but his and Banke's three young children had to share one bedroom, so what? Compared to his childhood, when he had landed his first job hawking newspapers at age nine, his offspring were living in paradise, with the very real prospect of far greater riches for the family a few years down the line if Jackson's real estate risks paid off as he anticipated. As he later recalled, "That sort of thinking is really the key, which is so simple and yet so often lost once the conglomerates move in. I was thinking in terms of where we would be five, ten, twenty years down the line, and then in terms of a one-hundred and two-hundred year threshold. I was operating, and always have operated, a family business, with principles that focus on building for the future, building something that endures beyond what the climate does to us and the economy does to us and what government does to us and what fashion does to us. I had no stockholders to answer to, no quarterly reports to leaven, none of the shackles that held back so many of our competitors from doing business in a long-term, strategic way. That's why we bought when they sold, expanded when they pulled back, and why we risked when they hedged. And more often than not, we won."

In the case of buying phylloxera-stricken vineyards, that risk was considerable. The organism was originally identified as the cause of a mysterious grape-wasting disease in nineteenth-century France, labeled then as *Phylloxera vastatrix* or, colloquially, as "the Devastator," which aptly summarizes its murderous impact on wine grapes. Phylloxera is a type of aphid that in its louse stages attacks the roots of grapevines. Its effects, though not the cause, were known as early as the sixteenth century in North America, where the creatures originated. Florida vineyards planted by the French with European *vitis vinifera* strains invariably withered and died, a pattern that would be repeated throughout the colonization of the New World. Only in California did the European vines survive, with growers concluding that there was something special about California soil and something wrong everywhere else in the Americas. This was incorrect; the only difference was that the phylloxera bugs had not migrated to the West Coast—yet. Elsewhere in the colonies would-be winemakers tried to make do with one or more of the six species of grape native to the Americas, most of which were highly resistant to the aphid's toxic bites, though the resulting wine was invariably deemed inferior to *vinifera* vintages.

Once a susceptible vineyard is infested by the Devastator, the voracious creatures spread inexorably plant by plant, each succumbing to the same symptoms. Each of the bugs lays several hundred eggs, with multiple hatchings and layings over the course of spring and summer months, a geometric progression that means a single phylloxera bug yields millions of hungry descendants very quickly. In their nymph stages of development, the bugs latch onto the grapevine roots, suck out nutrients, and inject waste and toxins back in, which causes the roots to wither and the plants to starve. They may continue to produce fruit for a time, but eventually the vines succumb. The aphids, meanwhile, after a complex series of sheddings and metamorphoses (each time producing yet more eggs), develop wings and fly farther into the vineyard—or neighboring vineyards. Because the bugs kill the roots first, then move on to new victims before the vines above the ground show the ill effects, the causal relationship between the killer aphids and the disease did not become clear for centuries.

This was how infected American grapevines could be brought to Europe for experimentation, either by Britons, who had made amateur botany a national obsession in the nineteenth century, or by French winemakers looking to try something new in their vineyards. The introduction of this invasive species probably stemmed from multiple sources. In any case, in the 1860s the creatures gained a toehold across the ocean from their American home and spread in a consuming epidemic through the vineyards of Europe, destroying upwards of two-thirds, perhaps more, of the cultivated grapevines there. Midway through the epidemic, with the French government offering an F 300,000 reward for a solution, several scholars pinpointed the tiny phylloxera bugs as the cause, after which a number of unsuccessful cures were tried. These ranged from thumping the ground around vines to scare off the bugs, to burying a toad beneath each plant, to dousing the ground with water to drown the parasites, and to applying toxic pesticides to kill the plant-killers. Numerous exorcisms were attempted as well. The day finally was saved when experimentation revealed that grafting *vinifera* vines onto American grape rootstock provided the best of Old and New Worlds—Europe's wine grapes tasted just as good, while beneath the ground their American roots resisted the fatal effects of the phylloxera's bite. Reluctantly, most French and other European vintners accepted this "reconstitution" of the grape, although by the time this cure was discovered, European vineyards had been decimated and the American wine trade, along with the Scotch whiskey business, had taken the world by storm as alternatives to European wines. Time to recover and rebuild France's vineyards, coupled with the wine-crushing fist of Prohibition in the United States, finally put the Yankees back in their proper place at the bottom of the wine hierarchy.

A century later, in the late 1980s and early 1990s, California Wine Country experienced a rude awakening when a new and tougher strain of phylloxera appeared in the wild. The widely used AXR rootstock strain—once believed to be resistant to phylloxera—began to shrivel and die from infestations of the Devastator. An expensive and time-consuming regrafting onto new and more-resistant rootstock followed for those in stricken areas who could afford to do so; those who couldn't afford it sold or suffered foreclosure to lenders like the Equitable.

Jackson decided to gamble on the fine *terroir* of the Salinas Valley, figuring that even without the infestation, he would have ripped out most of the misplaced Cabernet vines anyway and replanted had he purchased and paid full price for those Monterey fields. So the headache and expense of dealing with phylloxera didn't mean as much to him as it would to prospective buyers looking for vineyards with intact and healthy fruit. The disease meant the thousands of grapevines and their rootstock planted there would ultimately be worthless, with shrinking yields each year as the plants withered. Such vineyards would represent a considerable upfront cost with little return for years because the diseased land would have to be cleansed of the stricken vines and roots and the ground then would have to remain fallow for a season. So Equitable offered Kendall-Jackson 1,300 acres at a very low price compared to healthy vineyards in the area, knowing Jackson had been searching for exactly that Monterey *terroir*.

Jackson and Banke snapped up the land as a long-term project they believed would eventually have an enormous return on the investment by ensuring future supplies of Vintner's Reserve as well as other premium wine grapes. They ripped out the Cabernet right away but kept some sections of Chardonnay and Riesling grapes that were still producing even while the bugs devoured the roots. Those harvests, sold on the bulk market, defrayed some of the costs of acquisition. Each year after that Banke and Jackson planted a portion of the land with resistant vines with whatever surplus cash they had available. While waiting for these replanted vineyards to progress to the point of producing usable fruit again, Jackson purchased a thirty-year lease of an adjacent 1,200 healthy acres, which he planted with Chardonnay and Pinot Noir as well, ensuring a sustained supply of Monterey grapes, with their distinctive flavors of green apple and peach, that were critical to the Vintner's Reserve blend. They also formed the basis of several artisanal wines under another label Jackson launched, Carmel Road.

In 1992 Kendall-Jackson hit the 1-million-case sales mark, and the company churned its increased revenues into yet more land purchases. At a time when icons of family winemaking—Fetzer and Benzinger's Glen Ellen brand among them—cashed out and sold their brands and lands to conglomerates—Jackson was rapidly building the largest family-owned winemaking business not named Gallo.

This included the purchase of a twenty-acre vineyard and farmhouse just across the road from the new Stonestreet vineyards, on the banks of Franz Creek. It was a perfectly fine place for grapes, but that was not the property's main purpose. In 1992 the Jackson-Banke family—with Katie age seven and in first grade, Julia five and almost ready for kindergarten, and Christopher an energetic three-year-old—left their first family home in the Bay Area town of Tiburon and moved into the Franz Creek house. With that, the Kendall-Jackson transition to Sonoma County became complete. The Franz Creek home was what real estate agents call "cute": well made, pleasing in design, in a great location, and small. Very small. The two bedrooms were a tight fit for the family of five, with all three kids crammed into one room, though another bedroom would be added on within the next two years. For now cute would have to do; it was what the family could afford.

The commuting from the Bay Area had become intolerable, making home life even more chaotic than would otherwise have been the case with a demanding new business, a law practice still in motion, and three kids born in the space of four years. The place was cramped with dogs, chickens, a couple of llamas in the back, and plenty of nannies to keep three busy kids in check while Banke and Jackson worked. It was a time of little sleep, Banke would later recall, but she had a husband who, this time around, could be more engaged in the daily care of his later-life children than he had been with Jenny and Laura. When Julia wouldn't sleep through the night, it was Jess who piled her into the car and drove the dark, quiet roads of Sonoma, rolling hills and engine rumble putting the restless child to sleep. And it was Jess who marched the kids out in back of the house to plant the vegetable garden or feed the chickens or hike around the property looking for arrowheads or rabbits, the general directing his toddling troops. Once the three little ones were old enough, he brought each child into the vineyards, demonstrating how to prune and succor, how to smell the rich earth and feel it, how to taste a grape for ripeness, how to roll the juice across the tongue and taste the tart and the sweet. He wanted Katie and Julia and Christopher to love this new life as he was coming to love it, this wine business that he had never wanted to enter, that fate had tricked and trapped him into adopting, and that now he could not imagine being without, these fields where his dreams were unexpectedly coming true.

Which is why he had to have more.

In February 1993 Jackson bought the Vinwood Cellars Winery in the Alexander Valley town of Geyserville, a $10 million purchase from the Chevron oil company's land development division, which had bought the winery just a few years earlier as part of a massive land acquisition and development deal. The Vinwood purchase included fifty-eight acres of vineyards and a massive inventory of bulk wine, but the prize Jackson coveted was the 75,000-square-foot, 500,000-case winery. He'd been desperate for this kind of capacity in Sonoma County, as the facility near the airport he had proposed in 1990 remained locked in environmental review with county planners, balky neighbors, and environmental groups. Now he had an existing, fully permitted, enormous facility that he could load up with row upon row of oak barrels for his Vintner's Reserve. At last he could ease up on the constant, expensive, quality-impairing truck traffic back and forth to Lake County. There was a bonus, too, to this purchase: his successful bid for Vinwood had squeaked by a rival offer from Glen Ellen Winery, the main brand of the Benzinger family. (A few months after the Vinwood auction, the Benzingers sold their Glen Ellen brand to Heublein, a massive conglomerate that at various times owned Smirnoff vodka, Jose Cuervo tequila, Grey Poupon mustard, Kentucky Fried Chicken, and the distinctly low-end wine brands of Inglenook, Almaden, and Blossom Hill.)

Two months after the Vinwood deal closed, Jackson bought the financially stricken La Crema Winery in the Sonoma town of Sebastopol: a sixty-acre vineyard in the Russian River Valley with a small, 40,000-case winery and a once proud brand, which was the most valuable part of the purchase. La Crema, founded in the seventies, had produced one award-winning Pinot Noir after another. But the winery had been a money loser that slowly drifted into bankruptcy—though not before its management eroded the brand's reputation with poor mass-produced wines sold at bargain-basement prices in a desperate, futile effort to flood the market, capitalize on La Crema's good name, and restore cash flow. Jackson wanted the La Crema brand far more than its facilities. He felt he could restore its luster while also using the smaller subsidiary to keep Kendall-Jackson from losing the edginess and risk-taking that had defined Kendall-Jackson when it was still a small upstart.

He was delighted that his company was now considered a major player, but he did not want the fact that it now sold 1 million cases of wine a year to crush the spirit of a start-up that had infused the early years of his winery. He recognized the challenge before him as the classic innovator's dilemma, for now his signature achievement—the superblend Vintner's Reserve—was being produced in such great volumes that consistency year to year, rather than innovation, had become the primary path to success. Yet he wanted Kendall-Jackson to remain the innovator. He wanted to experiment with new *terroir*, to try the unexpected, to be the contrarian, because only a contrarian would have come out with that first 16,000-case run of Vintner's Reserve. So he decided to divide the company by creating a series of small, artisanal winemaking subsidiaries where experimentation and cutting-edge techniques could play out away from the pressures of the increasingly large Kendall-Jackson VR operations. La Crema would be among the first of these, but it would soon be joined by eight different labels under the umbrella of a new parent division, Artisans and Estates. Jackson attended the La Crema bankruptcy auction in Modesto and personally outbid the giant Constellation Brands conglomerate, bringing in the Sebastopol winery as a wholly owned subsidiary for $3 million. No matter how big he grew, Jackson told his winemakers, he always wanted to run a good part of the company like a risk-taking start-up. He said he expected every one of them to try something every season that pushed the envelope, something crazy or unexpected, the science experiment in the back room, that probably would lead nowhere but just might yield something spectacular.

The new vineyards came in rapid fire then, an unprecedented accumulation of Wine Country land between 1993 and 2001. Jackson bought Domaine Laurier in Forestville in Sonoma County for $2.5 million, renaming the vineyard Hartford Court for his daughter Jenny and son-in-law Don Hartford, who had left his law practice in Lake County to become general counsel for Kendall-Jackson—the promotion and raise Jackson had promised so long ago ten years late but more than Hartford had ever imagined.

Next Jackson bought a large portion of the Durell Vineyard in southwestern Sonoma Valley, with its rocky soil and cool winds that slowed the ripening and maintained the grape's acidity. Durell's Chardonnay fruit was special, but Jackson would never let on how much he wanted it, and back in the glut days, he had been merciless in negotiating contracts for those grapes in that mother of all buyer's markets. Never letting out how he could not have got by without Durell, or how cash poor he had been at the time, he had negotiated a ridiculous deal on the phone, telling the owner he'd take the grapes on spec, wouldn't pay a dime until the spring when the wine he made with them was ready, and if that wine was good— and only if it was good—then he'd pay top dollar. If the wine wasn't good, then Durell would have to pay Jackson to make the wine and sell it back to the vineyard. Ridiculous, vineyard manager Steve Hill thought—who the heck did this Jackson guy think he was? But in the end Durell accepted the terms, as did the other growers Jackson sought out during the glut. The wine that came from those Durell grapes had been amazing, Vintner's Reserve was a hit, and come spring Jackson paid a fair price as promised. Then he entered into a multiyear contract to make sure he'd get those luscious grapes in the years to come. And when Durell decided to sell, Jackson had been a welcome suitor.

Next came the Veeder Peak Vineyards in Napa Valley, Jackson's first property in the best-known part of California Wine Country, which he would rename Cardinale and establish as a producer of superpremium wines. Veeder Peak stood 1,500 feet above sea level in Napa's far corner of the Mayacamas Mountains, with poor, volcanic rock and loamy soil—the tough conditions that Jackson always said

sparked a response in grape DNA that commanded the vines to produce fruit, the plant's children, in intense, fecund bursts. In Veeder's
case, where the sixty-three acres of vineyard sat above the coastal
fog line, allowing a longer, warmer growing season well into November, that meant fruit with intense blueberry and blackberry flavors
and the aroma of violets, the backbone of some special Cabernet
Sauvignon blends that preeminent wine critic Robert Parker would
one day describe as "profound." Mount Veeder was its own appellation, and the Cardinale Winery soon expanded with the purchase of
the taller, colder Keyes Vineyard on Howell Mountain east of Veeder
Peak and a long-term grape contract with the independent grower
who controlled part of the century-old To Kalon Winery in Oakville,
where Napa's first premium wines had been made decades before
the first automobile or telephone or radio came along—an in-your-
face intrusion into an area that the Mondavis had long considered
theirs alone.

This entrée into Napa posed a bittersweet moment for Jackson,
who had chosen to make Sonoma the base of his empire but who
had passed on the chance back in the early seventies to buy one
of the finest Napa Valley wine properties at a fraction of its value.
Jackson had been representing the Bartoluccis in a foreclosure case.
The property had been their family business, the Madonna Winery
in Oakville, which they had sold a few years earlier to a partnership led by a former trucking magnate, W. E. Van Loben Sels. The
wines produced there were a critical success, but the business was
not, and the Bartolucci family ended up foreclosing on the property
and reclaiming it through Jackson's legal footwork. At that point
his clients offered to sell Jackson all six hundred acres of prime
Napa vineyards for $18 million—a property that, in a matter of
years if not months, would be worth several times that amount. The
deal included not just the land but also the Oakville winery and all
its inventory.

Jackson would later say he was not even tempted because he had
no interest in being a winemaker and even less interest in securing

that sort of financing to make such a purchase. "As a farmer, I love land, but I abhor debt, and that would have been too much debt for me then," Jackson recalled. "It was a beautiful property, and an enticing opportunity if you wanted to make wine. Passing it up ought to prove to anyone that I had no desire or intention of going into the wine business. Not voluntarily, anyway. Now, of course, I say, 'What a fool I was.' That property is worth more than 100 million now."

Purchased and held briefly by Inglenook, the property ended up becoming an important part of the then-growing Mondavi empire. Now, nearly two decades later, Jackson had his beachhead in Napa at last.

Jackson followed the Veeder Peak deal with the purchase of another old-line Napa brand, Robert Pepi Wines, to add to his artisanal collection. Then he made his next purchase to the south, obtaining another six hundred acres in the Santa Maria area of Santa Barbara not far from Cambria.

By then the company that had started out with 84 acres in Lake County had more than 5,000 acres of prime Wine Country property and ranked in the top ten California wine companies, with sales of 2 million cases a year. Jackson walked the hills and the vineyard rows of every one of those purchases, rubbing the soil in his big hands, tasting the grapes and the dirt, too, feeling the morning fog bleed into the blanching sun of California summer. He said he needed to know each place before he sunk his money, heart, and future into it. "This is one of the special places," he said atop Veeder Peak. "This is where the vines are stressed, the soil is thin, the nutrients aren't there. And so the vines can't have too many children. Their DNA is coded for that; the vines say, 'I have to survive, but how? I'll be making fewer children but making them more intense and flavored so the birds, bears, man, and bees will eat them and propagate the seed.' That's the survival technique coded into the vines, and it's activated only in this sort of special place. That's how the best and most intense flavors are created—not to please us or to feed us, but because that is how the grape ensures the next generation's survival."

Understanding and finding these "special places," as he called them, made it seem to those around him that Jackson was not merely assembling a real estate empire. He saw himself as playing with the grand forces of evolution, of allowing the grapes to realize their heritage and potential. This is how Jackson, the accidental winemaker, had come to think about grapes, how he anthropomorphized them as natural wonders endowed, if not with thoughts, then with will all their own.

AT THE SAME time Jackson angled to obtain holdings in every coastal *terroir* in California, he also lusted for another sort of property: he wanted to own his own barrel-making operation. And not just any barrels, but French oak barrels—unique, traditional, and, to Jackson's way of thinking, the gold standard. They were expensive to buy and import, painfully so, and impossible for a foreigner to own. These cooperages were part of the mystique and heritage of the French wine industry. So naturally Jess wanted one.

He had purchased barrels from a Missouri-based cooperage that handcrafted American oak barrels—fine barrels, Jackson told everyone, just beautiful. But they were not French oak. To most people, oak was oak: American, French, it all looked they same, cut the same, felt the same. But to winemakers, and to Jackson's taste, French oak held an ancient magic, a unique blend of weathered, toasty, earthy flavors, subtle yet unmistakable. The wine Jackson liked and wanted to make needed to sit inside barrels of French oak, soaking in the same magic they'd been using in Burgundy and Bordeaux for centuries, and he was spending a fortune for the privilege by importing copious quantities of barrels at up to $600 a pop, an insane expense at the volume he now maintained.

As early as 1990 he had been looking for a better, cheaper way to get those barrels, flying to France on business or for conferences, then slipping away to prowl the countryside where barrels were made, trying to learn how it was done. Did the French dry their oak in kilns, in a kind of industrial process that quickly leached out most of the tannins in the wood? Or did they weather and age the oak staves naturally, out in the field, for whole seasons, even several years, to get them just right? The French barrel makers proclaimed their methods a trade secret they'd never tell; the French government considered the country's oak trees a national treasure, not to be meddled with by foreign interests. These weren't conglomerates making barrels on massive assembly lines, but small village and town stave-making operations using time-tested methods that pre-dated the American Revolution, and the coopers were proud and protective. If you liked them, buy them, one barrel maker told Jackson. But don't pry into our secrets.

But he did pry. On one trip he and one of his executives, Tom Selfridge, were literally climbing through barbed wire fences to spy on a stave mill Jackson admired, his pants shredded on the barbs. But he saw how the barrel staves were made—not within a speedy kiln but with the slow and steady aging nature exerts on all things living and dead, the staves spread out on a field in the open air, exposed to sun and wind and storm. There the little bugs and bac-teria and the progress of seasons aged the wood naturally, the long rainy season washing out the heavy tannins over two to three years, a completely natural, unhurried process that fascinated Jackson, that linked those barrels to generations, to tradition, to something that for him went beyond process and chemistry. If the grapes had a voice, then the barrels carried a message, imbuing the wine placed in them with the molecules and mystique of the French countryside.

When he told of that trip, his daughter Jenny claimed he was a hopeless romantic. Her father shrugged. "What I know is we've got to have our own stave mill in France. We have to own a part of that."

No American winemaker had managed such a feat. None had ever tried as far as Jackson knew. But then no one had ever bought as many oak barrels as Jackson did. After several years of trying un-successfully to cut a partnership deal with a French cooper, Jackson asked the French national government for help, and to his surprise he got a favorable response. The government owned most of the oak forests in the country, and officials were amenable to a deal so long as it would not hurt French companies. They did not want a foreign company to come in and compete against local businesses in an already highly competitive, labor-intensive industry. Jackson swore he had no interest in selling barrels in France; he didn't really want to sell them at all. He needed to make wine with them and would use them all and only in the United States, he promised. The French trade officials green-lighted that concept, a winning deal all around—if they could find the right partner for Jackson, the right location and workforce. The French looked, but after six months the government liaisons hadn't been able to find a willing partner. A year later still no partner had stepped forward. Then, finally, a group of barrel makers in a small village outside the city of Epinal in a forested corner of northeastern France expressed interest. Their stave mill had closed down, and the whole village was out of work. This was a region with a proud, centuries-old tradition for making fine wood products: furniture, home siding, and, especially, barrels.

There were a couple of concessions Jackson had to make that no employees in the States would get: the fifteen key people at the now-shuttered mill were promised jobs for life, and when they died, their spouses would continue to receive their pay as pensions. Jackson also had to promise to pay for funeral expenses when these employees died. These conditions offended Jackson's free-market philosophy, but then again, he noted with a shrug, he couldn't make French oak wine barrels out of philosophy. He took the deal, and Merrain International, a barrel-building partnership, was born that brought together the French workforce, Kendall-Jackson, and a Missouri-based barrel maker, Independent Stave. The signing ceremony was televised, as the storyline—California winemaker pleading for French barrels—was a ratings winner for French television. A state-of-the-art facility soon sprang up outside of Epinal, updating the old mill with precision laser-cutting technology and an advanced computer tracking system that revealed the size, weight, birthplace, and aging time of every oak brought into the mill. But out in the yard traditional methods continued: the oak sat in the open, aging naturally, in the weather and sun.

The upshot: instead of paying $600 each for barrels with a useful life of about four years, Jackson's cost dropped to $300 for the same barrel, shipping included. Multiplied by 20,000, that represented a very substantial return on his investment. The French barrel company not only paid for itself time and again, but it also gave him a huge advantage over other winemakers.

"We are unique," Jackson crowed at the next national sales conference as he sought to rev up the troops to sell more wine. "We are the only American winery that owns a stave mill in France. That's a major point of differentiation against all the other guys. It's another hook for you to sell us."

Jackson wasn't done with Europe yet, however. If he was making barrels there, he told his family, then Kendall-Jackson ought to be making wine there, too. He and Barbara had vacationed in Italy, and she fell in love with the Chianti region of Tuscany, where wine had been made since the days of the Roman Empire. In 1994 they decided to invest some of their Vintner's Reserve income in the 2,000-acre property of Villa Arceno, with its vineyards, olive orchards, and villa, where the family could vacation as well as make premium Italian wines.

Jackson had also begun looking for vineyards in the grape-growing regions of Chile and Argentina, where the land was relatively inexpensive and the climate benign, and where he sensed an opportunity to expand the Kendall-Jackson brand and its reach. American winemakers had "discovered" Chile and Argentina as a source of fine grapes and wines in the 1990s, notwithstanding the fact that Chileans had been making excellent French-style wines there longer than Californians had. The imports had also caught on with some American consumers, so Jackson decided to tap into that market as well, figuring he could market Chilean wines in both hemispheres. He had made several trips there with Jed Steele and Don Hartford, who had worked as a high school Spanish teacher before going to law school. Those initial visits were most notable for wild rides down back roads in the Chilean outback, tastings at a host of vineyards and villages, followed by some severe intestinal upset for Jackson and Hartford that had them laid up for weeks. But the trips produced no new wineries. Then Jackson dispatched a young winemaker, Randy Ullom, to South America to find the right properties.

The lanky Ullom, partial to cowboy boots and blue jeans for all occasions, was destined to play a pivotal role at Kendall-Jackson, but back in 1994 he was the sort of quirky freethinker Jackson gravitated toward when looking for new energy and ideas for his staff. Ullom had been studying to be a geologist when he took a break for a ski vacation in Chile and ended up staying two years, falling in love with a girl whose family was in the wine business, then falling in love with winemaking, too. When he left Chile and the girl to return to the States, he retained his love of wine and switched studies to viticulture; he was working at the Sonoma County winemaker DeLoach when Jackson found out about his Chilean connection. Jackson hired Ullom to start up a new Santa Barbara–based vineyard, Camelot, but Jackson warned him he would have to split his time with other projects. Next thing Ullom knew, he was hunting for properties in Chile and Argentina; banging down country roads with Jess, Barbara, and Don; breaking down in the middle of nowhere; and walking miles looking for food and transportation. It was a typical Jess Jackson adventure that ended up with a borrowed school bus and an impromptu trip down a deserted Argentine road that ended at an amazing parcel of mountainous land perfect for a vineyard, where no one was making wine yet but where many would follow once they saw what Jackson had built there. The Tapiz Winery was born in the highlands of Argentina's Mendoza wine region, while across the border in Chile Jackson launched Vina Calina Vineyards in the Casablanca Valley in the Andean foothills. Suddenly, the little Lakeport winemaker was growing and bottling fine wines on three continents.

Jackson employed a curious marketing principle for most of these acquisitions. He called it the Rule of the Hard "C"—he liked names that included the phonetic hard C for his wines and wineries: Kendall-Jackson, Cambria, Camelot, Hartford-Court, Vina Calina, La Crema, LoKoya, Cardinale. With few exceptions (such as the family name Stonestreet), Jackson went with that particular sound for his wines, convinced that it resonated with consumers as memorable and pleasing. "It's not scientific, but it works," he said. "Names matter, and those names work for us. The hard 'C' is not a hard sell." His employees and winemakers shrugged noncommittally about this particular foible of Jackson's; this was Jess's theory, not theirs, but he was the boss, Ullom recalled. "Who's going to argue with him? He's only the most successful winemaker of his times."

By 1995, just a dozen years after his first run of Vintner's Reserve sold out, Jackson had expanded his wine business from one field of grapes and a remote hillside winery to more than 5,000 acres of California vineyards with three wineries in operation, one coming out of mothballs, and another in the environmental review stage—with another 1,000 acres of grapes and three wineries abroad. Kendall-Jackson by then had joined the ranks of the top ten winemakers in the country, reaching nearly 2 million cases sold and $250 million in annual sales. KJ's wines were the most requested in American restaurants, and for the previous two years Kendall-Jackson had led all US wineries in wine judging medals. No winery had grown so big so fast in the history of the California wine industry. And even though there were higher-volume winemakers such as Gallo churning out more than two-thirds of the gallons of wine produced in the state, Jackson had become a leader in superpremium wines ($7–$14 a bottle) and *the* leader in ultrapremium wines ($14 and up)—a segment of the wine market that was comparatively small in quantity and yet, because of the quality and the price it commanded, was seizing a majority of the profits.

Jackson may not have been the only one driving this change in consumer choices toward better, pricier wines and a new industry sweet spot, but his peers certainly saw him, for good or ill, as leading the charge—which was one reason *Wine & Spirits Magazine* named Kendall-Jackson the 1995 winery of the year and the *New York Times* branded him "the brash prince of wine country." But the capstone to this rapid period of expansion, acquisition, and accolades came that same year back in Sonoma County, the *terroir* Jackson had come to love best and to call home. He would purchase a property that entranced him with its beauty and potential more than any other he would buy or vie for, land that would come to define the entire Kendall-Jackson image and enterprise. Overnight that one purchase would almost double the company's real estate holdings—and bring Jess Jackson his very own mountain.

This property had first caught Jackson's eye in the late sixties, back when he had just started toying with the idea of buying a farm as a weekend getaway from his law practice and land prices in Sonoma County were a fraction of what they would be in the near future. This was six years before his chance meeting with the old winemaker Hank Bartolucci put Jackson on course to buy the Lakeport property and long before he had given serious thought to trading courtrooms for vineyards. Jackson had been looking for a property to buy in partnership with a golfing buddy, Nick Primiani, best known for leading the San Francisco office of famed architect Welton Beckett, designer of the city's milestone One Market Plaza and a host of other California landmarks. Jackson and Primiani had heard about a beautiful property for sale in Sonoma County, the sprawling J Bar B Ranch, where the owner had raised Irish wolfhounds, a stable of prize-winning cutting horses, and a herd of Hereford, Guernsey, and Holstein dairy cows since World War II. At 5,400 acres, the landmark ranch encompassed all of the 2,800-foot-tall Black Mountain—the highpoint in Alexander Valley—along with miles of rolling pastureland, making it one of the largest agricultural holdings available anywhere in the county. In 1969 Jackson's bid lost to a better offer from the founder of an upscale chain of Bay Area men's stores, Roos/Atkins. Edward Gauer had sold his share of that business for $16.5 million in

1965—$122 million in 2013 dollars—and decided to retire to the life of gentleman farmer on the gorgeous terrain of Black Mountain.

Gauer built a spacious, low-slung house in a muted, contemporary style with plenty of native redwood and stone on the outside, the interior designed with a strong Asian aesthetic he had come to love from his and his wife's travels abroad. The dominant feature was a stand of towering, rustling, century-old oak trees surrounding the house, cooling the grounds, framing the views. Once the living quarters were squared away, Gauer set to work trying to grow things on all that rich land stretching nearly as far as he could see from his hilltop vantage. But he knew clothes, not farming, and though he hired a procession of experts to find and raise the right crop or livestock for the newly christened Gauer Ranch, nothing seemed to work. Initially, he planted prunes; then he tried herding sheep and later raising cattle. None was self-sustaining; they all lost money. And while Gauer didn't need to be any richer, he didn't want his slice of Sonoma paradise to be a money pit either. Then he decided to plant grapes, and at last Black Mountain could strut its stuff.

The rich and varied soils of the many ridges and benches that wrinkled the mountainside like an old man's brow could grow just about any grape variety Gauer might like. Parts of the mountain remained warm and sun-soaked while other areas lay blanketed in a ghostly, cooling sea of fog for long, flavor-nurturing hours. A natural spring on the ranch put out seven hundred gallons of water a minute, more than enough to carpet the whole mountain with vines. Such a massive planting would be neither desirable nor possible (only about 20 percent of the mountain is physically plantable, which is a good thing, as the mountain is prime habitat for a host of native animal, plant, and bird species, including cougars, wild boar, and a variety of owls). By the mid-seventies Gauer had a mature harvest, and as Jackson would do in Lakeport, Gauer started selling his grapes to a number of wineries, where the fruit ended up in higher-end bottlings at such winemakers at Chateau St. Jean, then a well-regarded independent, though it would eventually be absorbed by a conglomerate.

Gauer's most famous contribution to the wine world came in 1982 when he planted Chardonnay grapes on a high ridge near the top of the mountain, an area dubbed Upper Barn. The fruit from that spot became famous among winemakers for its high quality, and Sonoma County winemakers Helen Turley and Sir Peter Michael produced some legendary handcrafted Upper Barn Chardonnay. (Even after Jackson bought the mountain, he continued to supply Turley and Michael with Upper Barn fruit, saying he felt Kendall-Jackson should support small, innovative, high-quality wineries by making its rare and finer fruit accessible. Those Chardonnays have sold for hundreds of dollars a bottle.) After a few years Gauer figured he ought to be making his own wine with some of his fantastic grapes and renamed his vineyard Gauer Estate Winery (though he did not actually have a winery until 1987 when he bought Vinwood, a few miles away in Geyserville). He put out a couple of well-reviewed wines, but he ended up bottling only a few very small vintages at his new winery, most of which were sold as private-label wines to wholesalers and brokers. The best wines out of Gauer's harvests were made by others.

At the same time Kendall-Jackson had taken off with a far less regal home base than Black Mountain, Gauer's winery was barely on anyone's tasting road map. At age eighty-five, less than two years after he had bought Vinwood, Gauer tired of the whole enterprise and sold what had become one of the most valuable pieces of real estate in Sonoma County to the Huntington Beach Company, the real estate development arm of what had been Standard Oil when Gauer bought his property but was by then, thanks to a merger with Gulf Oil, known as the Chevron Corporation. Chevron paid $35 million for the mountain, ranch, vineyards, the Vinwood Winery, and its stock of still-fermenting wine. Chevron announced that it would continue maintaining the vineyard in the short term but hinted strongly that the company envisioned developing the property with a golf course and up to 150 Wine Country mansions. At the time of the sale the county had already zoned the property to allow it to be subdivided into fifty-four "ranchettes" to be built on the mountain.

While Chevron entertained visions of a $250 million profit from developing such prime property into gentrified estates, conservationists and county politicians mobilized after Gauer sold out, promising to fight the conversion of a scenic landmark and valuable agricultural land into "McMansion-ville," as the locals took to calling it. Facing the likelihood that, in an increasingly green-minded Sonoma County, Chevron might never prevail in getting such a subdivision approved, the company began discussing with county officials the possibility of a conservation easement. Such a designation would preserve the land as open space in perpetuity while allowing Chevron to claim an enormous tax deduction and continue to earn money from the vineyard (most likely by leasing the operation to an actual wine company). But in the midst of the easement negotiations, Jackson, who had never forgotten how much he loved that property, swooped in, bought the Vinwood Winery for $10 million in 1993, and secured an option to buy the ranch should Chevron decide to sell it in lieu of the easement. A year later Jackson ponied up another $19 million, and the Gauer Ranch—redubbed Alexander Mountain Estates in honor of the valley's early pioneer and Jackson's grandfather's middle name—was his. Only the Gauer house and a few surrounding acres were held out, as Gauer and his wife continued living there after Chevron bought the rest of the mountain. Gauer died in 1991, but his wife, Marion, still lived there after Jackson bought the mountain and surrounding land. And suddenly Jackson had more than 8,000 acres of vineyard land.

As Jackson laid plans for expanding the vineyards and for building a home and satellite office complex on his new mountain, he and his viticulture experts began combing through the property, ridge by ridge, creek bed by creek bed. They found twenty-three distinct soil types, a dozen microclimates, and thirty-five abandoned, rusted hulks of old cars that had been dumped in creeks and canyons, some of them looking like they had rolled off the assembly line before Jackson was born. The property was pretty shabby in parts, overgrown, undermaintained—but it was a veritable laboratory for growing superior wine grapes, for creating new blends and flavors, and for experimenting with the next big thing for Kendall-Jackson to sell. Jackson and his viticulturists laid plans for about eight hundred acres of vineyards up and down the five separate ridges rippling across the mountain: Cabernet Sauvignon in one, then Merlot, Cabernet Franc, Sauvignon Blanc, and, finally, Chardonnay. Room was left for some very small plots of other varieties as well. Jackson insisted that all the coveted grapes on his mountain be grown with extra care and expense; the average grape was touched twelve times during the growing season, but Alexander Mountain grapes would get nineteen touches or more. They would be pampered like infants in the king's nursery, never left alone, never out of sight. This was Jackson's new playground. There would be no more trips to his old getaway in Lakeport. That was the past. Now he was hiking through his new domain, envisioning what it would look like after five years of work, and ten, and then twenty.

And even then he was not finished indulging his obsession for new properties. That year politicians and pundits were stoking fears of inflation and recession that scared off many investors. They'd be proved wrong in the end, as 1995 would be the year of a "soft landing" for the economy, heralding the start of consistent growth that lasted throughout the rest of the Clinton years. But at the time nervousness dominated the economy, real estate prices dipped, and everyone else in Wine County thought about selling, not buying. So, naturally, Jackson pushed to buy more. He leveraged his future profits and real estate for a couple more mammoth loans and scooped up three more vast, signature properties. The first was the opulent estate known as Graystone, a 1,200-acre Arabian horse farm in the Bennett Valley area of Sonoma County, south and east of Alexander Valley, with perfect cool, foggy conditions for Pinot Noir and Chardonnay but barely touched by the wine business. Bennett Valley had only 650 acres of vineyards and four wineries in the whole AVA (compared to 15,000 acres of vines and forty-two wineries in busy Alexander Valley). Jackson knew an opportunity when he saw it. The property had its own lake—an essentially limitless water supply—but there were no grapes grown there, just stables and an indoor arena for raising and training Arabians. A local hardware and home improvement store magnate, Bill Friedman, had built Graystone more than a decade earlier during a national craze for the fine horses. At the height of the fashionable horse farm, it hosted lavish celebrations and Hollywood weddings featuring elephants, hot-air balloons, paddleboats, and the ever-present, elegant Arabians. But the craze fizzled, and Graystone went on the market; Jackson paid $8 million, renamed it Jackson Park, and laid plans for vineyards, a winery, and, perhaps, conversion of the stables to the horse culture he most loved: thoroughbreds.

Next he bought the 1,250-acre Clegg Ranch in Knights Valley, on the eastern border of Alexander Valley, on a historic dairy farm property where the owner, Douglas Clegg, had invented the automatic milking machine. The land was gorgeous, perfect for wine, but the structures were dismal, an old adobe house and a lodge built of stones that Banke dubbed "the Big Ugly." Jackson renamed the place Kellogg Ranch, derived from the property's original 1870s incarnation as a mining center known as Kellogg. He laid plans for a winery and the valley's first tasting room, notwithstanding the shotgun-toting mob that had turned up a few years earlier to oppose (successfully) another winemaker's plans for Knights Valley's first tasting room.

Finally, Jackson scooped up a broad valley property known as Jim Town just a few miles south of his new Alexander Mountain estate. He immediately proposed building a sprawling, 500,000-case winery and vineyard on the Jim Town site to be dubbed the new Stonestreet Winery, replacing the little operation with the same name opened on Jackson's first Sonoma County land purchase, across the street from his Franz Creek home.

Every one of these purchases and Jackson's plans for them stoked some controversy and opposition. Kendall-Jackson had become something of a behemoth in its Sonoma County stronghold, and the era had ended in which he could expect the sort of free pass often given small businesses with small footprints. An era of constant battles began in its place.

10

Gallo, Gall,
Greens, and Growth:
Jess Jackson at War

J ESS JACKSON DIDN'T MIND GOING TO WAR. HIS LIFE AS
a lawyer was built on it, first on behalf of the state seeking to
construct a modern California, then on behalf of the property owners and developers he previously had battled for the state. In both
incarnations he saw not the seeming contradiction but a continuing,
if evolving, dedication to fight on what he called "the side of the
angels." It was simple enough in his eyes: he was creating jobs and
vital public infrastructure in the first instance, championing property rights and creating jobs and important private infrastructure
in the other. Who could argue with that? He saw his creation of a
major winemaking power and his simultaneous advocacy for small
and family wine companies in the same way. His detractors might
have seen cynical spin or conflicts of interest, but this ability to
maintain a moral certitude even as he tacked in a completely different direction was one reason so many friends and colleagues found
him such a compelling character to be around. "He inspires people,"

his chief winemaker, Randy Ullom, would say. "He's the irresistible force because he so clearly believes in what he's saying and doing."

In this new era of battles, some of the conflicts were a good fit for Jackson's preferred self-image as advocate for the rights of the oppressed. He was suing the biggest and most powerful wine company in the world, Gallo, and it wasn't just business—it was personal. He was suing state wine regulators in California and elsewhere in the country. He was warring with entrenched beverage distributors and the Wine Institute trade association, which, he believed, slighted family wineries in favor of corporate behemoths. These were the battles Jackson relished.

In other quarters, though, Jackson found himself in the unfamiliar position of being targeted by people who saw *him* as the face of a big, bullying corporation. He battled conservationists over his cutting of oak trees on land he wanted to plant with grapes. County planning and zoning officials delayed his winery construction plans with questions about traffic, water use, and pollution. And he had repeated tussles with neighbors who objected to the construction of wineries and tasting rooms in their quiet rural communities, where one weekly newspaper branded him Wine Country's top "robber baron." For years he had been cast as the brash and admirable upstart of Wine Country, the mystery man with the Midas touch for grapes and land. Suddenly, he was being portrayed as the corporate heavy, and it jarred him, even wounded him, though he hid this by reacting to the criticism with anger and intransigence. This is the flip side of his combination of idealism and certitude: a my-way-or-the-highway approach that, just as it helped end his marriage to Jane, also needlessly exacerbated some of his winery battles, particularly on the environmental front.

In any case, during this period in the 1990s the complaints, hearings, and lawsuits were flying around Kendall-Jackson like champagne corks. In most of these disputes the new and uncomfortable role of lightning rod didn't stop Jackson from making a pretty good case for himself—and in the end he would prevail in all but one. And even in the one conflict he lost, the public perception, if not the legal decision, ended up favoring him.

In Wine Country he became a polarizing figure. Other upstarts appreciated his flouting of the area's traditional veneer of gentility in favor of a more pugilistic approach. The old guard fumed. To them, Jackson had not only abandoned the winemaker's preferred behind-closed-doors, good-ol'-boy way of resolving disputes; he was also ignoring their accumulated, multigenerational wisdom about how to make, price, and market wine. Even more galling to them was the fact that his business model was not simply working; it was winning. So when lawsuits and conflicts arose, even some winemakers Jackson considered friends, or at least allies, would express shock at his tactics and take his opponents' side wherever possible.

In truth, Jackson's tactics didn't really surprise many in the business. It's not as if he hadn't been clear about who and what he was since he arrived in Lakeport and started showing up on the doorstep of the likes of Barney Fetzer, charming and elbowing and competing his way into the water with the big fish. He was a tough negotiator and lawyer harboring not a shred of shyness about asserting himself—or his rights in and out of court. The era of conflicts had been telegraphed for years, ushered in with Jackson's acrimonious parting in 1990 with his first winemaker, Jed Steele, a breakup that inevitably landed in Jackson's most familiar domain: the courtroom.

Neither man cared to speak of it years later, their breakup as difficult as any divorce and in many ways just as costly. The bottom line was that Jackson had started the 1990s aiming to sell 1 million cases of Vintner's Reserve a year (a goal he would soon meet and surpass). Steele, however, realized he didn't want to be that sort of winemaker. There was industry power and prestige in making and selling that much wine of that high quality—and money, too—but Steele made it clear he missed the more intimate brand of winemaking that he had known in his first job at Napa's Stony Hill Winery, then at Edmeades, and even in the early days of Kendall-Jackson. It seemed to others at the company that Steele liked the days of the old trailer at Lakeport, with its seat-of-the-pants winemaking, the giddy excitement when that call came in from the White House—a time when one call could transform the whole business. He liked a wine company where the owner had to throw on an aqualung to unclog the pump in the pond to save the vineyard.

But there was no turning that clock back—not on the company or on Jackson's ambition. To Steele, the issue boiled down to the old corporate model versus the lone craftsman laboring in his small wine cellar. He and Jackson argued over it time and again, with Jackson vowing to never compromise on the quality of the wine no matter how Kendall-Jackson evolved and grew, and Steele saying that he believed him but it was the quality of the winemaking experience that concerned him. Jackson wanted to build a vast warehouse and winery filled with thousands of individual oak barrels—handmade wine on epic scale, the winemakers relying on computers and robotics and software that would have to be written in-house from scratch because nobody had ever tried anything like it before. Jackson wanted to make history. Steele just wanted to make wine. Maybe Kendall-Jackson couldn't turn the clock back, but Jed Steele could, at least for himself.

So in August 1990 he and Jackson agreed to part company, though Steele agreed to stay on as a consultant and to train his replacement, John Hawley, whose departure from Clos du Bois had caused such acrimony between Jackson and the rival winery's owner. Steele wanted to start his own small wine company so that he could exert the level of control in his own shop that Jackson reserved for himself at Kendall-Jackson. This progression from novice to journeyman to master winemaker in the employ of others to independent winemaker is a traditional path in the industry—not the only path but nothing out of the ordinary. Winemakers, like CEOs, are control freaks, and if they're good, many eventually will want to have the final word on their wines. Steele would be only the first of many of Jackson's winemakers who would make that leap, and Jackson would take pride in that evolution—most of the time. Not so with Jed Steele.

The breakup seemed amicable enough at first. Steele was upfront about his plan to support himself by consulting with other wineries as well as Kendall-Jackson. This, too, was a long-standing wine-maker practice of collegiality and knowledge sharing that benefited everyone in the wine business, including Jackson, who had saved that first stuck fermentation and launched his breakthrough Chardonnay with a team of consultants from competing wineries. The agreement Steele and Jackson signed in 1990 called for a payment of $400,000 over the course of the contract, plus $10,000 a month during the winemaker training period, a generous severance package. But the deal and the relationship between the two towering, strong-willed men soon soured. After paying him only one installment of $125,000, Jackson told Steele, whom he once described as a "winemaking treasure," to get out, cutting short the consulting and the payments. Jackson accused his former top winemaker of giving competitors inside information on Kendall-Jackson and its sourcing of grapes.

Steele denied Jackson's claims and said he was the one being wronged by his former employer, and he sued Jackson for the rest of the promised $400,000. Such a contract dispute normally would garner little or no publicity. Neither would two of the countersuits Jackson filed in return: one accusing Steele of intentionally ruining a last batch of Chardonnay, the second alleging that the departed winemaker interfered with Kendall-Jackson's existing deals with other grape growers.

Jackson's third countersuit, however, became an unintended bombshell. To his surprise, it escaped the confines of the quiet back-water of the Lake County Superior Court to rivet and roil the wine industry, drawing press coverage from the *New York Times*, the *Wall Street Journal*, and the international media. In it, Jackson accused Steele of divulging trade secrets to other winemakers: the process and recipe for making and blending Kendall-Jackson's most import-ant product, Vintner's Reserve Chardonnay. The secret to that wine's success belonged to Kendall-Jackson, not Jed Steele, and Jackson in his third countersuit sought what amounted to a gag order against the man he had slaved beside for years in Lakeport.

The outrage over this move, genuine and feigned, spread faster than phylloxera as other winemakers rallied behind Steele and lined up to testify against what they asserted was a bullying and over-reaching Jess Jackson. This, too, took Jackson by surprise. He had assumed that other winery owners would agree with him because surely none of them wanted their winemakers to be free to trade inside information to their competitors the moment they walked out the door. That, in Jackson's view, would not be openness; it would amount to betrayal and theft of intellectual property.

Instead, a chorus of wine industry critics emerged to support Steele publicly. Many, if not most, were Kendall-Jackson competitors eager to claim a piece of the emerging premium wine market Jackson had grabbed for himself. Mondavi, Parducci, Buena Vista, and others all came to Steele's defense. They derided the notion that winemaking techniques used by hundreds, even thousands of winemakers worldwide could be classified as trade secrets. What would happen to the tradition of open exchange between winemakers that had helped California Wine Country advance to prominence in recent years? "If Kendall-Jackson prevails," Robert Mondavi told the *Wine Insider* newsletter, "and I don't think it will, a winemaker won't know what to do. How would he practice his occupation?"

According to Mondavi and the other big-name winemakers who sided with Steele, there really were no secret methods Kendall-Jackson could claim as its own. Yes, there were patented *devices* in the wine world—Gallo owned quite a few of them—but methods, recipes, the steps taken to turn grapes into wine, were another matter. On that level wine was all about the nose and the palate and the winemaker's artistry. Skill and panache were not trade secrets. Jess Jackson, in this view, was trying to patent poetry and to cripple Steele's ability to ply his trade outside of Kendall-Jackson's cellars.

This piling on included a basic assumption repeated time and again by these critics: that Jackson's argument with Steele primarily concerned the method of sweetening Vintner's Reserve and that Jackson was outrageously trying to claim ownership of a common and well-known technique for spiking a wine's sugar content. In speaking out, Steele's allies invariably referred to the not-so-secret story of Jackson's stuck fermentation and the methods Steele could have used to simulate it in subsequent vintages. Everyone knew that Vintner's Reserve was made a bit sweeter than previous incarnations of Chardonnay—a quality his newly outspoken critics would cite with an air of contempt, Jackson would recall, notwithstanding the rest of the industry's rush to copy the market leader. And his critics all claimed there were only a few ways to achieve that sweetening effect, none of them secret. Either the winemaker stopped the fermentation early for some of the wine in the VR blend, it was said, thereby preserving residual sugars and sweetening the flavor. Or he used the process of *Sussreserve*, the German term for holding back unfermented grape juice after the crush, then adding it to the final fermented wine to sweeten the flavor. This would also cut the dryness of the wine, which was why *Sussreserve* was most commonly used for dessert wines and considered a kind of cheat for other types of wine. The few other ways to sweeten a wine were all variations on those themes, and none were hush-hush. "After all these years of making wine," legendary winemaker John Parducci said, "I have never heard that there were any secrets to it."

Jackson had expected to be attacked by Mondavi, given their acrimonious dealings over Tepusquet in Santa Barbara. He figured the Mondavis would be happy to see him stumble in his battle with Steele and so appear diminished in the public eye. But Jackson was wounded by the stance of some of his friends in the business, particularly the venerable old founder of the Parducci Winery, who had been crushing grapes in Mendocino County since the 1930s and had bought some of Jackson's earliest grape harvests.

Nevertheless, Jackson refused to back down, saying the Steele faction had it all wrong. The real secret of his Chardonnay was not the sweetening; it was the blending: the proportions and identities of all the coastal wines he mixed to achieve a certain complex yet consumer-friendly flavor profile, part of a nine-step process, from crush to shipping to separation in stainless and oak, to achieve the right sweet-dry balance. He had spent years demonstrating with his blending seminars just how hard it was to duplicate his secret formula. That part of the process really was unique to Kendall-Jackson, he argued, and it was his, not Steele's, to hide or share as he pleased. Jackson submitted its details in writing to the court, under seal, so that a judge could see for himself that there was more to Jackson's trade secret than throwing sweet grape juice into the mix.

"Those comments about our unique process were just ridiculous," an indignant Jackson would later say. "And they knew it. They just saw a chance to tarnish our brand. I had not until that moment realized how much our success threatened the old guard."

Privately, Jackson hated being portrayed as the corporate bully going after his now-self-employed former winemaker. In Jackson's view, exactly the opposite was going on. It was Steele, Jackson asserted, who was teaming up with far more powerful corporate interests in order to undermine Kendall-Jackson. One of Steele's main clients was the Stimson Lane Company, owner of Chateau Ste. Michelle Winery in Washington, and a newer acquisition, Villa Mt. Eden in Napa Valley, which was gearing up to make premium wines in direct competition with Kendall-Jackson. Steele had become their hired gun, Jackson complained. Stimson Lane was a subsidiary of the giant multinational company Phillip-Morris. Jackson had been furious with Steele over this and felt his old winemaker had to be stopped—by court order, with the threat of heavy financial penalties— from revealing Kendall-Jackson secrets to Stimson Lane.

To help make his case, Jackson hired attorney Jeffrey Chanin of San Francisco, who had won a similar trade-secret suit to protect the proprietary recipe of Mrs. Fields chocolate chip cookies. But Jackson, who hated to delegate any task that he was actively interested in, pulled the legal strings and directed the strategy at the Lakeport trial and even heatedly lectured Chanin during breaks in the trial. The whole three-week proceeding was defined by the bitterness between Steele and Jackson, each man feeling betrayed by the other. They would snipe at each other in the courthouse hall-ways; Steele had to spend days being questioned on the stand. After the trial decades would pass before they spoke again, and even then their conversation would consist of only pleasantries exchanged at a chance meeting.

The judge on the case, Lake County Superior Court judge John J. Golden, eventually decided the case for both men, though the key victory went to Jackson. Steele prevailed on his claim that Jackson owed him another $275,000. This finding was blunted, however, because Jackson won monetary damages, too: the judge agreed that Steele had interfered with Jackson's relationship with grape growers by trying to negotiate his own deals for the new Steele Winery. More importantly, Judge Golden, in a detailed forty-one-paged opinion, agreed with Jackson on his claim that there was a trade-secret and unique winemaking process that had to be protected, and he banned Steele from disclosing it to other winemakers.

The industry mavens who had belittled Jackson's claims as preposterous early in the case now asserted that the matter was deadly serious, arguing that the ruling would have a chilling effect on the entire industry. "Ruling Stuns State Vintners," the *San Francisco Chronicle* headline read. "A Cork on Chatter: Court Ruling Could Chill Free Flow of Winemaking Data," the *Los Angeles Times* headlined its report, adding that Steele was "flabbergasted," then quoting him as insisting, "There are no secrets in this industry. What we did at Kendall-Jackson was widely known by a lot of people." The Associated Press, meanwhile, warned in its headline, "Trade Secrets Ruling Could Discourage Sharing Among Wineries." Wine-makers around the state would no longer be able to share ideas and discoveries, it was said. The "Yeast Police" would be checking up to see if winemakers were sharing fermentation tips. This would spell the end of collegiality in the industry, several opined, and a new cold war of wine would erupt.

Nothing of the kind happened, Jackson would later note. It was all hype, silly and wrong on a number of counts—an attempt, as

Jackson saw it, by his critics to try the case in the media after it had been lost in court. The over-the-top fears were, by any measure, unsupportable. Because the case had been tried in a county-level court rather than a higher "court of record," the ruling had no legal effect beyond the boundaries of Lake County; absent an appeal, it set no precedent and had no real effect on the California wine industry. Furthermore, the ruling had been narrowly focused on Kendall-Jackson and Steele's relationship and contracts, coupled with Jackson's evidence of a specific proprietary process. It set no sweeping limit on Steele's (or anyone else's) ability to confab with other winemakers about their own techniques and experiments. Besides, Jackson noted, if other wineries wanted openness and sharing with competitors, and if they truly felt there were no secrets in the making of wine, this ruling did nothing to stop them or alter their supposedly collegial ways. Share away, Jackson told them. Just stop going after *my* trade secrets. Indeed, Steele continued consulting with other wineries even as he built up a small and respected operation of his own, Steele Wines. After the initial flurry of media attention, the ruling in the case faded into obscurity. Steele initially vowed to appeal, but it was never filed, and the case ended up having exactly no effect on the way wineries in California did business, though it would be cited for years as evidence of what Jackson's critics alleged were his paranoid and bullying ways.

But the case had been an edifying experience for Jackson. When so many other winemakers and competitors came out of the woodwork to line up against him, it suggested to Jackson that they were afraid of what he was building—afraid and jealous and, he believed, willing to strike below the belt. He began to anticipate another attempt to uncover some vital company secret or to infringe on his trademark or brand.

He didn't have long to wait. A squadron of enormous yellow Caterpillar D-9 bulldozers soon arrived in Sonoma County, surplus earthmovers that had been used to build the trans-Alaska oil pipeline. Now they were in the service of Ernest and Julio Gallo, the biggest wine company in the world, which was moving into Sonoma like an advancing armada. No longer would Gallo farm only the Great Central Valley, Jackson's inferior interior. They had bought up huge swaths of Sonoma's coastal geography and were spending years plowing it under in the biggest conversion of wildland and forest to farmland in Wine Country history. More than 6,000 acres were scraped clean, hilltops leveled, streams dammed. Near Healdsburg, with its emerging locavore food scene and quaint and leafy downtown, Gallo constructed a $100-million, eight-building winery complex with an aging cellar bigger than a football field and bristling with loading docks and mammoth fermentation tanks. The facility was designed to produce nearly 5 million cases of wine a year.

Gallo sold a fourth of the wine consumed in America at that time, but that volume was almost all bottom shelf and cheap. Gallo's share of the premium wine market, where Kendall-Jackson so profitably led, was virtually nonexistent in the early 1990s. Ernest Gallo, then the eighty-three-year-old leader of a $2 billion winemaking dynasty, who was still known to wander into markets and rearrange shelves to expose bottles of Gallo while hiding competitors' labels, was determined to seize a major piece of that premium space. And for that he needed premium grapes with a premium address. The Modesto-based company with its roots in John-Steinbeck-*Grapes-of-Wrath* country needed a new base, a new division: Gallo of Sonoma, a bid to rule premium wine sales just as Gallo had long ruled screw top and Thunderbird. "He's looking at that and just salivating," Michael Mondavi, CEO of the Robert Mondavi Winery, told the *Los Angeles Times* in 1994. Of course, Mondavi, which had no great presence at that time in in the $10+ premium market either, was also about to take aim at Kendall-Jackson's dominance with its own high-end Sonoma line of wines, Mondavi "Coastal" Chardonnays and Cabernet Sauvignon.

Initially, Jackson was optimistic about the threat posed by Gallo. The brothers could buy all the land they wanted, put up massive wine factories, plow through the county from Cloverdale to Santa Rosa. "At the end of the day, there will be no handcrafted methods, no individual barrel aging. Gallo would still be Gallo," Jackson predicted. The wine would be mass-produced and mediocre, he figured, but even if the wines were good, they would lack the complexity and craft of true premium wines owing to the bulk-production techniques. He felt it would take one miraculous makeover for any consumer to believe Gallo could make a great premium wine.

Jackson's prognostication seemed, at first, on the money. Gallo spent a fortune marketing its initial line of premium wines released under the Gallo Sonoma label in 1994, but they did poorly with both wine critics and consumers. The next year, however, Gallo launched a new brand of premium Sonoma wines—a coastal Chardonnay, a Pinot Noir, a Zinfandel, and a Sauvignon Blanc—and everything changed.

As Jackson saw it, the label and the bottle style bore a startling resemblance to those of Kendall-Jackson's Vintner's Reserve. Strong enough, Jackson fumed, to confuse consumers into thinking they were buying Jackson's wines when they were actually about to guzzle Gallo. Indeed, the name "Gallo" was nowhere to be seen on the label or logo. Instead, the brand was called "Turning Leaf." Priced on the low end of the premium scale, Turning Leaf landed on the same shelf as Kendall-Jackson, but priced several dollars less. Turning Leaf sold 1 million cases in its first year, moving from 649th place in Chardonnay sales to the number 2 spot—right behind Kendall-Jackson Vintner's Reserve.

The lawsuit was filed within a matter of months.

GALLO AND JACKSON already had a long history of mutual animosity stemming from Jackson's representation a decade earlier of Joseph Gallo, the younger brother of the more famous Ernest and Julio Gallo. Joseph had worked a while for his brothers in the wine business, but he had never been considered part of the ownership or leadership at Gallo. Instead, he had launched his own successful cheese company based in California, which he called Joseph Gallo Cheese. His own brothers sued him in April 1986 for using the family name, and after a protracted battle of trademarks, the older brothers prevailed. Ernest and Julio had a long history of suing others for using the Gallo name, including an Italian chianti maker that had been in business longer that the Gallo brothers (they wore out the Italian firm with endless, costly legal filings), but their attack on their own little brother shocked even Gallo's supporters. Joseph Gallo had to rename his business, "Joseph Farms," though it remained successful despite the brand change. He was so upset, however, that long before the trade name case was resolved, he countersued his brothers, claiming they owed him a third of their wine company—and the billions that went with it—having allegedly cheated him out of his inheritance. The lawsuit portrayed a family history and business success story based on betrayal and double-dealing. Jess Jackson was Joseph Gallo's attorney early in the case, though another lawyer would eventually take over.

"He had a pretty good claim," Jackson recalled years later. "And I learned quite a bit about the Gallo family history. I felt for Joe."

Joe maintained that the Gallo grape and wine business began not with Ernest and Julio but with their and Joe's parents, which, he argued, meant that he should have inherited the business that Ernest and Julio had always claimed as solely their own.

The Gallo Wine Company, as it is known today, began in 1933, when Jess Jackson was three years old, and just a few months after the violent deaths of Ernest, Julio, and Joseph Gallo's parents, Joe Sr. and Susie. A coroner's jury ruled that Joe had shot his wife and then himself, a murder-suicide. The circumstances of the case were murky. The gun was found three feet from the outstretched hand of the elder Gallo, who had been shot in the temple and lay prone on the dining room floor. There was no suicide note. His eldest son, Ernest, told authorities that financial pressures were the likely motive, but just before the shooting, Joe Sr. had left a check in the mailbox to pay his taxes ahead of schedule. Joe Sr. had no will, but Susie left one, and it made clear that the three boys—Ernest and Julio were adults; Joe Jr. was thirteen at the time—were to share equally in the inheritance, which included Transamerica stock, vineyards, a farm, and cash. The older brothers were made legal guardians of Joe Jr., but when they took the inheritance and formed what would become the world's leading wine business, their little brother was not included. Only Ernest and Julio would own it and profit from it. Joe complained that he had never seen a penny of the inheritance. He claimed it all had been used to build the new business. Which meant, he argued, that he was entitled to a third of the multibillion-dollar wine business his brothers had built with it. His lawsuit sought $200 million in damages as well as the right to use the family name in his business, just like his brothers.

Before the trial Ernest and Julio offered to settle for $20 million, then rescinded the offer. By then Jackson was no longer on the case. The suit was later dismissed—by a judge who, it was later revealed, had business and financial ties to the Gallos. The same judge had been slated to preside over the Gallo's trademark lawsuit against Joseph Gallo Cheese but was forced to withdraw—only to be replaced by yet another judge whose old law firm had worked for the elder Gallo brothers. Joseph lost that trial, too; lost his company name; and lost his appeal of both decisions despite the evidence of judicial conflicts of interest. He suffered several strokes during the legal proceedings. Outside the courtroom the victorious Ernest Gallo told reporters his little brother's cheese was "garbage." They never spoke again.

That was Jess Jackson's introduction to the Gallo wine juggernaut, and it formed a lasting impression. He learned that the division of responsibility at Gallo was simple: Julio was the farmer; Ernest was the strategist and marketer and the brother most feared in the industry. "He was brilliant, but totally unethical," Jackson said of Ernest.

When Jackson began investigating Turning Leaf, he uncovered a range of allegations about Gallo's supposedly unethical conduct that included alleged sabotage of rival products. The Federal Trade Commission had investigated Gallo for alleged anticompetitive practices in 1978. Now Kendall-Jackson sales reps accused their Gallo counterparts of going into stores to rearrange the stock so that the new Gallo wines sat right next to Kendall-Jackson. Jackson's sales force would then move the two brands as far apart as possible, but the Gallo staff was much bigger, and so the shelving war became a losing battle for Jackson.

Then the calls started coming in—just a few, but enough to convince Jackson he had to act. Customers, he learned and later alleged in court, were complaining about the poor taste and quality of that new Kendall-Jackson line of budget wines, Turning Leaf.

THE JACKSON-GALLO lawsuit filed in San Francisco federal court garnered far more publicity—and provided better courtroom theater—than the Jess versus Jed trial five year earlier. There were two main media and spectator takes on the drama. To Jackson's supporters, it was David versus Goliath. To his detractors, the storyline was a less sympathetic Clash of the Wine Titans. Who would the wine old guard rally behind this time, given the industry's antipathy toward both Gallo and Jackson? And what were the wider industry implications? Again they were said to be huge. This time, unlike the overblown and largely silly claims in the Steele case suggesting that a Jackson victory would somehow put a cork in winemakers' ability to talk shop, *Kendall-Jackson Winery v. E. & J. Gallo Winery* had real potential to affect the industry. The decision could provide some firm guidelines in the largely gray area separating legitimate competition from copycat packaging—"palming off," in industry parlance, a "trade dress" violation in legalspeak. A jury would have to decide which version best fit the facts.

From the beginning Jackson had sketched out on one of his ubiquitous yellow legal pads all the ways the Turning Leaf wine seemed designed to resemble Kendall-Jackson: grape leaves turning from summer to fall hues of yellow, orange, and green, exactly the same shades; the same bottle neck with a broad flange; the same medallion; the same wax topping; the same clear view of the cork in the bottle because of the absence of foil. And unlike all the other Gallo wines to that point, including the Gallo Sonoma wines so heavily promoted a year before the Turning Leaf debut, this one carried the name Gallo nowhere. "That's no coincidence," Jackson said.

His attorney, Fred Furth, an antitrust expert, close friend, and fellow winemaker, thundered to the jury, "When they copy our label in such great detail, did they just forget to use the Gallo name? . . . Obviously what they're trying to do is trade on the Kendall-Jackson name."

Jackson was blunter in his emotional testimony. "They are stealing our business," he told jurors.

Furth pointed to internal Gallo memos and testimony, which he said proved the company had studied the premium market primarily by studying Kendall-Jackson, then sought to replicate its success. The minutes of one meeting quoted Ernest Gallo telling his advertising and marketing staff, "We want to do in one year what took Kendall-Jackson ten years to do in a field they had to themselves."

Furth argued that the company had no choice but to try to disguise its Turning Leaf wines as something they were not in order to snatch market share from Kendall-Jackson. "By making Night Train and Thunderbird, low-cost, high-alcohol wines that fry people's brains, it caught up with you when you tried to get into high-priced wines, didn't it?"

Gallo called the suit a "publicity stunt" by Jackson and issued a taunting prepared statement as the trial was about to start. "The suit is nonsense. Turning Leaf bears no resemblance whatsoever to Kendall-Jackson. The only explanation that makes any sense is that Kendall-Jackson has become very concerned about the dramatic success of Turning Leaf."

And Gallo had its defenders—some of the same wine industry titans who sided with Jed Steele against the "corporate bully" Jess Jackson now took Goliath Gallo's side. Leaders of three major California wineries, Mondavi, Sebastiani, and Wente, all testified for

Gallo, dismissing any similarities between Turning Leaf and Vintner's Reserve labels and bottles as involving iconic imagery and designs no individual could claim as his own trademark.

"Wine is made from grapes. It's reasonable for someone to put a grape, vine, or leaf on the label," the CEO of Sebastiani Winery, Don Sebastiani, told jurors.

Michael Mondavi, CEO of his family's winery, said he used fall-colored leaf imagery on some of his wine, too; hundreds of vintners did, he said. As for the flanged bottle, Mondavi added, that look had been pioneered by Mondavi wines, not Kendall-Jackson. Jackson took angry exception to that claim, saying he had let Mondavi "pretend" to be first with this new look because the bottle manufacturer that both companies used had given priority to the order from the larger Mondavi, even though Jackson's had been first. Winemaker Eric Wente said all that was beside the point: he testified that the flanged bottle with clear neck and visible cork had become such a common design that it had been nicknamed "the California Look" and was used by wineries all over the state. Nobody else was screaming about being copied, the Gallo camp suggested. To them, the case was really about Jess Jackson showing the same paranoia about protecting his brand image and secrets that had provoked the suit with Jed Steele.

Furth and Jackson offered no apologies for vigorously defending their brand from what they saw as illegal and unfair competition. Besides, they said, it wasn't any single element of the Vintner's Reserve "trade dress" being copied that posed the problem. Anyone with eyes could see that many brands shared some common elements in their design and marketing, they argued. The problem was the entire package of features and images that Gallo had assembled for Turning Leaf mimicked what the company saw as Kendall-Jackson's unique look in order to confuse consumers. "The colored leaf is our logo. Our corporate statement," Jackson pleaded to jurors. "It's who we are. I felt they were deliberately targeting our logo and giving our consumers the impression it was our wine and not theirs."

Proving that claim, however, was not so simple. Each side had dueling experts and polling to suggest that there was or was not significant consumer confusion between the two brands. Each side brought in accountants and spreadsheets, with Jackson's showing losses of many millions of dollars and Gallo's showing that in the most important head-to-head competition—Chardonnay—Turning Leaf had been a money loser for Gallo.

Certainly, money lay at the heart of this battle, not just for the litigants but also for the other industry players taking sides, such as Mondavi and Sebastiani. For the previous ten years Kendall-Jackson had been seeing 25 percent growth year to year, reflecting the phenomenal rise in consumer interest in premium wines. Gallo's much larger business, in contrast, had been shrinking year to year as cheap and screw-top wines stagnated. Gallo was still Goliath, selling 55 million cases a year in 1995, the year Turning Leaf debuted, while Kendall-Jackson had reached a sales total of 2.5 million cases of its various wines. But the two companies' revenues were far closer because of the much higher margins for premium vintages: revenues ran about $1.2 billion that year for Gallo, more than $200 million for Kendall-Jackson. Jackson sold less than a twentieth of the cases, but his revenues were a sixth of Gallo's. That was why Gallo felt such an urgency to compete in Kendall-Jackson's segment of the market and why Jackson felt even greater urgency to beat Goliath back however he could. Turning Leaf had gone from zero to 1 million cases in a year—1 million cases Jackson felt should have been his to sell in a year when his growth suddenly went flat for the first time ever.

"It's great drama," Bill MacIver, co-owner of Matanzas Creek Winery in Santa Rosa, told reporters at the time. He was a Jackson supporter (who would eventually sell his winery to Jackson). "Kendall-Jackson is getting in the ring with a 1,000-pound gorilla used to having his own way. . . . Gallo has been copying anything that is successful for the twenty years I have been in the wine business. I don't put it past Gallo to copy the Kendall-Jackson label because it was so successful."

Testimony in the case left little doubt that Gallo was trying to replicate Jackson's success with Vintner's Reserve and that the bigger company's tactic was to bring to market a very similar product and package to compete with the market leader. This is an age-old retail tactic that, intentionally or not, may also have blurred the distinction between a Gallo product and a Kendall-Jackson wine in the hands and eyes of consumers. Certainly, this left Jess Jackson beside himself. But as Apple would learn more than a decade later, when its litigation efforts failed to stop rival manufacturers from bringing waves of nearly identical iPhone and iPad clones to market, imitation, no matter how slavish, is not necessarily unfair—and certainly not necessarily illegal. There's only so many ways to make a touch-screen smart phone or a bottle of wine with grapes and leaves on the label. And absent using an actual photocopier on a rival's label and logo, or a brand name that sounds or is spelled nearly the same (something like Kenneth-Johnson Vintner's Reserve, say), a company may be able to embrace striking imitation without running afoul of the law. And so Gallo won the case.

"Gallo shouldn't be excluded from using a grape leaf, which is a valid representation of wine," the foreman of the seven-person federal jury said afterward, summing up the two days of deliberation in matter-of-fact shorthand. Like most of the jurors, the foreman said he was not a wine drinker. He added that he and his fellow jurors were most swayed by the seemingly impartial testimony of Mondavi and Sebastiani. This infuriated Jackson to no end, as he felt they had their own axes to grind, considering Kendall-Jackson more of a threat and a barrier to their success in the premium market. He believed they were happy to see Jackson lose out to Gallo.

Jackson appealed and lost and decided against taking the case for a final round before the US Supreme Court, having already thrown $2 million into prosecuting the case. He didn't like it, but Jackson knew pursuing the case further would be a bad bet: if he couldn't convince a more liberal Ninth Circuit Court of Appeal, his prospects before the High Court were unlikely to improve. He couldn't help imagining Ernest Gallo gloating over putting the upstart in his place. But as it turned out, Jackson ended up dishing out a bit of payback—not from his suit but from another filed by the Gallos.

In a postscript twist the makers of Turning Leaf sought to turn the tables on Jackson by following up on their courtroom vindication with a countersuit. Gallo accused Jackson of malicious prosecution and, with ill-disguised glee, trade-secret violations of his own. According to the suit, Jackson had enticed the former chief marketing officer for Gallo to betray company secrets, which Kendall-Jackson then used to gin up a lawsuit that he knew all along was false and unsupported by proper evidence.

It seemed Gallo wanted to rake Jackson over the coals—and recover its own $2 million in legal costs—but the countersuit ended up as Gallo's one great tactical blunder in the case, a fit of hubris that would taint its legal victory in the original trial. By filing the new suit, Gallo opened up more investigation into its own business practices, and the revelations were not flattering for the giant winemaker. In responding to the countersuit, Jackson not only denied doing anything wrong; he also asserted a defense known as the "doctrine of unclean hands," which essentially meant that for Gallo to file these charges against Jackson, the company had to be innocent of any related misconduct of its own. And Jackson's investigation had unearthed evidence that Gallo's hands were anything but clean. The opinion from the California Court of Appeal recounted these findings in embarrassing detail in its published ruling in the case, *Kendall-Jackson Winery v. Superior Court of Stanislaus County:*

(1) Kendall-Jackson has learned that Gallo has numerous representatives working for chain stores who are involved with shelf schematics for the stores or are otherwise involved with moving wine products. Alternatively, Gallo representatives have directed non-Gallo employees to make schematic changes for Gallo.

(2) Gallo employs a technique which it calls "piggy-back adjacencies." The technique involves training its distributor/

salesperson to place an inferior, lower-priced Gallo product adjacent to a higher-priced category leader. The category leader's display attracts the consumer's attention. When the consumer reaches for the well-known product, he or she will see the lower-priced Gallo product, and may buy that product instead.

(3) Gallo employees have admitted moving Turning Leaf wines next to Kendall-Jackson wines, which would require them to move a non-Gallo product in violation of federal and state regulations.

Kendall-Jackson identified a number of documents that described conduct supporting its unclean hands defense. The documents contain direct and circumstantial evidence showing that Gallo used its influence to have retailers place Turning Leaf wine next to Kendall-Jackson Vintner's Reserve wine. The documents also reflect that Gallo representatives or employees moved Kendall-Jackson products, provided free labor to retailers in exchange for favorable product placement, prepared shelf schematics for retailers, maintained offices in some retailers' stores, wore retailer badges while stocking product, removed Kendall-Jackson wines from a retail store, participated in retailer resets which involved handling a competitor's product, and interfered with Kendall-Jackson's marketing displays.

According to the appeals court opinion, Gallo admitted this conduct occurred, but the company argued that this evidence was irrelevant. For the unclean hands defense to be used, Gallo argued, Jackson would had to have known about all this manipulation of shelving, placement, and interference with Kendall-Jackson displays *before* filing the lawsuit. Instead, the information was not uncovered until much later. The trial court actually agreed with Gallo and barred Jackson from using the unclean hands defense in the case; Jackson immediately appealed that ruling, and the appeals court took Gallo to task for trying to evade responsibility and to engineer yet another legal victory despite evidence of its own misconduct.

By filing the countersuit, Gallo ended up making public extensive evidence that supported Jackson's allegations that Gallo had improperly sought to confuse Turning Leaf with Vintner's Reserve. Had Jackson based his original suit against Gallo on what was happening in stores rather than on a comparison of the labels on the bottles, he could have had a far more straightforward case to present to the jury. Every winemaker might, as jurors concluded, have a right to stick a grape leaf on a label. But none had the right to shove a competitor's wine bottle aside.

After the appellate court sided with Jackson on Gallo's malicious prosecution claim, the case settled and was dismissed, ending the Jackson-Gallo legal feud for good.

Jackson claimed vindication, and this final twist gave force to his long-standing denial that the original lawsuit had been, as Gallo asserted, a publicity stunt. But there was no denying the trial's publicity value for Kendall-Jackson. Gallo may have won the primary court battle, but the coast-to-coast media coverage proved far more effective than any advertising Jackson could have bought at making clear that Turning Leaf was a Gallo product, not a Kendall-Jackson creation. If there had been confusion before about who made what wine, there was a lot less after the trial.

"We lost the verdict," Jackson would later assert. "But no one was fooled. Not after that."

Christopher Silva, president and CEO of St. Francis Winery and Vineyards, saw Jackson's decision to file the lawsuit as an act of genius, concluding, "He turned the entire lawsuit into a national argument about Kendall-Jackson's quality, and it almost didn't matter that the jury ruled in Gallo's favor. What mattered was that in covering the story, the *Wall Street Journal* and virtually every newspaper in the country carried a front-page picture of Kendall-Jackson's Vintner's Reserve label, as well as quotes from Jess Jackson about his superior wine quality. You couldn't buy that kind of publicity. Regardless of his motivation, the lawsuit and how it was played out in the media was the single most brilliant act of wine marketing in the past thirty years."

ENGAGING IN THE tense courtroom confrontation with Gallo didn't stop Jackson from opening other battlefronts at the same time, picking more fights even as he tried to focus on day-to-day operations at his growing, often unwieldy company. Those operations included wrapping up the purchases of Graystone and the Clegg Ranch properties, overseeing the completion of his vast new Stonestreet Winery complex, and laying plans for yet more wineries in the region, which already were arousing opposition. His cluttered, book-filled office at Kendall-Jackson's new Santa Rosa headquarters took on the aspect of a Pentagon war room, his massive desk piled high with legal pads and papers, an easel with a giant tablet of poster paper on it displaying his latest bullet points, and printouts showing, among other things, that the dip in sales that followed the introduction of Turning Leaf appeared to be over. Premium wine sales in the United States set an all-time record at the end of 1996.

With all that going on, this would be the time Jackson chose to go after the hidebound 1930s post-Prohibition distribution system. That system had rankled him from the moment he opened his winery. He hated having to plead with one distributor after another in state after state just to get them to carry his Vintner's Reserve. And while he struggled to reach a national market in those early years, with distributors telling him that they had enough wine, that they didn't need to take on some other California unknown, the same old guard wines, regardless of their quality, received favorable treatment, display, and marketing from these same seemingly untouchable and entrenched distributors. They wielded godlike power—indifference being the worst—that could make or break a winery, Jackson complained. His long battle against the distributors was an extension of his even longer war with the Wine Institute, dominated by Gallo and Jackson's other detractors in the Wine Country old guard. A new lawsuit Jackson and other winemakers filed ultimately killed the California Wine Commission, a state agency that taxed every winemaker, then gave the proceeds to the same Wine Institute so many of them had rejected for its preferential treatment of just a few big companies.

"Together these pieces of the wine business were assembled to favor the established players, the incumbents, the good old boy network, and the huge and financially powerful corporations, to the detriment of entrepreneurs and family businesses who are trying to innovate and build something good," Jackson would later say. "Something had to change."

That same year he fought Gallo in court over Turning Leaf, Jackson ended his exclusive California distribution deal with Southern Wine and Spirits and gave the business to his previously small in-house distribution department, Regal Wines. In the space of one day Regal became one of the largest wine distributors in the state. The move was years in the making, but it finally gave control of Kendall-Jackson's most important market to Kendall-Jackson—and immediately saved the company the 10 to 25 percent commission previously paid Southern.

The main impetus for this move had come during a contentious meeting between Jackson and the head of Southern Wine, Harvey Chaplin, which had left Jackson rankled and in the mood for a change. The two men had been tooling around Sonoma in a limousine with heavily tinted windows, Chaplin's preferred setting for business meetings. Jackson complained that his higher-priced, smaller vintages, such as the Stonestreet label of artisan wines, needed more attention and marketing at the wholesale level in order to reach customers. Only his high-volume Vintner's Reserve was getting the level of distributor "tender loving care" he expected from Southern Wine. So he had a proposal.

"Harvey, we want to take Stonestreet and go sell it ourselves because you're not doing it well," Jackson said. "I'll partner with you, and we'll make a fine wine division for Southern."

Chaplin turned him down flat. He liked the idea of a dedicated staff for fine wines, including Stonestreet, but the distribution piece of the pie was his and his alone, he said. There would be no "equity interest" for Jackson—no partnership. And if Jackson tried to go it alone, Chaplin threatened, "we'll resign the Kendall-Jackson line."

There was the age-old reality of the three-tier supplier-distributor-retailer system erected to protect the nation from unregulated sales of alcohol after Prohibition: the distributor held the power. Jackson had his vineyards and his wineries, he had amassed a trucking fleet to ship his products, he had built sales and marketing teams that were the envy of the industry, but he still was in thrall to distributors like Southern. They had the contacts, the network, the retailer relationships—the power to say no. Chaplin's refusal carried with it an implicit challenge: What was Jackson going to do about it? Try to distribute all by himself? Would he amass a staff, train its members in a side of the business in which he did not have expertise, go to all that expense and time, and run the risk of being crushed by the system?

Jackson's answer was yes, that's exactly what he would do. And when he had his Regal staff, led by Mike Haarstad, start wholesaling the Kendall-Jackson wines, Chaplin made good on his threat and stopped distributing all of Jackson's wines. Then Jackson had no choice. He had not wanted to be in the distribution business alone without a partner, but necessity drove him to put a team of thirty people onto the street doing wholesale work. "It turned out to be the best thing we did," Jackson would later reflect. "We controlled our own destiny."

After a rocky start Kendall-Jackson, Stonestreet, and the company's other brands got the tender loving care that Jackson wanted and that no outside distributor had ever offered. Placement with California retailers improved so much that sales rose 100,000 cases in the first year Regal Wines became the in-house distributor. What he had always shied away from as a costly headache turned out to be a revolutionary move for the wine business. Chaplin had pushed Jackson in a new direction just as the grape glut had done years before. Now Kendall-Jackson had achieved a rare "vertical integration" that left the company in the unique position of controlling the grapes, the crush, the winemaking, its own trucking, its own sales force, and, finally, the piece where control had eluded Jackson, the distribution of his wine into the world. The idea of controlling the "whole widget," whether the product was wine, cars, or computers, was compelling but difficult and prone to painful costs and failures. But when it worked, Jackson saw, the competitive edge in terms of quality and cost could be like putting a business on steroids. At the time the only other winemaker with similar vertical integration was Gallo, which had built its own distribution machine in order to become the industry leader.

"We were our own masters for the first time at least in California," Jackson recalled. "So of course we said, 'Why stop there?'"

State by state Jackson began to sever ties with other distributors that failed to meet his expectations. Wherever he could, he took over distribution or partnered with more agreeable distributors willing to work together and grant that equity stake in the operation rather than lose Kendall-Jackson's business entirely. This didn't work everywhere: twenty-one states banned interstate wine sales, forcing wineries into distribution deals. Kentucky went so far as to make it a felony for winemakers to sell directly in the state. For a time Jackson and other winemakers boycotted Kentucky over this issue.

In Illinois Jackson and two other winemakers took the lead in suing over a measure passed by the state legislature in 1999, the Wine and Spirits Fair Dealing Act, which was designed to block winemakers and brewers from selling directly to retailers or consumers. The law barred Jackson from firing a distributor in Illinois, Judge & Dolph, for poor performance; another winemaker, Sutter Home in Napa Valley, was compelled against its will to renew a contract with a distributor it wanted to drop. "It was as if Illinois had become a banana republic," Jackson raged. "Instead of president for life, it's distributor for life." The measure was so anticompetitive that as soon as it passed, all distributors in the state raised their prices, knowing that they could not be fired.

The law was so egregious that Kendall-Jackson, Sutter Home, and Peak Wines in Sonoma County (which had been bought out by

Jim Beam Brands) won an injunction against the Fair Dealing Act almost immediately on the grounds that it violated the Contract Clause of the US Constitution. As Jackson was fond of pointing out, this very clear provision barred states from meddling with contracts, which the founders considered sufficiently important to cover in the Constitution before they got to the part about enumerating the powers of the presidency. The Illinois law was nicknamed the "Wirtz Law" after Bill Wirtz, head of Judge & Dolph, who was among a group of distributors who had donated $700,000 to legislators prior to passage of the act. The courts kept it from taking full effect and eventually struck it down completely. The measure is frequently cited as an example of the corrupting influence of unregulated campaign donations and a prime example of the need for campaign reform.

The upshot of all these distributor battles was that within a few years Kendall-Jackson controlled 55 percent of its distribution, with plans in place to achieve 80 percent in time. This proved to be a transformative move that radically boosted revenues, as the cost of staffing an in-house distribution company was offset by the elimination of those 25 percent distributor commissions. Plus Jackson built a distribution force loyal to Kendall-Jackson alone, which measurably boosted sales.

Jackson capped these "battles of the middleman" by becoming a founding member of a new organization of winemakers, the Coalition for Free Trade, whose lead counsel was none other than President Bill Clinton's impeachment nemesis, Kenneth Starr. The coalition filed a lawsuit that led the US Supreme Court to sweep away legal barriers to direct interstate sale and shipment of wine. At last, all those wineries with no access to out-of-state distributors— more than half the family winemakers in California, who struggled to find outlets for their wine and who found exporting from California to Illinois more difficult than shipping to Paris or Beijing—could now reach millions of potential customers by mail and online.

THE LAST SERIES of conflicts during this period in the mid-1990s, the environmental battles, were the least costly for Kendall-Jackson in terms of dollars and cents. But they were the most damaging to the company's public image and the most painful personally for Jackson. He leaped into the others with relish, eager to take on Gallo and the distributors and the old guard. But these fights over Kendall-Jackson's environmental impact gave him no joy, win or lose, and in retrospect Jackson seemed to realize they could have and should have been avoided.

They began with his impatience. His first big winery construction project had been held up for years, and though he had bought and built other facilities in the interim, this plant was to be a centerpiece of his Sonoma operations. And he was tired of waiting.

"If we don't get started, we won't be done in time for the harvest. We have to break ground now," Jackson told his staff. People might wait for bureaucracies, he said, but grapes did not wait. They were ready when they were ready, which meant his winery had to be ready. "Let's move."

The problem was that, after jumping through many regulatory hoops, writing reports, weathering multiple inspections, and waiting six years since submitting his first set of plans for his big winery near the Santa Rosa Airport, Jackson had only been allowed by the county to grade and pour a foundation. Everything else remained at a standstill.

The Sonoma County Building and Permits Department had twenty-nine major environmental, safety, and health conditions that needed to be accomplished and approved before further construction commenced. As harvest time neared, Jackson's team had got formal approval for meeting twenty-eight of them. The last of the twenty-nine, a sound study of the winery's external machinery, which did not yet exist, had been conducted and submitted in mid-February 1996. County officials told Kendall-Jackson staffers they would get back to them—in three months.

Jackson could not believe it. His builders had informed him they would have to start construction right away if there were to be any hope of opening the winery for that year's autumn harvest. A three-month wait would be out of the question. A three-week wait would be too much.

So Jackson told them to start immediately. He figured completion of the sound study, which had produced unremarkable results, fulfilled the twenty-ninth condition. He did not, however, share his thinking on this with the county. He just went ahead and put the construction crews to work, assuming that the building permit, though not formally issued as yet, was little more than a formality at this point.

He was wrong. Inspectors showed up at the building site on March 1, halted construction, and "red tagged" Kendall-Jackson. He faced a $44,000 fine for building without a permit.

In isolation, that might not have been a very big deal. In fact, Jackson and his staff discussed the possibility of a fine before breaking ground and figured that it might be worth moving ahead anyway. The cost of not having the winery open in time for harvest and continuing for another year to truck record amounts of grapes and juice to more remote locations, such as Lakeport, would be far more expensive. The delays in constructing the winery had, in Jackson's estimation, cost him millions over the years.

But the building permit dust-up did not come in isolation, as Kendall-Jackson's critics were quick to point out. It was the capstone to a long and acrimonious process that marked the first serious opposition to a proposed winery in Sonoma County history. The new winery was a big and complex project, and the homeowners who lived nearby worried about noise and traffic, waste and pollution. Sonoma County had embraced farming and viticulture without reservation, and officials were delighted to see vineyards expand across the terrain, rather than strip malls or housing for Bay Area commuters. But gigantic wineries were another story, more industry than agriculture, at least from the perspective of people living just down the road. This is where Jackson wanted to line up a 10,000-barrel army of French oak, another of Jackson's signature winemaking achievements, of hand-stirring and hand-testing his bestselling Chardonnay on an epic scale so that his wine would taste small but sell big. This was the vision that Jackson had pursued obsessively since first proposing the winery in 1990 and that had driven Jed Steele from Kendall-Jackson in search of a more intimate winemaking style.

The opposition from neighbors and local environmental groups had been bitter. They insisted the project was too big for the site and its surroundings, and their tenacity led the county to do something it had never done before: require Kendall-Jackson to prepare a formal Environmental Impact Report for the winery project. This is a costly and detailed scientific study of all the potential environmental, social, and economic impacts of a project on air quality, water supplies, traffic, home values, noise pollution, local businesses, and infrastructure. It triggers a process that requires lengthy review, public comment, public hearings, responses to public comment, and a plan by the builder to mitigate the project's negative impacts either by changing the plans; finding new, less harmful ways to do business; or repairing any inevitable damage (for example, planting new trees in a different location to replace existing ones that might be cleared for construction). The only other winery project to be subjected to similar scrutiny for the next decade would be the massive winery Gallo built to produce Turning Leaf.

The main change the neighbors sought from Kendall-Jackson was a reduction in size, knocking the plant's capacity to less than a quarter of what Jackson wanted so that it could produce at most 80,000 cases a year. That would be a deal breaker for Jackson.

Instead, the company worked for the next four years to address the twenty-nine problems identified in the report by county planners, culminating with an emotionally charged Sonoma County Board of Supervisors meeting in April 1994. Opponents of Jackson's project and fellow grape growers packed the meeting, the former calling for the project to be killed, the latter expressing bewilderment at huge delays and hurdles that faced the sort of winery project that in the past would have received easy approval.

Jackson made an impassioned plea to the board, calling for common sense and recognition of the jobs and money, as well as a way of life that preserved the region's character and beauty, that vineyards and wineries brought to Sonoma. "If you can't build a winery in the heart of Wine Country," he asked in a ringing voice, "where can you build one?" After all that time the board, declaring the long process a model for public-private partnership in protecting both environmental and economic interests, voted unanimously to approve the winery construction.

And yet that didn't end it. The political process gave way to a bureaucratic one, and because this was a first such environmental review in Sonoma, the process was halting at best. Nearly two years later Jackson lost patience and started building without the permit in hand, leading to extensive press coverage and protests from critics who felt their worst fears about Kendall-Jackson had been confirmed.

In the end the county admitted it had moved too slowly and promised to accelerate the review process in the future. Jackson paid the fine, which the county later partially refunded, knocking it down to an even $20,000. County officials decided that, even though Jackson had broken the law and moved forward without a permit, the company really had met all the conditions set for it. Board members scolded Jackson publicly for not following the rules but added the caveat that he had good reason for impatience. A side effect of the uproar was that the county did not take three months to review the sound study after all, but instead quickly issued the building permit. Construction resumed, and the winery opened just in time for the harvest.

In a long column in the local newspaper, the Santa Rosa *Press Democrat*, business editor Brad Bollinger sided with Jackson on the controversy. "With four years of government vetting behind it and believing the issuance of the permit was assured, K-J started building. In the end, it got the permit and K-J paid dearly for what amounted to a misunderstanding—$20,000 in fines. But the entire episode should never have occurred. Sonoma County is a wine region with some of the world's best wineries. Wine is arguably the

region's chief competitive advantage. Government's role in maintaining that advantage is to be the world's best in the planning,
processing and permitting of what wineries need—vineyards and
buildings included."

Had Jackson stopped poking the region's burgeoning green sensibilities for a while, "Permit-Gate" soon would have been forgotten.
But another controversy was unfolding in the county at the same
time over vanishing valley oak trees. This signature species was (and
is) unique to California, long-lived, a majestic a symbol of Wine
Country with its broad leaves and rough-hewn bark. These oaks
were also a regular victim of the wine business, routinely cut down
by the dozens, sometimes the hundreds, to make way for grapes. The
county had been considering two possible measures, one to severely
curtail the ability of property owners to remove healthy old-growth
oaks or a second, in a compromise, to require replanting of seedlings
when old trees were chopped or bulldozed. Farmers and vintners
opposed such measures as interfering with property rights, as well
as making life hard for the already challenging economy of farming.
The growers also argued that they needed no regulations to be wise
stewards of the land; their livelihoods already depended on it. In the
end the County Board of Supervisors agreed, voting 4–1 against any
regulation of oak tree removal, reasoning that the county's farmers
understood that the public wanted a balance struck between the oak
and the grape and that therefore farmers could be trusted to avoid
heedless deforestation.

It so happened that right around this time, Jackson had acquired
seventy acres of open land in a rural neighborhood north of Santa
Rosa near the small town of Windsor, California. It was a good spot
for Pinot Noir, and Jackson bought the land to plant it with vines.
A month after Permit-Gate, and shortly after the vote against oak
regulation, residents in that neighborhood awoke on a Saturday
morning to the scream of chainsaws and the crash of splintered
tree trunks. More than fifty oak trees, some of them two hundred
years old, had been felled by Kendall-Jackson crews to make way

for the orderly rows of Pinot Noir. The felled trees represented about 15 percent of the oaks on that property.

Upset at the unexpected tree removal, the neighboring landowner told a newspaper reporter that the destruction was sad and unnecessary. "Indians, grizzly bears and elk wandered beneath those trees," Rick Daniels said. "There is a lot of history here and now part of it is gone."

The oak destruction outraged most of the neighborhood. The trees had been visible to passersby, as were the oaks' broken carcasses. "They did this sneakily," one neighbor complained. "They came early in the morning and didn't give us any warning."

"We own the property," Randall Clifton, the senior vice president of farming and development for Kendall-Jackson, snapped to a reporter when told of this comment. "How much notification do you have to give the neighbors before you do something on your own land?"

Clifton's comments aroused as much anger as the actual tree cutting because they seemed to some to reflect an attitude that the company now had carte blanche to do as it pleased, having won its winery approval, skated by with a reduced fine on Permit-Gate, and successfully opposed any oak tree regulation. The winemaker received hundreds of telephone calls from unhappy residents upset by the loss of trees and by one particular comment by Clifton, who was quoted in the newspaper as saying, "There's hundreds of trees on the property. We could have very easily cleared the entire property and yielded much more land but we chose not to."

The smart play in that political climate would have been to announce the planned tree cutting in advance and hire an arborist to do a quick report on how many of the trees were being removed, how many were diseased and how many were healthy, and how Kendall-Jackson was committed to preserving the vast majority of healthy trees on the site. The company could have accomplished the same result, while making the case that it was sensitive to public concerns and acting as a good steward of the land. Instead, the winemaker came off looking defensive, arrogant, and uncaring. Later Kendall-Jackson officials pointed out that those seventy acres had once been slated for high-density development with three hundred homes and a shopping center, but the winemaker preserved the land for open space and agriculture instead. The adjacent land had been cleared of oak trees years before for a subdivision, playground, and athletic fields, and no one had objected to that. But by the time these points were made, opinions had been hardened: Kendall-Jackson was, according to the *Press Democrat*, being viewed as "a cross between a scofflaw and Sonoma County's own Charles Hurwitz." Hurwitz, one of the most vilified businessmen of the late twentieth century, was infamous for trying to log vast swaths of the country's last remaining old-growth redwood forests after he acquired the Pacific Lumber Company.

Jackson cemented that reputation for years to come when he inexplicably repeated the blunder in Santa Barbara County, where he chopped down nearly nine hundred oak trees on newly acquired land to make way for a vineyard. The clear-cutting was too much for a neighboring winegrower, Richard Sanford, who had been championing sustainable winemaking for many years, urging growers to preserve habitats and native trees alongside their vineyards. Now he joined a coalition of environmentalists and nature lovers sponsoring a voter initiative that would have heavily regulated oak tree cutting in Santa Barbara. It would have passed, but farming interests, including Jackson, used California's wide-open initiative system to their advantage. They placed a watered-down alternative measure on the ballot that, as intended, confused voters because both purported to protect oak trees. The strong oak regulations failed by a very slim margin of votes.

Jackson's initial reaction was outrage at the outrage. How dare people try to interfere with his right to do as he pleased on his own land. And how dare they suggest he had no appreciation for nature. Jackson loved nature and wanted to be a good steward of the land. But his first love, even more than nature and the outdoors, lay with the soil, with growing things, with the miracle of the grape, clinging to life, straining to produce fruit. Farming was about partnering with nature to make something special. That was the magic, the thing he loved most about wine. "My high," he once said, "is going out and pruning my vines. That is where I find peace and content-ment." And it was true: he appreciated and admired wild nature and knew it was vital and should be protected—somewhere. But what he loved on his land was the tilled earth, bringing forth his own cultivated interpretation of the natural world. He loved the grapevines and the fact that his farmland meant there would be no drive-through fast-food restaurant or sixteen-theater multiplex or cracker box condo complexes on that piece of property. There would be rolling hills and orderly grapevines and, yes, where pos-sible, those beautiful ancient oaks. But planting around oak trees was inefficient, and grapes didn't like the shade. So some trees had to go. And, bottom line, his attitude in that era was: *It's my land. Deal with it. You want to preserve oak trees? Buy your own damn land.*

Still, the Santa Barbara tree "massacre," as the locals called it, marked a turning point. The fact that Californians knew Kendall-Jackson not for its fine wines but from statewide news reports about the oak trees in Santa Barbara left an impression on Jackson. That was not a legacy he cared to carry. So little by little, and with en-couragement from Banke, he began to turn toward more sustainable practices with growing and winemaking: woodland preservation, water conservation, elimination of pesticides and herbicides. Many of these moves turned out not only to be environmentally responsible but also to save money for the company, and soon Jess and Barbara were donating millions to the University of California to research sustainable winemaking and to design new low-impact wineries. They started to work on preserving endangered and threatened species on their land and began a tree-planting program to replace trees they had to cut down. When they developed the sprawling Al-exander Mountain estate into vineyards, their home, and Jackson's office away from the office, he boasted that not a single tree was cut down, other than those that were dead or diseased.

But he would not stomach anyone trying to compel him to do such things. "We don't do sustainability because we have to. We do it because we want to."

He expanded on this theme in a 1995 interview with *Wines & Vines* magazine after he was taken to task by conservationists for developing mountaintop vineyards: "People don't have a brain if they don't understand the relationship between open space and agriculture. Open space IS agriculture. There's no one who is a better protector of open space than a farmer. The population thinks food comes in plastic at Safeway. They don't know how to kill a chicken. Citizens who live in the city and never experience growing a crop live in a Disney fantasy. Everything on earth eats something else! I love Bambi as much as the next one, but the coyote and the cougar need Bambi as food. All that seems so crass and crude to the average person."

Jenny Jackson said the need for balance between farming and conservation was her dad's blind spot for many years. What he did with the oak trees in Sonoma and Santa Barbara was legal, sensible, and common practice for vineyards. That did not, in Jenny's mind, make it okay, however. She had argued with him about tree cutting for years, dating back to their first harvests in Lakeport back in the 1970s. From the start she had pleaded with her father to preserve the gorgeous old stands of still-productive walnut trees that had been on the Lakeport property for a hundred years. "Please, Dad, don't cut them down," she begged him. "They're visually beautiful when people drive on the property. We have plenty of room; we can plant around them."

But he would have none of it. He wanted efficient, straight blocks of vines, uninterrupted by those hulking old trees, and so the bulldozers swept through while Jenny watched in tears. "They were beautiful. But to Dad, they were beautiful obstacles."

11

Family Man, Part II— and the Retirement That Didn't Stick

As Y2K APPROACHED—ALONG WITH THE SEVENTIETH birthday of America's last major family winemaker not named Gallo—Jess Jackson started planning a radical move he had last contemplated a quarter century earlier: he started plotting his retirement.

He put out few overt signs of this at first. The hectic pace of land purchases, winery construction, vineyard planting, and brand expansion continued and even accelerated as he began dishing out ever-greater piles of cash to purchase high-quality but financially struggling rivals. The search for new properties and markets abroad didn't slow either, part of the push to evolve Kendall-Jackson from the leading purveyor of good affordable wines into a winemaker also known for high-end, high-priced vintages. Although his signature Vintner's Reserve had made him rich and enabled all his other endeavors in the wine trade, Jackson dreaded the thought of retiring as the maker of "that sweet Chardonnay." Transforming Kendall-Jackson into America's version of Tuscany's Antinori family dynasty, into a multigenerational winemaker that did it all (except stock the cheap shelves he happily ceded to the bulk producers), was his final mission.

And so Jess's fourteen-hour workdays continued uninterrupted as well, regardless of occasion or location. He, Barbara, and the kids flew off on the reconditioned private jet the family bought (not so affectionately dubbed "Old Smokey") on a month-long tour of the world, a trip that was designed for adventure and enjoyment but that could not separate Jess from his work. Every touchdown in Europe became an opportunity to scope out estate vineyards and wineries. A visit to Tahiti saw him at vanilla bean plantations, scribbling on yellow legal pads, working out his personal formula for the costs of goods and services, then excitedly declaring to Barbara that they needed to get into the vanilla business. He also became enamored of truffles as a side business during their travels, certain that they owned the right *terroir* for the high-priced delicacies back home. (Ultimately, the vanilla idea died owing to daunting transportation costs, but the truffle business eventually took root in Sonoma years later.) Back home executives received nearly daily faxes of questions, commands, and new ideas from the boss abroad, and they were expected to respond by the end of the day—not dropping their normal duties but adding to them. At Kendall-Jackson the staff tended to dread Jackson's so-called vacations.

"You'd think when the boss is away, life would get easier," former chief operating officer Randy Clifton would later recall. "But not at KJ. We used to say, 'Oh no, Jess is going on vacation. Now it's time to really get to work.'"

Even as such business as usual continued, Jackson quietly engineered a new web of holding companies and a complex network of family trusts that shifted assets away from his personal ownership so that on paper he owned very little of the company outright, though he and Barbara had complete control of the trusts. On its face this corporate makeover served a common and obvious purposes of taking advantage of various tax, liability, and inheritance laws. But

Jackson had more in mind, as the reorganization also enabled two mutually exclusive goals he did not announce, his own Plan A and Plan B. Plan A not only created a seamless succession of power to Barbara, then his children, then their heirs, but it also locked in his vision of an enduring family wine dynasty—his ideas to be carried out after his retirement without his needing to be there every day (or to be there at all).

Then there was Plan B: the same restructuring could also be used to put Kendall-Jackson on the auction block. This could take place with Jackson still at the helm by selling stock through an initial public offering (IPO) while maintaining a controlling majority of shares for the family, à la the Walton clan and Wal-Mart. Or the new structure of the company could serve just as well as a prelude for a very lucrative outright sale of the business, creating a Kendall-Jackson with no Jess Jackson in the corner office. The Plan B option had multiple scenarios: Jackson's holding companies could be sold entirely, putting the whole enterprise from Lakeport to Santa Barbara up for sale; or they could be decoupled with ease, allowing him to part with the moneymaking machine of the Kendall-Jackson brand and Vintner's Reserve, while keeping his Artisan & Estates high-end brands and all the invaluable *terroir* he had accumulated over the years to play with. This was an era of rapid consolidation in the wine business, and there were plenty of potential suitors lined up, eager to dangle billions for the Jackson family enterprise, all or part of it.

Either plan would enable a triumphant second retirement for Jackson—the first retirement being from the law, the second from wine—by the start of the new millennium. Not even those closest to him felt comfortable predicting which direction he would take in the end, if any. Jackson himself wasn't sure. But there were those who felt certain that he would never pull the pin on either option, that he could not bear to sell his beloved company or his even more beloved land, and that he would be retired only by the grave. Don Hartford occupied that camp, assuming that even then Jackson would probably figure out a way to have his orders carried out for years after his passing.

Asking him did no good. He'd just smile and shake his head and fall back on generalities or platitudes. "My focus is on making the best wine in the world," he'd say. "If we pursue that goal, everything else will come in due time." He loved variations of this stock comment because it could mean almost anything.

Kendall-Jackson had its own coterie of Jess Kremlinologists endlessly trying to divine his intentions: sales head Mike Haarstad, COO Clifton, Vice President Paul Ginsburg, who had risen from being Jackson's divorce lawyer to become a senior executive and was a strong supporter of the let's-sell-and-get-rich plan. Periodically, they'd meet among themselves when Jackson was absent, debating what to do about their boss's latest decision to acquire a new label, develop a new marketing plan, or, his most controversial move, up the price of Vintner's Reserve Chardonnay above the "$10 barrier" to improve margins and raise brand prestige.

This was a big deal at the company. The psychological impact on consumers of adding even a penny to $9.99 was roundly feared by his lieutenants. They felt Jackson's higher price would stall sales rather than grow margins. Jackson dismissed such concerns as "Wal-Mart thinking." He still maintained that his founding principal should hold firm: he didn't want to drive sales volumes with rock-bottom prices. He wanted to drive profits by charging a premium price for a premium product, the wine that consumers perceived as a good value rather than as a cheap one.

The command to cross the $10 barrier sparked a secret meeting. Word of it got back to Jackson, however, and he was incensed to learn that one of those in attendance had characterized the purpose of the gathering by declaring, "We've got to save Jess from himself."

This was neither the first nor the last time those words would be uttered, Don Hartford later recalled. But it was the first time Jackson had heard about them in the context of a secret meeting about the future of the company, and they left him livid. He assembled the company leadership the next morning, fuming about cabals going behind his back. What really bothered him—hurt him, Hartford believed—was the implicit lack of confidence in his leadership and decisionmaking that he felt lay behind this meeting. Nothing brought Jackson down faster than the perception that his people lacked confidence in him. For a tough and forceful leader at home and at work, Jackson had always been extremely sensitive to such slights and easily wounded. He saw this one as the height of disloyalty, something he found unbearable.

A similar perception had sparked the rift between Jess and Jane, at least on his end, and had driven him to exact what his eldest daughters believed to be an overly harsh divorce settlement. The property settlement gave Jenny and Laura shares of the company in trust and enough cash to each buy a house, but Jane received a flat $1 million (Jackson had to borrow heavily to make the payment) and relinquished all ownership of Kendall-Jackson. As Jenny and Laura saw it, their father took such a hard line because he felt that his first wife's lack of confidence in him and his business plan—what he saw as her disloyalty—disqualified her from profiting from the success of the business or retaining a share of the company after the divorce. Jess and Barbara, however, recalled that he gave Jane the option of retaining her interest in Kendall-Jackson, which would eventually have been worth hundreds of millions, and that it was she who insisted on cashing out for what turned out to be a relative pittance that overwhelmingly favored Jackson. He certainly wasn't sorry it had worked out that way, but he always chalked that up to Jane's insistence, not his. Either way it was Jackson's perception of a hurtful, maddening lack of confidence in him that had had such a ruinous effect on the marriage. Few of those taking part in the secret meeting to "save" Jackson from the price increase understood the perilous ground they were occupying, until Jackson's reaction was to go nuclear: he banned meetings of his executives except when he was present.

Such a policy would be extraordinary—and extraordinarily counterproductive—for most CEOs of large companies such as

Jackson's. By the year 2000, Kendall-Jackson had become the leading employer in Sonoma County, with more than 1,200 workers and a growing global presence. Yet that was the new rule: "No meetings without me or my okay."

"The typical CEO, the saying goes, flies at 30,000 feet," Hartford observed. "Jess operated at about 3 feet. Other CEOs delegate. Their subordinates *have* to meet separately. That's how they take care of the detail work. They are empowered to make decisions. But that wasn't how Jess operated. His great strength was that he had a mastery of so many of the details and lines of the business, he could actually pull it off. But that was also his weakness. He hated to delegate. He would have had the janitor report to him if he could. That's one reason why he had to work so many hours. He could do it because he had the energy and the commitment to keep his people in meetings for three days as he explained what he wanted and how he wanted it done, until everyone finally would just give in and say fine, it's his company, he's got the successful track record, we'll do it Jess's way."

And, bottom line, he just didn't want his executives meeting about him or his business without Jess Jackson in the room.

Yet at the same time he had fashioned a corporate culture most of his staff described as exceedingly open, where anyone with an idea or a suggestion felt free to voice it, often directly to Jackson. Rigorous debate and questioning—which Jackson distinguished from doubt and dissent—weren't just permitted; they were expected. This was part of the Socratic method of discussion and decisionmaking Jackson had preferred since his law school days at Berkeley. He encouraged a vigorous debate even about the touchy subject of price increases, though it was equally clear that once Jackson made up his mind, he almost never changed it. A willingness to discuss the merits of an $11 VR versus a $9 one was not evidence of democracy at the company, merely of Jackson's desire to explain his position, counter arguments from the other side, and basically wear down the opposition to the point of capitulation. When Mike Haarstad pushed beyond that point during heated discussions of the $10 barrier, with the two men shouting at each other from opposite ends of the conference table while those in between cringed, Jackson finally told him enough debate.

"Stop talking now," Jackson warned, but Haarstad, veins bulging in his neck, kept talking about stalling sales and pricing the signature brand into competitive vulnerability.

"Shut up," Jackson shouted, but Haarstad kept gesturing and arguing.

"Shut up or you're fired, Mike," Jackson said, but Haarstad, every bit as stubborn as his boss, kept on arguing.

"You're fired, Mike!" Jackson yelled, and still Haarstad kept talking.

"You're fired!" Jackson repeated, but to no avail. The meeting broke up, and everyone else fled, but the two men continued railing at each other.

Only Haarstad, whose sales acumen had been pivotal in transforming Kendall-Jackson from a Lakeport curiosity into a global powerhouse, could get away with this. The next day Haarstad was still at his desk, the firing apparently forgotten and the price increase put on hold. Jackson eventually punched through the $10 barrier two years later, and though sales briefly contracted, profits did not, and soon the volume rose as well. Jackson had been right, but so had Haarstad, who had counseled the more gradual approach to pricing that Jackson eventually accepted.

Jackson's autocratic tendencies were balanced by the value he placed on the good ideas of others. He went out of his way to seek the opinions of his staff. He wanted the entire workforce to be educated about wine, its culture, taste, and language so that all his employees, in turn, could become Kendall-Jackson's apostles. When he first started out, he had his law office staff taste and rate his early vintages. This was formalized over the years at Kendall-Jackson headquarters, and he would gather conference rooms full of employees to taste Kendall-Jackson's latest wines, new and established, in blind comparisons to competing brands. "I wanted to make certain we did not develop a house palate so that we could be aware of where we stood with the competition," Jackson later recalled. "Our wines always scored very well in those blind tests, but they were honest comparisons."

These were serious occasions, somber and high stakes. Wine-maker experiments were tried out here first. House brands could live or die here. Jackson demanded library silence on such occasions, and each participant would have to write his or her impressions down, detailing the qualities of the wines, their fruitiness, their tannins, the mouth feel and finish. And only after each had made those silent, secret ballots was open discussion permitted. Jackson wanted honest impressions from a variety of palates and wine expertise, confident that a cross-section of his employees was representative of the larger population, and he did not want his tasters influenced by the opinions of peers or managers. These tastings assumed the aspects of ritual, comforting and inspiring, intimidating yet unifying.

"We all loved that part of working here," marketer Teresa Mattingly recalled. "It was one of the ways Jess inspired us because he so obviously wanted our input and took it seriously. It made us all feel valued. Our opinions mattered. In a way, we *all* were winemakers."

IF FEW OF his staff or workplace confidants sensed any desire in Jackson to slow down or exert less control over his business as the quarter century anniversary of his winemaking enterprise neared, his first two daughters saw possible movement in that direction—on the home front. It seemed to Jenny and Laura that their father had mellowed with age in his parenting approach. The second time around he seemed both more hands-on and more relaxed as he raised a new set of kids in his sixties during the nineties (versus his first go-round, which began in his twenties during the fifties). At least it seemed so to Jenny and Laura, if not to their younger siblings, as they remembered a father more stern than playful, who worked nearly around the clock as an attorney, his labors punctuated by busy family vacations and extended car trips. This time around Jenny saw little evidence of the trial-by-fire parenting methods that she remembered so vividly from her own childhood: being asked to memorize amortization tables while in grade school; learning how to drive with clients' cast-off cars, including a sports car with failing brakes; getting dropped off at an advanced ski slope while she was just learning, her dad calling over his shoulder, "See you at the bottom," as he glided away, leaving her to slide down on her butt the whole way, crying. "How else are you going to learn?" he asked at the bottom, seemingly perplexed by Jenny's tears.

Jenny and Laura—and many of his employees—came to see this sort of approach to learning as Jackson's trademark: put a person in a challenging position, sometimes with little or no preparation, and let her or him learn under pressure. Whether it was selling wine, tasting wine, or driving a brakeless sports car into a garage for the first time, he believed that learning under pressure brought out the best in workers and children, pushing them to do things they might otherwise never attempt. He once explained to Don Hartford that he had learned from similar situations when he was young, and Hartford assumed that his father-in-law felt that if it had ultimately benefited him, then it would be do the same for his kids. But Jackson seemed to back off that approach with his second set of children.

"I think Katie, Julia, and Christopher were spared some of those experiences," Jenny would observe. "Although that may be less about Dad changing than because Barbara wouldn't allow it."

It was Barbara who, invoking safety concerns, insisted that the kids learn to drive not in Jackson's beloved rattletrap VW van (which was shipped off to Hawaii to the condo they bought in Kauai in 1990), but in the late-model Volvo that served as the family car in these more affluent years. Yet Jackson still put his own twist on driver's ed: he insisted on providing the lessons personally, and he let his kids start practicing behind the wheel on the lightly trafficked roads around Alexander Mountain when they turned fourteen.

When his daughter Julia asked, "What about the police?" Jackson shot back, "I was a cop. Don't worry."

Growing up in a family who lived and breathed the wine business rather than the law was a very different experience for the three youngest Jacksons, a more relaxed agrarian environment supplanting city life. By the time Katie was five, the family had already left the Bay Area home in Tiburon and settled in the first house in Sonoma County, the two-bedroom place across the road from the original Stonestreet Vineyard. Instead of sitting quietly in the law firm's office, as Jenny and Laura had when visiting their father during business hours, Katie's earliest memories of her father at work were of him leading the way through vineyards, showing her how to prune, having her pick up, smell, and even taste different clumps of soil. See, he'd ask, how the *terroir* can vary across just a few rows of vines? Just a few feet and the world changes, from the little grape's point of view. See that red dirt? Red means it has more iron in it, and grapes growing in it will taste different. She was too young to remember much more than that, though he'd repeat it many times, a familiar refrain: the primal joy of good earth, this mysterious element called *terroir*, the ancient strain of mountain grapes brought here from distant lands. It was the sensual nature of those vineyard walks that always stayed with Katie, the vivid leafy colors, the smell of freshly turned soil, the mounting heat of the day, and the feeling that her family was involved in something magical because when her dad described farming—that's what he called it, not viticulture, not winemaking, but farming—he made it sound like magic, passed down from a time long before the pyramids.

Only one clear memory of her father predated those childhood strolls through the rows of grapevines: the bunk bed in the bedroom she shared with her siblings during those first lean years in Sonoma and the night she fell from the top, shattering her clavicle on the hard wooden floor. She was four, lying terrified and in pain, afraid to move except to scream and cry in the dark, when the light in the hallway flicked on, impossibly bright. Then her dad appeared, huge, warm, and comforting, haloed by the lightbulb behind him as he stooped to pick her up as if she were weightless, telling her it was going be okay. "And I remember his voice was so deep and so calm, I believed him. I felt so safe. That's my first specific memory of Dad—me in pain and Dad swooping in to fix it."

Katie was the most outwardly sensitive of the three youngest Jacksons. Only ten-year-old Katie ran into the house and hid her face when their father decided it was time they all learned to slaughter a chicken, pluck the bird, and butcher it. Young Julia and Christopher stoically participated, watching the dreadful headless chicken spouting blood and staggering around the yard before flopping over. "You need to learn about where food comes from. It doesn't just appear in the grocery store. Someone has to grow it. And some day, if things were to change, you need to know how to raise and grow your own food and what to do with it." And then there was a long explanation about how bartering with neighbors could work. There had to be a big vegetable garden for that, he explained. Jackson regularly marched the kids to the backyard with shovels to plant and care for lettuce, beans, carrots, and other green things. With vegetables and chickens for eggs and meat, they could always trade for whatever else they needed: milk, cheese, bread. "We can be self-sufficient here if we need to be," Jackson told them, not speaking as a potential survivalist but as a true child of the Great Depression. "I want you to learn this, just in case. If you have some land and know how to farm, you'll never go hungry."

Katie's main takeaway from this lesson, however, once she had been so viscerally schooled in the origins of drumsticks, was to give up eating all meat and poultry, much to Jackson's consternation. For some reason only he seemed to grasp, he had chosen this occasion to share the story of his own pet chicken being slaughtered and served to him for dinner at his father's behest. Too late, Jackson realized it had been a mistake to link his how-to lesson on poultry butchering to the loss of his beloved pet and his father's cruelty, which Katie quite correctly perceived as a terrible and traumatic event despite

Jackson's attempts to backtrack and put the gloss of a hard lesson learned on that awful tale. The whole chicken-wringing scene had been at odds with how Katie normally perceived her father, whom she called the "animal whisperer" because the cats, dogs, goats, and llamas that roamed the grounds all tended to flock to Jackson. Her father loved animals and loved being around them, and Katie saw they responded in kind. Even ensconced in the big yellow easy chair in the living room, absorbed in his yellow legal pads and highlighters—the signal his children knew well, that he was not to be disturbed—the big old tabby cat would boldly perch on his shoulder or on the top of the chair, purring down at him, the dog stretched out at his feet. The chicken butchery had shaken her. It would be years before she'd touch a piece of chicken at the table.

Katie—everyone called her that, except her dad, who usually called her Katherine—described herself as the bookworm of the three, fond of hiking and swimming but generally more comfortable with a good book than athletic competition. She would be reading while Julia and Chris climbed trees or went swimming, which left Jackson fretting to her about the need for both a healthy mind and a healthy body. In his sixties and continuing into his seventies, he went running daily. He was so fit and energetic, it didn't occur to Katie that she had an older dad until one day a schoolmate's mom said innocently, "Oh, is that your grandfather picking you up at school today?"

This was a revelation to Katie, as she hadn't really thought about her father's age before, and now she was seeing him through new eyes. The comment offended her a bit, but mostly she was worried that her dad would hear it and be hurt. It didn't bother her that her father was different from the other parents; she had always known he was unique in a multitude of ways, age being the least of them. She routinely got straight As on her report cards—making her the standout of all five of the Jackson children, rivaled only by Jenny's daughter, Haley, a Jackson grandchild though she was actually only five days younger than Chris. Jackson's reaction to his daughter's report cards were classic contrarian Jess, the opposite of all the other parents at the prep high school she attended: "I'm proud of you," he told her, looking over a set of perfect grades. "But you don't have to work so hard. Bs are okay, too. I worry that you don't have a life."

If Katie was the book-loving dreamer, Jess's next daughter was the house rebel. Katie reacted to the chicken incident by running. Julia endured it, then struck back the next day when, at all of six years old, she set the remaining chickens free. As her usually sweet border collie proceeded to maul and attempt to eat the birds, she realized her prison break was turning out to be counterproductive. She saw her father was furious with her and only many years later learned he had been secretly pleased by her gumption and by the fact that she had stood up to him in a way he had not done with his own father until he was many years older.

Julia and Jess shared a strong physical resemblance as well as some key personality traits that were more obvious to others than to themselves, namely, their mutual fondness for argument. They debated and quarreled lustily and often, leading to frequent shouting matches. Whereas Katie dated sparingly and when she met her future fiancé, Jackson quite liked and welcomed him, Julia's taste in boyfriends worried him. Julia was more outgoing than her older sister, and her dates led to a series of mutually embarrassing lectures and disagreements. There were his pronouncements on the evils of sex before marriage, which Jackson pointedly forbade (with Julia barely able to resist pointing out that her and Katie's births had preceded Jess and Barbara's nuptials). There was his threat to pull out his shotgun if one particularly disrespectful young man ever showed up again on the property. There was the time they argued, and Julia snuck out to spend the night at another boyfriend's house. This had been done under his parents' supervision, but Jackson nevertheless next greeted him by saying, "You're corrupting my daughter," then turning his back on him.

In time Julia figured out how to crack the boyfriend code with her dad because it turned out that his problem with teenage boys in general (and those who wanted to date his daughter in particular) was grounded in their tendency to speak barely beyond a grunted hello and good-bye with the intimidating, towering father of an already intimidatingly attractive girl. He saw them as disrespectful and doltish and didn't hesitate to make that clear, his customarily warm welcome to any visitor quickly freezing over. When she finally couldn't bear this ritual bashing of a date any longer, she began counseling boyfriends to sit and chat for a minute with her dad, look him in the eye, shake his hand, and express interest in his business and activities—in other words, to engage in a little respectful sucking up. The transformation was dramatic the first time she had a date try it. There was no freeze. No shotguns. She realized her dad wanted to be wooed along with his daughter.

Julia was the youngest of Jackson's four girls, and he most often called her "Princess JuJu" (a nickname based on toddler Katie's imperfect pronunciation of her little sister's name). They shared a gift for music that was unique in the otherwise tone-deaf family. Julia inherited Jackson's ability to hear a tune once, then play it on the piano. Jackson always kept a piano in the house, and when the family moved into larger lodgings on Alexander Mountain, Jess had an office designed in a particularly scenic spot, Bear Point, which he equipped with a Steinway grand piano. Julia would sit on his lap when she was very young and place her hands atop Jackson's as he played, and it felt to Julia as if she, too, were making that beautiful music.

He wanted Julia to join him in the wine business—he wanted that for all his kids—but Julia felt particularly pressured to conform to her father's wishes and to choose a business course of study in college. She was interested, but art was her passion. She might have gone with a business major and an art minor in college, but she felt trapped by her dad's desire to bring her into the business, and this evoked the contrarian instincts she shared with him. So she chose a school and a program with a major in art. This became another source of battles between the two. She was turning her back on him,

Jackson would say. Art was impractical; she was wasting her time and neglecting everything he had taught her about the work ethic, how he had worked so hard at so many jobs at her age and how that was a key to his success. By that he meant he would not tolerate a spoiled rich girl for a daughter—the greatest fear that his newfound wealth brought him.

Julia shot back that if art was so impractical, who designed Kendall-Jackson's labels and logos and brochures and packaging? And while they were talking practical, just how practical was it to give up a lucrative law career and risk everything to start a winery?

He relented a bit then, saying, "I do want you and your brother and sister to be well rounded. So fine, go out and try things. As long as you come back and work for me."

Julia made no promises. For all his ranting about art being a waste of her abilities and education, she also knew that the well-wrought original drawings she gave him every birthday were among his most treasured possessions.

Chris, the youngest and Jackson's only son, grew up a dead ringer for his dad: tall, broad shouldered, athletic. Jackson became a fixture at his son's varsity basketball games, part of a league of small high schools that required spectators to take long drives all over Wine Country, where some of the towns were so competitive that the family cars from the Sonoma Academy were all keyed during one contentious game. Another town harbored such enmity to the visitors from Sonoma that they needed a police escort. Jess's vociferous cheering and willingness to shout questions about referees' eyesight during such games didn't help, though Chris's teammates loved him for it. One of Jess's great resentments in life had been his own father's absence from his football and basketball games, and so Jackson seemed determined to be clearly present and engaged for his own son. His enthusiasm soon became local legend, including the occasion he was ejected from the stands for shouting about bad calls and later could be seen with his face pressed against the gymnasium window watching the end of a pivotal game in which the hometown bias he perceived in the referees' calls had infuriated him. Of all the kids, Chris grew up to be the most similar in outlook and world-view to his father, drawn to business and law and fascinated by history. Whereas Julia and Katie identified themselves as politically liberal in most respects, Chris came to share Jackson's conservative–libertarian–socially moderate live-and-let-live political philosophy. In the summer of 2011 Chris would head off to Washington, DC, where he would work as an intern for Speaker of the House John Boehner. His roommate and best friend would serve as a White House intern for President Barack Obama.

As with Jenny and Laura before them, Jackson one by one pressured all three of his youngest children to leave college before graduating to come work for the company. This baffled the kids. When he needed help from his first two daughters, his wine business had been new, understaffed, and struggling, and money for tuition was scant. It was a harsh but at least understandable reality when Laura left school to work at the business and Jenny had to pay her own way through the law school education Jess begrudged her. Laura never did go back to get her degree. But a quarter century later the company and the Jacksons' bank account had a radically different posture. By the time his next generation of kids was ready for college, the company had a huge workforce and Jackson was buying villas in Tuscany. Still, he made his plea: he needed his kids to come learn the business and help him run the company. Except it was really less a matter of needing them and more a matter of missing them—and fearing that they would go their separate ways and leave him. And that he could not bear.

Katie ended up doing as he wished, leaving school before graduation to work for the company. But she said that was primarily because she ended up disliking the East Coast liberal arts college she had chosen to attend (over Jackson's Berkeley-centric recommendation).

Chris and Julia resisted, however. They made it clear that they adored their quirky, opinionated, accomplished father, who could be so tough on them one moment, so demanding, and the next sit them down on his lap on the piano bench and make them feel as if they were playing a concerto. The three best gifts Julia treasured most were from her dad, who did not give presents often, who disliked on principle the commercialization of holidays and the organized gift shopping of Christmas and birthdays. But now and then he enjoyed finding special, unusual gifts for his kids. The first and most favorite for Julia was a collection of CDs of his thirty favorite classical composers. He gave this to her at age eight. The second was a gift of stock the year she turned twelve (Katie and Chris received the same). The portfolio featured shares in Pixar and Krispy Kreme, and to Julia, owning that stock, those small pieces of incredible real businesses she knew about and admired, seemed powerful and important. And the third most treasured gift Julia received was a precision instrument called a refractometer, calibrated to be taken into the vineyards to measure the sugar level of grapes—the Brix, as it's called. (A close runner-up was a gift of cattle; Jackson took the kids to Knights Valley, where cows grazed next to vineyards, and each of them picked out a head.) Julia could not understand how the father who was so thoughtful and discerning in choosing such unique and personal gifts could be so insensitive as to demand that she leave college in her junior year to come work for him. When she unequivocally refused, she was surprised to observe that *he* was surprised, and so she told him that he had to stop treating her like one of his forty-five-year-old male employees. "I'm a twenty-year-old girl in college. I know you want me to catch up with you, but that's impossible. You have fifty years of experience in business and as a lawyer. I need to graduate. I need to find my way, just like you did."

Grudgingly, he relented. In retrospect, it seems Jess's desire to bring his kids home was very different this time around. It was easy to overlook in so vital a person, who seemed to defy time, who ran fifteen miles a day, and who outpaced and outworked colleagues half his age, but in truth he was feeling the accumulation of years. What he wanted was quite simple: he wanted to teach his children the business he had built and loved, to put into place his legacy before his time ran out.

THAT JACKSON MIGHT be headed not toward building a family dynasty, but toward retiring and putting the company on the auction block finally became a subject of public and media speculation in Sonoma County in the fall of 1998. The news soon spread to the pages of the *Wall Street Journal*, which had been covering the rapid consolidation, IPOs, and conglomerate gobbling of family wineries that had begun churning the US wine industry. The first sign of Jackson's shift in focus was the splitting of his wine business into two division: Kendall-Jackson Winery, LTD, where Vintner's Reserve had carried the company to $300 million in revenue that year, and a now separate Artisans & Estates division, which by then consisted of fourteen small, independently run wineries and brands. These boutique wineries collectively made a tenth of the revenue of the main division, but they held all of Jackson's prestige labels and pricier vintages. Jackson developed this line of the business as a reputation enhancer, creating a halo of perceived quality that extended to even his lowest-price wines, and also as a growth opportunity of its own. Jackson believed the nascent market for high-end wines would evolve into a high-profit opportunity over time if Jackson could crack burgeoning international markets, particularly in Asia's rapidly expanding economies, and persuade them to embrace California's ultrapremium wines.

The artisan business also owned all that beautiful vineyard real estate Jackson had been accumulating for decades, which meant his wallet might reside in the Vintner's Reserve offices, but his heart was with those high-end labels and mountaintop *terroir*. If there was a deal to go public or to court a buyer, it almost certainly would be for the big moneymaker division, while Jackson would hold on to the boutique wineries and glorious land to play with in his "retirement." Or so the speculation in the press and among the wine cognoscenti went in those last years of the century, though even they admitted their predictions were nothing but guesswork. Jess and Barbara were obliged to attend the winemaker galas and social scene, but they let nothing slip about such plans. Jess had always been obsessively private about his business dealings anyway, one of the advantages of a family-owned company that a publicly traded one could not share so easily. For that reason alone, some of those closest to Jackson doubted that an IPO would ever happen. They knew how he hated to be second-guessed and being forced to justify himself and his decisions—something he'd have to do regularly as head of a publicly traded company. "Jess could never stand for that," Hartford said to Jenny at the time. "It's not in his DNA." Others saw the huge infusion of capital an IPO would bring and figured Jackson would hold his nose and cash in because it would empower him to do more and buy more than otherwise would be possible. The best guess at that time was that the Kendall-Jackson division could fetch at least $500 million if it went public.

Much was made of the fact that Jackson handed over day-to-day control (at least on paper) to two new CEOs, one for each of the newly cobbled divisions. There had never been a formally titled chief executive officer at Kendall-Jackson before, much less two of them; Jess and Barbara had most often described themselves as "proprietors," although they also alternately held titles of chairman and president. Now there were CEOs. Newly in charge of the Kendall-Jackson piece was Leonard Cairney, a former top executive at Heublein Spirits, which for many years had been a liquor and wine-making giant, only to be bought out, broken apart, and dissolved by the even bigger R. J. Reynolds Tobacco conglomerate after the cigarette company merged with food giant Nabisco. Jackson's veteran executive Randy Clifton took over the boutique wineries of Artisans & Estates, which he had been unofficially overseeing for years. Both of the new CEOs reported to Jackson, but though he retained ultimate control, the hiring of a corporate player such as Cairney was widely interpreted as the first step in prepping the company for Jackson's retirement and for an IPO of stock. Jackson fueled the speculation with a purposely ambiguous press release that quoted him as describing the moves as marking "our ongoing planning for succession." Then he had the company PR person issue a pointedly weak denial that the company was going up for sale: "We're always looking at options. There are no plans, in the next sixty to ninety days, to go public."

It seemed, then, that Jackson was joining (or wanted everyone else to *think* he was joining) a trend in the California wine business: companies printing stock to go along with bottling wine. Robert Mondavi had started the movement when he staged a massive IPO in 1993, setting off a chain reaction of me-too stock sales, including the then largest to date, Beringer's 1997 offering. Winemakers were increasingly turning for financing to Wall Street investors instead of conventional bank loans as the wine business exploded in the 1990s. The shift in consumer interest, particularly in the once anemic red wine category, was in large part attributed to the television news show *60 Minutes*, which in late 1991 featured an attention-grabbing piece about wine consumption entitled "The French Paradox." The program quoted scientists who had investigated why the French population, whose diet featured high amounts of fat and dairy, had extremely low occurrence of heart disease (the opposite of the US pattern of high fat intake and correspondingly high heart attack rates). The scientists credited moderate consumption of red wine and its possible health benefits as the explanation, as the French liked to wash their butter-soaked foods and cheese plates down with vino, whereas Americans' favorite beverage was soda.

That year *60 Minutes* was the most watched series on television (twenty years later the reality singing competition show *American Idol* would occupy that spot, while *60 Minutes*, still the most watched news show, stood in sixty-ninth place—which may be the most revealing statistical comparison in recent US cultural history). In 1991 *60 Minutes* could galvanize the nation, and in the year following the French paradox broadcast, sales of red wine in America shot up nearly 50 percent. Never mind that the most beneficial substances in red wine—compounds known as antioxidants—could also be found in nonalcoholic grape juice, broccoli, and a variety of other foods. The notion that a good belt of red wine could be a virtue rather than a vice had obvious appeal, a marketing godsend for winemakers who raced to plant more Merlot and Pinot and Cabernet grapes as the new "health food."

By 1995 the US Food and Drug Administration's position on wine had morphed from a bald claim that it had absolutely no health benefits to a statement that a healthy diet could include moderate amounts of wine at meals. This reversal on the official word on eating healthy in America brought the modern medical establishment back to a position first espoused by Hippocrates, the father of Western medicine, who had sung wine's virtues back in 400 BC and whose position was accepted as an obvious truism throughout most of the rest of human history, right up to the point that Prohibition cast wine as terror rather than tonic. Now wine was hot again, which explained part of Kendall-Jackson's sustained and rapid growth in this era—as well as the need for wineries to amass cash to keep pace with demand and to finance planting new vineyards. The national economy was on the upswing in the late 1990s, and stock offerings were a pathway to large piles of cash without the need to sell the entire company or to give up complete control. Jackson's moves signaled he was about to follow Mondavi and Beringer down that same path.

But the signals were mixed because Jackson, not his newly hired CEOs, continued setting the overall strategy of the company. And that strategy was continued acquisition, growth, and vineyard expansion—aggressive, debt-inducing moves that offered great returns down the line but were rather risky for a company trying to sell itself as a sure-thing investment to Wall Street. Yet the race to plant more vineyards continued unabated at Kendall-Jackson. On Taylor Mountain above Santa Rosa, on land that had once been an Arabian horse showcase, Jackson planted fields of Merlot for a new upscale brand, though this time, thanks to some

painful lessons, the stands of beautiful tall oak trees were left un-
touched, with the vines carefully laid out to avoid any tree removal.
This was premium land that would yield premium grapes, which
were selling in 1999 for as much as $2,500 a ton, four times the price
in 1989. Prime vineyard real estate was fetching as much as $50,000
an acre by then; the imperative for Jackson to plant his own grapes
rather than buy someone else's had become overwhelming.

So growth on the vineyard was not just an option in Jackson's
view; it was a necessity, which was why he snapped up yet another
property in 1999, a five-hundred-acre cattle ranch in Sonoma County's dairy belt west of Petaluma. This area had always been thought
to be too chilly and windy for quality grapes, which meant Jackson got the land comparatively cheaply: $2.4 million, or $4,800 an
acre, dairy farm dollars rather than vineyard prices. But Jackson
had his vignerons studying the climate and soil in the area for two
years prior to the purchase, quietly testing what sort of fruit this
particular climate could bear, and their findings backed up Jackson's initial hunch that the new property could be a mini-Caucasus,
the birthplace of the *vinifera:* land that could produce top-quality,
cold-loving Pinot Noir. He snapped up the ranch and laid plans
to put grapes down on more than half the terrain. The cattlemen
in the area were stunned, convinced by long-standing conventional
wisdom that grapes couldn't grow there. But Jackson's vines took
to the *terroir* there, and his coup meant the land tripled in value
very quickly. "We are planting where no man has planted before,"
Jackson crowed.

Less than a year later, just a few steps across Bennett Valley Road
from the old Graystone horse farm with its new Merlot vineyard,
Jackson spent considerably more money—$45 million—to make
another purchase. This time it wasn't raw land, but one of Wine
Country's elite boutique wineries and small vineyards. The property,
Matanzas Creek, had been built from a broken-down dairy bought
at an estate sale in the 1970 by Bill and Sandra MacIver. The novice
vintners converted the dairy barn to a makeshift winery, learned

winemaking as they went, and planted fields of lavender around the property to draw tourists to this remote corner of Wine Country (their annual wine and lavender festival now draws thousands every year). The small winery's reputation for high quality left Matanzas a perennial sellout, unable to meet eager customers who demanded more than the 40,000 cases the little winery produced each year. This demand came despite premium prices—the cheapest wine, a Sauvignon Blanc, was $22 in 1999, and one of Matanzas's most popular wines, a Merlot, sold out at $155 a bottle. Matanzas Creek, grape for grape, was one of the most valuable wine properties in the nation, and Jackson had long coveted it.

Bill MacIver had become a close friend and ally; he and Jackson worked together in the California Family Winemakers trade group, which MacIver cofounded, and the Coalition for Free Trade, the group that fought repeated legal battles to crack open the wine distribution business and permit direct sales across state lines. When the MacIvers decided to scale back and move out of Sonoma, they saw Jackson as the natural choice for buyer, both because they believed he shared their values and would preserve what they had built, and because the grapes Jackson was already growing in the same *terroir* across the street could be used to increase Matanzas volume without compromising quality.

"This is the jewel in the Artisans & Estates crown," Jackson said in announcing the sale, promising, among other things, to keep the current winemakers in place. "You don't fix what's not broken."

Not long after the Matanzas Creek deal concluded, new rumors began circulating that Jackson and his representatives had been meeting secretly with the leadership of the much larger Beringer Wine Estates of Napa Valley. Beringer had been bought by Nestlé decades earlier, changed hands several times, and returned to majority US ownership in the mid-1990s with the arrival of the Texas Pacific Group, the world's largest private equity investment firm, owners of such diverse companies as Ducati, Burger King, and Metro-Goldwyn-Mayer. Later the group launched a lucrative IPO.

When word of the meetings between Jackson and Beringer got out, the immediate assumption was that a merger or sale was in the works and that the larger fish was going to swallow the smaller fry. Kendall-Jackson tersely denied that any sale of the Sonoma winemaker was in the offing, which was true. But the rumor had a basis in reality: Beringer wanted to discuss buying Kendall-Jackson. But that was just a foot in the door for Jackson, who wanted to flip things and try to buy a major piece of Beringer's Wine Country properties, if not the whole company. "It was classic Jess," recalled Don Hartford, one of the few who knew what Jackson was trying to do. "We were somewhere between a tenth and quarter of their size at the time. They had a spirits business and a wine business, and Jess had it in his mind that there was a way to leverage Kendall-Jackson's assets to make what would have been a mammoth acquisition."

Beringer as a brand had taken a hit in terms of the quality of its wine after years of foreign corporate ownership, but it wasn't the label that drew Jackson. There were the once storied family wineries in Sonoma County that Beringer had bought out over the years, including Chateau St. Jean. More than that, however, was the land. Beringer owned 10,000 acres of Wine Country vineyards, and Jackson saw that real estate as a premium wine jackpot that was being squandered to make mediocre wines. He would know what to do with those vineyards, he told Hartford, if only he could get his hands on them.

It didn't happen, though. Just a few weeks after media reports discussed a possible Beringer purchase of Kendall-Jackson, Beringer itself was bought out by mammoth Australian beer, spirits, and wine conglomerate Fosters, for $1.5 billion. The huge purchase price set an industry record that seemed to usher in a new age of globalization in the wine business. Analysts predicted that other companies—notably Kendall-Jackson and even larger players, such as Mondavi—would be pressured, perhaps forced, to sell, merge, or find strategic global partners with the immense Foster's level of clout in order to stay competitive. One wine industry analyst, Sonoma-based broker Mario Zepponi, predicted, "The Beringer deal will open the floodgates for consolidation in the wine industry."

A marriage of Beringer and Kendall-Jackson would have created the largest premium wine company in the country, if not the world, a formidable global competitor. But the move by Fosters also strengthened Jackson's position. With Beringer gone, there were only so many other targets ripe for merger or buyout, and when increasing demand meets dwindling supply, prices rise. The sale of Beringer instantly doubled, at the very least, the potential sale price of Kendall-Jackson.

"Jess Jackson is in the catbird's seat," Zepponi told a reporter for the Santa Rosa *Press Democrat*, "because the value of his company just went up in a big way."

But what, exactly, was the value of the company? Jackson wanted to know, needed to know. He had the financial ability to swoop in and buy a Matanzas Creek whenever the opportunity arose, but if he wanted to make serious overtures to buy something big, something like a piece of Beringer, he needed to know what he was worth on the open market. But no one, not even Jackson, could put a firm dollar figure on the value of what he had built. Like a house, KJ's true value was whatever someone was willing to pay for it on a given day, and circumstances could radically change that amount from one day to the next. Beringer got sold, and the $500 million price tag Kendall-Jackson wore in theory suddenly jumped to $800 million or $1 billion, or maybe more. What would it be after the next big sale or the one after that? What if Mondavi sold out? Where would Kendall-Jackson's price top out then? What would the company be worth when it was the last of the old-line family winemakers left standing?

The only way to learn would be to actually put the company up for sale. And so, driven more by an obsessive curiosity than financial necessity, along with a thirst to acquire epic amounts of vino real estate, Jackson decided to do just that. "I want to know," he said simply.

After the Beringer sale, the will-he-or-won't-he phase of speculation and ambiguity ended, and it became very clear, inside and
outside Kendall-Jackson, that the company was being prepped for a
sale. The web of trusts that held ownership of the company for the
family and the formal splitting of the company in two had made
the sale a possibility. But now Jackson was taking concrete steps to
make it happen, right down to giving top employees stock options, potentially worth a great deal if the company sold or went public. "No
one really knew for sure if a sale would go through or not," Hartford
recalled. "The company was divided internally, with some—mostly
those who stood to make a lot of money—all for it, while others were
very upset by it. I don't even think Jess knew what would happen at
that point."

Next came a new hire right out of the Wall Street IPO playbook,
introducing a level of corporate ability and experience unprecedented
at Kendall-Jackson—or anywhere in the California wine business for
that matter. Handpicked by Jackson as leader of his entire wine enterprise, Lew Platt had just left the CEO position at computer giant
Hewlett-Packard, where he had achieved 187 percent revenue growth
during a seven-year tenure at the top. Even so, his progressive policies toward the workforce and his preference for planning for the
long-term health of the company doomed him at Hewlett-Packard,
where the board of directors had grown eager for a more aggressive,
short-term-profit-focused leader. That was the new way of the tech
industry back then: quarterly churn, cost-cutting, layoffs, outsourc-
ing. Platt was seen as dated in his insistent clinging to the old-school
values espoused by the company founders, tech legends Bill Hewlett
and Dave Packard. Platt's successors accumulated disastrously poor
and often scandalous records as the HP brand lost its luster; in retrospect, Platt came to be viewed as the last really successful leader
at HP and his replacement as one of the worst corporate personnel
decisions in the history of Silicon Valley.

Jackson saw that long before the tech industry revised its col-
lective opinion and he made Platt an adviser at first, then chief

executive. The marriage of silicon and grapes might have seemed an unlikely one for a Wine Country CEO, but the fifty-eight-year-old Platt lived in Sonoma County, was an avid wine collector, and was a proven corporate leader known for high principles and his ability to build consensus. He had managed the transition at Hewlett-Packard from control by the founders to a more typical management hierarchy, and that experience matched up with what would have to happen at Kendall-Jackson if it were to be sold or go public. Platt's management style was to solicit input from company managers, then reach consensus rather than impose a strictly top-down decisionmaking process, as had been the case under Jackson. "You can give people lots of freedom," he said in an interview shortly after taking the job. "I do not like to micromanage. I like to talk about where we are headed, and then give people the freedom to go out and do the job."

This was a polar opposite management philosophy from Jess Jackson's; it was the difference, as Hartford put it, between flying at 30,000 feet and flying at 3 feet. A good boss, Platt liked to say, is not necessarily the one who gives the most orders. Hartford and others found it fascinating, if not outright inexplicable, that Jackson not only admired such a manager but also hired him to be his successor. Yet Jackson, who stepped down as chief executive once he lured Platt to the job in January 2000, seemed smitten with his new hire. "I couldn't think of a better leader for the future," he gushed. "He has a passion for learning and a passion for wine and a curiosity that won't stop."

Jackson, who still held on to his job as chairman of the company, told others he saw Platt as an extraordinary and deep leader, whom he expected to take Kendall-Jackson to "the next level." This was widely interpreted as Jackson wanting to move from an entrepreneurial family business, albeit a very large one, to a professionally managed corporation capable of expanding into international sales, able to continue expanding in California even as costs and environmental concerns rose, and, finally, able to prepare the company for the granddaddy of all Wine Country IPOs, if not an outright sale. At that time Kendall-Jackson's international sales comprised but 3 percent of the company's revenue, despite KJ having four marvelous foreign wineries. Their wines, like those produced in the United States, sold here. Platt's goal was to set plans in motion to raise foreign sales to 30 percent. But Jackson also made it clear that he was in no rush to force this transition, which, in retrospect, was probably his way of hinting that this vision of rebooting his company was in no way a done deal. He said publicly that he wouldn't consider going public for at least year after Platt's arrival. "We have to get all our ducks in a row."

As this conversion proceeded, as Platt broke down the silos that Jackson had built to separate departments from one another and keep them under his direct control, it appeared for a time Jackson really was stepping back from the business. Nine months after Platt took over, in November 2000, Jackson gave up his role as chairman of the company. "I'm available as a resource," he told a reporter. "But I don't think they'll need me much."

Few who knew Jackson well thought he could tame his über-competitive, workaholic tendencies. They figured that he'd never be happy walking away from his company, that he didn't know how to shut off the spigot of ideas and vineyard purchase schemes that had kept him busy and kept him young for decades. But he swore to limit himself to one two-hour lunch meeting with Platt a week. He'd let the man do his job, and though Jackson's daily absence felt like a vacuum to his staff, most also felt Platt brought a much-needed reorganization. Even rising stars under Jackson's reign, including top sales executive Rick Tigner, a Haarstad and Jackson protégé, thought the changes and discipline Platt was baking into the company would strengthen Kendall-Jackson no matter what happened with ownership or stocks down the line.

Jackson tried to devote his new freedom to rediscovering how to relax—to hike Alexander Mountain, where he and Barbara had designed their dream homestead, rustic, simple, gorgeous. And he wanted to spend more time with his two teenaged daughters and his son, Chris, then eleven, which he managed to do. But later, when the kids remembered that time frame, the image of them returning from a walk with the dogs and sitting down to relax together at home almost always included a yellow legal pad and a jar bristling with colored markers. Even relaxing, they said, Jackson's mind returned to work. And he still actively engaged in plotting the course of his artisan wineries, a branch of his business he decided to rename Jackson Family Farms.

But his everyday work began to take different directions, too, more commonly associated with a retiree with wealth. Jackson became more actively involved in philanthropy and good works, donating money to the University of California to back its famed wine program at the Davis campus and backing efforts to make the industry more sustainable and lower its environmental impact. With three more huge wineries in the works in Sonoma, Napa, and Monterey, Jackson commissioned designs that put the buildings mostly below ground level, lowering the visual impact that might disturb neighbors, as well as incorporating water and energy conservation into the designs.

Jackson also teamed up with a group of Sonoma County's wealthiest and most influential families to fund a $50 million private high school, Sonoma Academy, the first in the county, slated to open in temporary lodgings in fall 2001, with a newly built facility in place by the following year. Jackson, Banke, and Pixar filmmaker John Lasseter and his wife, Nancy, were among the donors and trustees (and all the Jackson children signed on for their high school educations there). The fund-raising included a $6 million endowment for scholarships. When the trustees of the new Sonoma Academy were trying to lure a doubtful Massachusetts educator to become headmistress, Jackson took on the task of convincing her to relocate, spending the day squiring her around Sonoma County in his private helicopter, explaining how he and his fellow trustees intended to build the best and most innovative school in the country, how they would make sure the school would be open to the children of vineyard owners and fieldworkers alike, and how they were certain she was the woman for the job. By the time he was done, Janet Durgin, who had mostly decided against taking the job before Jackson coaxed her aboard that helicopter, was saying yes, was saying she couldn't wait to get started, was saying thank you to Jackson. As he had charmed and sold so many others on his various visions, so he sold Durgin on the as-yet-nonexistent Sonoma Academy, she recalled. A force of nature, she called him, caring and committed but irresistible.

Forbes magazine, in its year 2000 compendium of the 400 richest people in America, gave Jackson an unwanted seventieth birthday gift by anointing him "America's first vino-billionaire." Ranking him 223rd on the 400 list of richest Americans—ahead of Oprah—*Forbes* pegged Jackson's net worth at $1.3 billion. Jackson reacted in a fury, writing an angry letter to the magazine for failing to recognize that the network of trusts and holding companies he had created were the actual owners of all that wealth, not him personally. This was legally true, but a bit of a technicality that *Forbes* chose to ignore for many years, making Jackson's complaint to the magazine a kind of annual ritual. "I typically have about $7 in my wallet," he griped. Which was true. Jackson was a generous fellow in many ways— donating to the Sonoma Academy, paying for expensive hospital care when a vineyard worker's insurance maxed out, and always picking up the check at restaurants. But out and about, when he might eat with others at roadside stands or diners where plastic wasn't an option, he was always borrowing cash from friends and employees. It was a standing joke. "He was one of the four hundred richest men in the country," Harford laughed, "but we were always buying him lunch."

It would be an overstatement to say Jackson was on the sidelines during this period—he still had final say on the big decisions—but he had definitely backed away during the Platt tenure, as corporate suitors circled, bankers and auditors alighted at company headquarters to certify the books and assets for a possible IPO, and speculation about the end of family winemaking in Sonoma County, if not all of California, became a near-daily preoccupation. The entire wine industry watched and laid bets on whether the lawyer-turned-iron-willed-vintner who had achieved success by flouting conventional wisdom for a quarter century would finally submit to a sale or the eternal scrutiny that would accompany the riches of going public.

The jockeying was complicated by a difficult and disappointing sales performance in 1999 by the winemaker. Jackson's propensity for raising prices with impunity backfired that year as sales stalled. A rapid series of price increases had not only obliterated the old $10 barrier but had also raised the price of Vintner's Reserve Chardonnay to nearly $15 a bottle. The precipitous increases had so dented sales that major retailers had large stockpiles of wine that had failed to sell; the Safeway grocery chain had so much inventory that the company didn't have to place its first order for the year 2000 until mid-May. The result was a marked drop in the company's revenues, its long-standing record of double-digit annual growth ended, and its potential sales price drooped. But within a year sales and revenue bounced back and set new records—more than $350 million earned on the sale of nearly 4 million cases of wine. Far from a misstep, Jackson's pricing strategy had succeeded in establishing a new baseline for Kendall-Jackson's most successful wine that would ensure future profit margins hard for any rival to beat.

That others agreed with Jackson's assessment became clear in February 2001 when two British conglomerates, Diageo PLC and Allied Domecq Holdings PLC, emerged as leading bidders for Kendall-Jackson. The two companies, not exactly household words in the United States, nevertheless were the number one and two liquor companies in the world. Diageo owned such brands as Guinness, Seagram's, Smirnoff, Tanqueray, Moet & Chandon, Johnnie Walker, and Sterling Vineyards in Napa Valley. The company, with sales in 180 countries, also owned Burger King at the time, though it would soon sell to the same investment group that had bought Beringer. Allied's many brands included Beefeater, Courvoisier, Mumm, Perrier-Jouet, Kahlua, Stolichnaya, and the once family-owned Sonoma winery Clos du Bois. When the *Wall Street Journal* found out about the secretive negotiations, it portrayed Kendall-Jackson as a wine industry crown jewel that could fetch $1.5 billion to $2 billion if Jackson were to sell everything, including his land and small labels, to one of the competing conglomerates. Diageo had the deepest pockets and was aggressively expanding its presence in California Wine Country, and the handicappers at the *Wall Street Journal* pegged the Burger King owners as the favorite. Another conglomerate, Australian winemaker BRL Hardy LTD entered the fray, along with massive US wine and spirits company Brown-Forman. All wanted a shot at Kendall-Jackson.

Although company vice president Paul Ginsburg had talked up the possibility of a deal getting close in media interviews, and investment banker Morgan Stanley had been brought in to analyze the offers, which seemed to indicate a readiness to sell, Jackson in the spring of 2001 began publicly expressing doubts. Yes, he said, he'd seriously consider an extraordinary offer—by which he meant at least $2 billion—but what he really seemed to be saying was that his family and friends had been right: Kendall-Jackson was his life and his legacy, and he wanted it pass it on to his kids, not shareholders in London or investment bankers in Sydney. He had watched the destruction of the culture and quality at other family wineries that cashed out to conglomerates that put profits first, and he feared for Kendall-Jackson's image, its workers, and its place in the community. Even as he was trying to sell the company, in public statements to the press Jackson was using such words as "horrendous" to describe some of the companies approaching him. He also told reporters, "I don't expect something to happen. We are perfectly happy doing what we are doing."

But he didn't call the whole thing off. Instead, Jackson set a deadline of May 4, 2001, for bids to buy the company. BRL Hardy, which was smaller than Kendall-Jackson, and the giant Diageo submitted offers that included substantial shares of stock in the new merged enterprise and that allowed Jackson to retain his artisan wineries and coveted *terroir*. Brown-Forman also placed a bid. The offers ranged in value as high as $1.6 billion and that was just for the money machine of the main Kendall-Jackson brand, the Vintner's Reserve and its sister varietals. Jackson now had what he wanted. He knew what his business was worth on the open market; add in his artisan wineries and all that land, and he had a $2 billion+ baby built out of eighty-four acres in Lakeport and a maxed-out mortgage on his family home.

"Not too shabby," he told Barbara. "Now let's take down the for-sale sign. I'm not letting any of those guys near my company."

He called off the sale, as Banke always knew he would, even if Jackson himself didn't. Nor would there be an IPO. Kendall-Jackson would stay a family business.

"Wasn't going to happen," Banke would later recall. "He never really wanted to sell, but he had to go through that process to realize it."

12

Bluegrass Hurricane: Mr. Jackson's Wild Ride

T HE FALLOUT FROM WALKING AWAY FROM CORPORATE takeover turned out to be surprisingly mild. Lew Platt left Kendall-Jackson on good terms a few weeks later, pronouncing his work complete after eighteen months in Santa Rosa. He had run Kendall-Jackson as the big, established company it had been for years but never quite admitted. He had used the same approach, admired but abandoned, that he had adopted at HP: humane, consensus building, risk averse, focused on long-term gain, and seeking to perfect the lines of business already in place that had been, in some cases, left half-baked for years, such as the anemic international sales division. This represented a major change for the wine company. Even as it became a huge and profitable enterprise, Jackson had continued to run the business like a start-up: edgy, risk-taking, always looking for the next innovation, leveraged to the hilt, and animated by his vision, decisions, and will, subject to turning on a dime on his say-so. Jackson's way had led to big wins that Platt might never have achieved, but the corporate man's vino version of the late, lamented values-driven "HP way" of doing business left behind a better-organized and better-functioning company leadership and a decisionmaking structure that did not have to rest solely with a single mercurial visionary named Jess Jackson. Kendall-Jackson was now a hybrid of the two philosophies. Most of Platt's colleagues there, including Jackson and Banke, were pleased by his accomplishments. Platt left on a high note, to be missed and admired.

For his part, Platt seemed delighted to return to the retirement from which he had been lured, and he appeared neither surprised nor upset by Jackson's decision to continue the family business rather than squeeze money from its dismemberment. If the Jacksons concluded that was the best thing for their family, community, and enterprise, Platt said, then they made the right decision. It had been his job to bring the company to that decision point without being invested in either outcome, and so he considered his tenure there a success. (Two years later Platt would be coaxed from retirement once again to take charge of the Boeing Company after the aerospace giant's previous CEO was forced out by an ethics scandal. In the midst of fixing Boeing, the sixty-four-year-old Platt died in 2005 of an undiagnosed aneurism while driving home with his wife.)

Meanwhile, the conglomerates that had stalked Kendall-Jackson soon found other prey as the march of winery consolidations continued elsewhere. The Australian bidder, BRL Hardy, launched a $100 million joint venture with mammoth Constellation Brands in order to crack the US market. Predictably, Constellation ended up gobbling up its smaller partner within two years as it made a major push into Australia. Allied Domecq snapped up Sonoma's historic Buena Vista Winery, family owned since before the Civil War, for $85 million. A dozen other California wineries changed hands in the following years, with Robert Mondavi, bigger than Kendall-Jackson but apparently not as valuable, sold to Constellation for $1 billion in 2004. With each sale, Jackson figured, his company became that much more rare and valuable—should he ever wish to sell it.

As for the reason the Kendall-Jackson sale fell through, the take from the outside suggested two simple possibilities: the offer hadn't been high enough, or Jackson simply couldn't bear to part with his baby and so set an impossibly high price once the bidding got serious. From the inside, the consensus was different: Jackson had never intended to go through with a sale under any circumstances. In this view, Jackson had nothing more complex in mind than putting a real-world value on his creation, and this was the only way he knew how to do it, which meant playing the part all the way and keeping silent about his true intentions.

"That's my take," Don Hartford said. "Everyone kept saying it was a go, that there's no way Jess would spend all this money, prepping the books, bringing in Wall Street people, hiring Lew, issuing stock options—all of which was very, very costly—if it wasn't real. And I tried to tell people, don't get your hopes too high. Jess was willing to spend a lot of money in order to satisfy his curiosity. But he never wanted to sell."

Jackson never admitted to this view, but neither would he deny it. When pressed, he would just slip on a Cheshire Cat grin and simply say, "Constitutionally, I seem unsuited to retirement."

But neither did he seem to want to return to full-time leadership of the company after Platt's departure. At seventy-one, Jackson decided to make his retirement official and permanent, or so he said. Banke, at age forty-seven, became CEO and chairman of Kendall-Jackson Wine Estates—the main part of the company that had been put up for sale. One of her first priorities was to ramp up the low-impact sustainable farming techniques that she had championed for years but that Jackson had not always raced to adopt. She also imposed a policy that no forests or woodlands would be cleared for future vineyards. No more oak tree battles, she said, putting an end to a bad practice that always garnered bad press. And to consolidate the business as a fully family-run enterprise, Don Hartford, who with wife, Jenny, was already co-owner of one of the boutique wineries, Hartford Court, producer of highly rated Zinfandels and Pinot Noirs, became CEO of the entire artisan wine division.

The company settled in for a new reality in which Jackson was cast as a guiding figure, but at a distance. Within a few months, though, Jackson started appearing at the office with greater regularity, calling meetings, issuing orders, and slipping back into his old ways. Banke showed him the door and reminded him that he had agreed on a new order—demanded it, actually. "Get a hobby," she suggested.

"I have been thinking about horses," Jackson answered. Banke pointed out that he had pined for owning some thoroughbreds for years, that he was always mentioning his brief partnership with his uncle in a small stable of stakes horses so long ago. He had the time. God knew he had the money, she said.

"I'll think about it."

Hartford, who knew Jackson went all in as a way of life, be it at a casino or a winery, was only half joking when he quipped, "What are you going to do, Jess? Go out and win the Kentucky Derby?"

Jackson laughed. But he didn't shake his head no. Hobbies were serious business for Jess Jackson, which was why he had hesitated before jumping in. His last hobby, a little farm in Lakeport that was supposed to be his retirement project and escape from work pressures when he left the law, ended up making him the nation's first vino billionaire—with even longer work days than his legal practice had required. Now a quarter century later he was beginning a second retirement by digging into the world of thoroughbred horses, reading voraciously, talking to experts, browsing at horse auctions, and pondering the strange history that had brought modern thoroughbred racing to a difficult position and a fading glory in its American incarnation. It would be a momentous retirement project, and he was anxious to do it right rather than rush in and have to recover from disaster as he had with his Lakeport winery.

The only problem was that, in fairly short order, horses stopped being a *retirement* project because by 2003, Jackson had *un*retired himself from winemaking. He could bear being away from the company no longer. "I work. I love to work. I live to work, and

Kendall-Jackson is my creation. The grapevine puts all its energy into its fruit, its seeds, its children. That is my way, too." And who could argue? In 2003 Jackson was fit, trim, strong, still jogging every day, hiking across the mountain property he had claimed as home with his beloved German shepherd Buddy, and he looked more sixty-three than seventy-three, and a youthful sixty-three at that.

So he returned to the CEO position, with Banke remaining as chairman. Returning wasn't the problem. The problem was Jackson could admire, but could not adopt, the Lew Platt model of managing from 30,000 feet and delegating the details. As he dug back into the daily flow of the wine business, he put horses on the back burner and returned to his micromanaging ways at Kendall-Jackson: diving into the business's daily details, coming in before everyone and staying later than anyone, and in essence driving his top people crazy. (*Thank God he's in his seventies*, the familiar plaint went, *because if he were still in his fifties, he'd be killing us*.) Banke finally called him on it, as no one else dared. The micromanagement was not good for the business, she told him. "You need to focus on the big picture, set the strategy, and then get out of the way so your people can take care of the details. That's why you hired them. Get that hobby. Split your time. Save the micromanaging for the horses."

To her surprise and the rest of the executive team's relief, Jackson offered only a token resistance. Behind his grousing, he felt relieved to be jogged out of his old habits. Yes, he could back off a bit, trust his people, trust his wife. The micromanaging was a habit, not a necessity, he realized. He could focus on larger vino strategy for the company, on acquisitions and development of vineyards, rather than bogging down in COGS charts and daily sales reports. He promised he would try to strike a better balance between wine and horses, and he found that it was a promise he wanted to keep. Jackson had not tired of winemaking as he had the law, nor was he facing a change in the wine business that limited his chances to succeed, as had happened with his legal specialty of inverse condemnation. If anything, the opportunities for his vision of the wine business were on the upswing. His embrace of *terroir* and his insistence on vertically integrating his company so that he could control the entire winemaking enterprise from field to distributor were paying off with robust annual growth. And he would still pursue even more opportunities to expand his holdings and labels, promises to back off be damned.

But he loved horses, too, had been around them since childhood, all those visits to his grandparents' farms, that memorable, exciting race he watched of the great Seabiscuit, an eight-year-old Jack perched on his uncle Luke's shoulders. He wanted to own a piece of that world, to be part of it, to crawl inside it and learn how it ticked. And for that he had to split his time better and let his managers at Kendall-Jackson do what he paid them to do: manage. They'd still come to him for the big stuff—they dared not do otherwise. But he needed time to pursue his true ambition on the horse front: to find the next Seabiscuit, the hero that inspired not just with strength and speed but also with character and courage. For some reason, he knew, humans found their most admirable qualities within certain other species. Dogs were one such animal. And horses were another. A horse could be a hero, could embody the qualities that humans hope to find in themselves, and could do it purely, Jackson believed. "They can shine the best of us back at us," he once said.

So that was his secret plan: find the next Seabiscuit. It was ambitious. It was crazy. And, Jackson believed, it was one more thing: "It was possible."

So Jackson began in earnest to scheme to build a world-class racing and breeding stable, one that could match the achievements of his wineries. Only faster. He knew he couldn't live forever. If he was really going to invest time and energy in thoroughbreds, he wasn't interested in buying a horse or two and dabbling. He had ideas about how to improve, change, and reform the elegant-on-the-surface, seamy-on-the-bottom world of high-stakes horse racing. He had ideas about breeding, about mating European and American bloodlines. His yellow tablets began filling up not with

COGS calculations for his latest fine wine but with entirely different calculations of the prize money, breeding fees, and sales prices
of premium foals the he could expect to command. And he would
eventually get there. As he had done with wine, he would rise higher
and faster than any horseman before or since.

But first he got taken for a ride.

JACKSON KNEW A Sonoma County horse breeder, Tom Bachman,
who owned the eight-hundred-acre Pegasus Ranch for thoroughbreds near Sebastopol, along with about fifty acres of vineyards.
Bachman was fifteen years younger than Jackson, but the two got
along well, they shared a love of wine and horses, and Jackson appreciated the younger man's equine expertise. They decided to fly down
to Southern California together aboard Jackson's private jet so that
Bachman could introduce the winemaker to the Two-Year-Old Sale
at Barretts Equine in Pomona. Commonly called "the May Sale," it
is the largest annual thoroughbred auction in California and one of
the most anticipated. Jackson was interested in several horses, but
Bachman had pointed him toward a filly sired by an Australian
champion named French Deputy. The promising youngster was expected to fetch a premium price of $250,000, and Jackson took one
look at the beautiful animal and had his heart set on possessing her.

But another horseman had his eye on the same animal, a veteran trainer named Bruce Headley, and the resulting back and
forth pushed the price up to $375,000 for the untested filly, not
even named, yet bearing only a numerical designation: "Hip #256."
Jackson eventually backed off—the price turned out to be a record
for the May Sale—and then second-guessed himself, unconsoled by
the two other lesser horses he had won. "I want to talk to him,"
Jackson groused, pointing at Headley.

Bachman made the introductions. Jackson still wanted a piece of
the filly and suggested to Headley that they go in as partner on the
horse. Headley looked at the tall, broad-shouldered man, his shock
of straight hair now silver-white, his eyes sharp and bright above a

broad, open smile, and the horse trainer stuck out his hand. Sure, they could partner on the filly: Headley would board, train, and race the horse from his stables in the Los Angeles suburb of Arcadia, home to the state's premier race course, Santa Anita. And Jackson would bear half the costs and have the privilege of naming the filly. He chose a moniker drawn from the Santa Barbara vineyard that his wife loved best, Cambria, naming the filly Cambria Gold.

Although he had asked Bachman to be his adviser, over the next weeks and months Jackson increasingly turned to the affably crusty Headley for advice and tips. To Jackson, Headley appeared to be the real deal. He had been training horses since the Eisenhower administration, and he'd had a good measure of success, particularly in California stakes races at Santa Anita and Del Mar near San Diego. And Headley, unlike the cautious Bachman, encouraged Jackson's ambitions to go big and move fast: if he wanted to be a presence in the racing game, be a presence. A close relationship soon evolved that went way beyond Cambria Gold as the winemaker and horse trainer went into business together. Headley would choose the horses to buy, with the goal of acquiring a stable of active racehorses, foals to be trained, and other horses to be bred. Jackson had the cash to buy the horses, and Headley would receive a commission or a minority share in the animals; his main contribution was to be training and boarding the horses and prepping them to race. And this was not about just a few horses. Jackson went after a veritable herd of horses, as Jackson became the trainer's most important client and partner. The work was big and busy enough that Headley introduced Jackson to a colleague, a muscular young horse trainer and agent named Brad Martin, who was hired as a coordinator and assistant to Headley.

The first big purchase came when Headley and Martin brought Jackson in September 2003 to the Keeneland Yearling Sale in Lexington, Kentucky. Jackson was excited. He had thought he'd do most of his buying, stabling, and racing on the West Coast at first, then expand overseas, where he believed stronger, heartier bloodlines could be used to invigorate America's more fragile thoroughbreds. But when he arrived in Kentucky, he found the scene captivating. He was at the epicenter of thoroughbred horse culture, in the heart of Bluegrass Country, at the world's largest and most storied yearling sale, with a history dating back to 1935. This would be the start of something great, he told Barbara. It was like starting the winery all over again, something small and beautiful that would yield a great deal. "Just have fun with it, Jess," she told him before he left.

He had fun, all right. He wrote a check at the auction for $3.4 million for sixteen yearlings favored by Headley and Martin, who told Jackson they had scoped out the best buys and the most promising juveniles. Jackson was delighted with his haul. The old hands at Keeneland watched, knowing that it was unusual even for the very rich to throw down so much money so quickly on untested horses, most of which, statistically speaking, would likely never win a race. Indeed, many would never *enter* a race. But the veteran horsemen shrugged it off and kept silent. Jackson was an outsider, a California wine guy, and he was loaded. Rich guys who thought they could parachute into the good-ol'-boy world of horse racing and buy their way to the winner's circle were a fairly common spectacle in Bluegrass Country, and they generally were left to learn the hard way that there was more to the thoroughbred game than writing checks.

Jackson thought he knew that much (though he later admitted what he didn't know just about ruined him). As he was just getting started with the most impressive bout of big check writing in recent horse-racing history, he wanted to assemble a well-rounded team of experts to guide his entry into the thoroughbred big time—an equine version of his old Lakeport Chardonnay skunk works, who had helped him bring the first Vintner's Reserve to market. At that same auction Headley introduced Jackson to Emmanuel de Seroux, a French-born bloodstock agent who specialized in scouting horses outside the United States. A bloodstock agent's role in the horse-racing business is to evaluate the likelihood that a particular thoroughbred foal or juvenile will become a top racer or produce one if older and purchased for breeding. Basically, the bloodstock agent decides if a horse is worth its price or worth anything at all. Like winemaking, this process is as much art as science, an attempt to predict the performance of an unknown, untested, or even unborn horse. Once a thoroughbred competes on the track, its record, not its bloodlines and physique, are what matters most and the bloodstock agent's role is essentially done. But the agent's clients always come back because mixed in somewhere amid all those foals and yearlings sold each year, most of which won't ever win a race, there's also a future Kentucky Derby winner and a Belmont champ and a Breeders Cup victor and a Horse of the Year. The trick is figuring out which ones they might be, a task not much different from identifying the champion potential of a Roger Federer or a Michael Jordan when he is in kindergarten. That's why the thoroughbred crystal-ball-gazers with a record of succeeding in this unlikely task are in high demand, and millions of dollars change hands on the advice of elite bloodstock agents. Jackson wanted to find a good one.

Headley told him that de Seroux was one of the premier bloodstock agents in the business and that he was the right man for the team. In short order Jackson retained him to work on commission with Headley and Martin to select horses in private sales, many of them overseas. These three men formed the core staff of Jackson's racehorse enterprise, with Jackson filling the Daddy Warbucks role of deep pockets and outsized ambitions.

A year later the team returned to Keeneland, where Jackson shocked even the most moneyed horse owners by sweeping into town and buying ninety mares for $19 million in order to establish a full-scale breeding operation. De Seroux identified another thirty horses in private sales abroad for another $12.8 million. Jackson purchased a retired champion, Got Koko, as a broodmare prospect for $1.5 million, a horse who had been trained and raced by Headley and co-owned by his wife. Jackson was also advised to pay $350,000 for Danzig's Beauty, the mother of a well-regarded stallion, Distorted

Humor. Then he bought a half share of a $575,000 colt born of a champion, True Integrity. Next he flew to the Ocala Breeders Sales auction in Florida and broke the price record for the most expensive filly ever sold there: Yankee Million, for $575,000.

In all, Jackson's team guided him to the purchase of 130 horses at a cost of more than $60 million between May 2003 and May 2005, as well as helping to engineer his purchase of one of Lexington's showcase horse properties, the 469-acre Buckram Oak Farm. Jackson paid $17.5 million for mansion, grounds, stables, and guesthouses on the vast horse ranch, which he renamed Stonestreet Farms. Jackson lived in rustic comfort back in California, but this property was beyond opulent, featuring a centerpiece mansion, seven other houses, five barns, office buildings, private lakes, streams with stone bridges, and, cushioning it all like living satin, those heartbreakingly green fields and hills of Kentucky bluegrass, wooden horse fences marching across. Jackson was used to fine things. He was friends with Wall Street titans, with the creator of Pixar, with people who could afford anything, anytime—and he was one of them. But this was the grandest thing he had ever owned or imagined he could own, a slice of history, a flavor of Scarlett's Tara, a proper place to claim membership in the sport of kings. He had looked at twenty different properties, a few gems and many dogs, but none could compete with Buckram Oaks.

The trade journal *Blood-Horse* in February 2005 portrayed Jackson's burgeoning "horse empire" by noting, "One of Jess Jackson's employees called the California wine tycoon a whirlwind. But based on what's been happening in Central Kentucky lately, that description was an understatement. Jackson, 75, is roaring through the Bluegrass with the strength of a Category 5 hurricane."

Or as Jackson would later put it: "I was not interested in merely getting my feet wet. I was—I am—passionate about horse racing. So I wanted to dive all the way in. I can be impatient that way sometimes."

Jackson was an accomplished handicapper, a savvy gambler, and he had been around horses throughout his life. He had owned and raced horses with Doc Ballenger back in the sixties, and they had won some big races in California. But Jackson's knowledge of racing, breeding, and training was that of an astute novice eager to learn and wildly enthusiastic about returning to the sport. In interviews he extolled the virtues of *equus ferus caballus*—"The horse is the most athletic and beautiful animal that is compatible with man!"—and explained how his goal was to focus on quality in his training and breeding, just as he had in wine. He spoke loftily of pursuing a new breed of champion, sturdier horses that could last more than a season, as in the old days when the immortal Seabiscuit's racing career spanned five years. He opined that the modern racehorse industry was too focused on breeding fragile freaks of nature incapable of excelling without being propped up by steroids and stimulants and coronary meds. He called for a campaign against doping and poor breeding. Great champions were being pulled from competition after a handful of races in order to cash in on their value as studs or broodmares, he said. "We should be breeding to race, not racing to breed," he proclaimed.

Many in the thoroughbred industry agreed with Jackson and liked his fresh perspective, energy, and ideas. But just as many resented this outsider for his lecturing and meddling. They sat back and waited for him to fall on his face, like so many other men who brought their millions late to racing, who didn't understand the system or how to quietly work from the inside for what they wanted, rather than calling press briefings and posting on the Internet and speaking out of turn. Win something, his critics suggested, and then maybe we can talk.

For all his innovations and risk-taking, Jackson was in many ways an old-fashioned businessman at heart. He believed in the handshake deal and in sizing up a person and deciding if he or she could be trusted. He always considered himself astute at making this call about people. But sometimes, he admitted, in matters about which he felt passionate and engaged, as he was with his horses, his notions about honor subverted the more cynical, lawyer's side of his brain, the part that was supposed to remind him to take nothing at face value. So despite some clear warning signs—and warnings from those who cared about him—Jackson gave the benefit of the doubt to Headley, a man who had dedicated his life to working with and caring for those noble, beautiful thoroughbreds. Two years into their partnership, Jackson had nothing but praise for Headley. "Bruce is an authentic original, and one of the best horsemen I've ever known," he said in early 2005, just before things fell apart. "He's also a partner, and working with him is a pure pleasure. I don't think there is anyone who breaks or trains a horse—or even selects a horse—who is equal to Bruce."

Others, however, had begun to harbor doubts, Barbara among them. When she questioned why the land they owned in California already, including properties in Santa Barbara Horse Country, couldn't be used for breeding and training, Jackson's experts said no, the soil and climate weren't right. Another part of California, perhaps or, better yet, Kentucky. When she questioned why the horses they were buying almost never made it to the track, Banke was told to be patient; they need a chance to develop. Some had injuries and were being rehabilitated, Headley reported. And when she questioned the high prices being paid for some horses, the answer was always "That's what the horse is worth." In other words, Banke said, "they were saying they're the experts, not me."

"I didn't really care for that, but Jess was having a lot of fun, and that was good," Banke would later recall. So she didn't push it.

Tom Bachman also harbored misgivings. He felt that Jackson was spending too much too fast and that his eagerness meant others might be tempted to take advantage of him. Early on Bachman told Jackson some horror stories about neophytes being fleeced, about rigged auctions and planted bidders whose job was to drive up auction prices in order to part newcomers from their money. But then Bachman backed off once Jackson showed no interest in slowing down. A year later, in mid-2004, Bachman again traveled to Southern California with Jackson, this time visiting Headley's place in Arcadia to see some of the horses Jackson had bought. Bachman was horrified by what he saw: horses being trained in a residential area near Santa Anita Park, in a backyard ringed with cages containing fighting cocks. "Jess, this is crazy. This is a circus," he said. "You shouldn't have million-dollar yearlings going through this. It's not how it's done."

But Jackson shrugged off the concerns, continuing his partnership for another year. Then a horse named Maggy Hawk changed everything—not just for Jackson but for the racing industry as well.

The Maggy Hawk deal began with a different horse: Afleet Alex, a promising stallion who had been hampered by illness early in life but whose speed and multiple-stakes race victories had made him a Triple Crown contender. Twice in 2004 Jackson instructed the bloodstock agent de Seroux to try buying Afleet Alex, but each time the agent reported back that the owner wouldn't sell. (Jackson's, not to mention the owner's, instincts were good: in 2005 Afleet Alex would win two legs of the Triple Crown—the Preakness and the Belmont Stakes—after placing third by a single length in the Kentucky Derby.) But Afleet Alex's breeder, John Silvertrand, was willing to part with the champion's dam. De Seroux reported to Jackson that the fine, healthy mare who had given birth to Afleet Alex, Maggy Hawk, could be purchased for $750,000. In August 2004 Jackson okayed the deal and wired his agent the money.

Nine months later, in May 2005, Jackson heard from Silvertrand, who told him flatly, "I think you've been had."

Silvertrand had just learned that Jackson paid $750,000 for Maggy Hawk. The problem, the breeder explained, was that he had received only $600,000, which is what de Seroux paid him on Jackson's behalf. Yet de Seroux had invoiced Jackson for $750,000, apparently keeping the extra $150,000 for himself. A fraction of that could be accounted for as the agent's 5 percent commission, traditionally subtracted from the sale price, but the rest of it was, in Jackson's view, sheer fraud and theft. But because Jackson and Silvertrand had never actually met, the discrepancy had gone undetected all these many months.

Even before this revelation, Jackson had finally started to wonder if there was something to Banke's and Bachman's doubts about his thoroughbred team. A month earlier he had hired Bachman to manage Stonestreet Farms and to give a professional, unbiased assessment of the horses, the training, and the breeding operation. The first thing Bachman sought to do was to have a team of veterinarians from the University of California, Davis, examine the horses at Headley's training yard in California to find out why, after two years and $60 million in purchases, Jackson's stable had run only three races. And this paltry record had been compiled despite Jackson's directive that all the horses be tested in real races in order to assess their true potential. But when Bachman reported back to Jackson, instead of an explanation for the poor results, he said Headley refused to give Bachman access and had padlocked horses in stables to keep him away. Jackson was furious. He owned 90 percent or more of each horse stabled there, he fumed. Headley had no more than a 10 percent share.

"He can't refuse you access," Jackson shouted. "They're my horses, and you are there on my orders!"

With Jackson's lawyers circling, the trainer finally gave into the demands for access. The report from Bachman on his personal examination of the horses was grim: they were overweight, out of racing shape, and hardly trained, if at all. When the vets did a close examination, they reported no evidence of injuries keeping some of the horses off the track.

"It's bad," Bachman told him. "Worse than anything I imagined. I don't know what they've been doing. Nothing good."

Jackson launched an investigation of every horse transaction his team had made, digging up records in Argentina and Europe as well as in the United States and removing the horses from Headley's control. Jess was mortified to learn that he had been a patsy from day one. He supposed they had seen him coming a mile away, with his California clothes, his sprawling vineyards, his billion-dollar fortune, his grand sweep into the insular, clannish Kentucky horse society. So he had received "the treatment": a kind of initiation reserved for rich outsiders who thought they could just waltz into Bluegrass Country and simply join people who had been at it for generations. There were the rigged auctions, the strawmen bidders, the kickbacks, the foals supposedly bred to greatness who turned out to be anything but. In retrospect, Jackson could see how one of his three agents would always be with him at the auctions, keeping him busy while their colleagues lined up deals—and, Jackson suspected, worked their double deals and kickback schemes. The old, established stable owners—"the Central Kentucky elite," as Jackson called them, and it was no compliment—could have warned him that he had misplaced his trust, that he was being fleeced. But they didn't. And when he finally found out, they figured this businessman from California with a reputation for canniness would do one of two things: quietly absorb the loss, avoid the public humiliation of admitting he had been taken so badly, tuck his tail, and run back to California. Or come crawling to the good ol' boys and beg the advice and help of his betters. Either way he would know his place.

Except he would do neither of those things. Instead, he went to war. Jackson went public all right, but he was determined it would be those who abused his trust who ended up humiliated. He fought with lawsuits, press interviews, and testimony before Congress. He assembled a team of lawyers, led by a Kentucky-based former gang prosecutor, who began lobbying legislators, deposing industry leaders, and asking some very uncomfortable questions about widespread abuses in the thoroughbred industry. Jackson railed about the fraud, the payoffs, the performance drugs, and the scams that had eaten away, like cancer, at a noble sport, with a minority of cheats ruining racing for the honorable majority. He was invited to join the Thoroughbred Owners and Breeders Association task force to reform the horse sales market, but he declined when it was made clear that a condition of his membership would be to stop criticizing the industry in public. He noted that the task force was dominated by industry players who wanted nothing more than to maintain the status quo, including sellers who had paid kickbacks to Jackson's agents, who in turn cheated him. So he banded together other reform-minded horsemen to form the Horse Owners Protective Association, which drafted legislation to go after corrupt practices.

And he won. He had predicted back in 2003 that he would find a way to win big at the horses. It's just that he never expected his first big victories to take place in state capitals and courtrooms instead of racetracks.

In his lawsuit and testimony, an embarrassed but coldly angry Jackson accused his team members of ripping him off horse by horse through overcharges in all thirty private sales they had arranged. He also said he had learned that his three agents, who were supposed to be providing him impartial advice about the quality of horses, had been receiving kickbacks and payoffs from the sellers of horses that they were urging Jackson to bid on at public auction sales—which was why, he said, he had spent millions on horses of dubious value. The very first horse he bought overseas, Rhythm Mad, had cost him $850,000. But when contacted, the former owner told him the price he charged was $750,000, out of which de Seroux was supposed to keep a 5 percent commission—$37,500. Instead, by inflating the purchase price, de Seroux made an extra $100,000, earning the equivalent of a 20 percent commission. This sort of skim, Jackson alleged, had happened in one of the horse sales. In all, his investigation found that he had been ripped off for $3.2 million in overpayments and that his agents had received another $450,000 in kickbacks and payoffs from the sellers of horses his agents were recommending that Jackson buy. This process of serving both sides of a deal, called dual agency, is dubious enough when it's disclosed and the buyer understands the ulterior motives that may come into play. But in Jackson's case, the double-dealing was kept secret from him. Sometimes, he complained, his agents used dummy corporations to keep it concealed.

Jackson was astonished to learn that the practice of accepting kickbacks was not illegal in Kentucky and that it was so deeply embedded and accepted by the thoroughbred industry that even the former governor of Kentucky, Brereton Jones, a horse industry lobbyist, had paid $130,000 in commissions to Headley for horses he and de Seroux convinced Jackson to buy. Jones defended the practice. "That is the beauty of the free-enterprise system, that you have the right to reward people who do business with you," Jones was quoted as saying in the *Lexington Herald-Leader* newspaper. "I have done it on a few occasions. Quite frankly, I will continue to do so." Jackson could only shake his head in wonderment when he read that.

Finally, Jackson learned that his beloved Stonestreet Farms could have been purchased from the seller for $15 million, but that his agents had kept him away from the property until the listing expired and the price could be raised to $17.5 million. Their efforts earned a $500,000 payment from the seller. "I found there was a corrupt tradition of cheating the new guy on the block," Jackson would later observe. "They have cohorts bid just to push up the price. They take kickbacks to talk up a horse as more valuable than it is, and buyers get soaked. The problem is that every part of the industry is profiting from the corruption—the sellers, the agents, the auction houses. So you have a culture of silence. But they picked the wrong victim this time. As anyone will tell you, I'm rarely silent when my rights have been violated and my trust abused. And certainly not when my pocket's been picked."

Jackson's lawsuit against the "dirty secret" of the horse industry created a sensation, as did Jackson's successful lobbying for legislation in California and Kentucky that imposed greater buyer protections on horse sales. A new code of ethics called for disclosure of dual-agency dealings. Some applauded him for coming forward when so many others had stayed silent. Arthur Hancock, a breeder with three Kentucky Derby winners to his credit, told the *New York Times*, "Honest sellers can't compete with those who cheat. I'm a fourth-generation horseman, and I'm ashamed that a winemaker has to clean up our sport."

Anger at Jackson was just as common a reaction, however. Multiple death threats led to police investigations, and for the first time in his life Jackson had to hire personal bodyguards for himself and his family. Headley and the others had their defenders in the industry, including former governor Jones, and there was considerable outrage at the "billionaire bully" who was airing horse racing's dirty laundry. Horse trainer Laura de Seroux, wife of Jackson's former bloodstock agent, told the *Wall Street Journal* that Jackson had made himself a pariah in the industry. "Pretty much everyone in Kentucky hates him," she claimed. Jackson saw the article and scribbled a note in the margin: "Hated by crooks."

There even were attempts to paint Jackson as the villain and the cheaters as the victims. The attorney for de Seroux issued a written statement excoriating the "Jackson litigation machine"—even as he agreed to settle the case by paying Jackson damages shortly before the trial was set to begin. "The wrath of billionaire Jackson was vented in a well-funded effort to destroy Emmanuel de Seroux professionally and personally," the lawyer wrote. "Learning our lesson from how Jackson spent years battling Gallo in a losing effort, a conscious decision was made to pay the ransom fee."

The statement made Jackson laugh out loud, literally, while his lawyer called it the rant of "an out-of-work attorney." Jackson pointed out that the privilege of issuing "that bitter, ridiculous statement" cost de Seroux $3.5 million: the amount the bloodstock agent had to pay Jackson to settle the case and avoid a trial. Headley settled by paying Jackson back $900,000 and promising to cooperate with the investigation and testify if necessary, while Brad Martin paid $250,000. By settling, the three men admitted no wrongdoing, but the result, reached after court-ordered mediation, seemed a clear victory for Jackson.

The case involving the Stonestreet Farms purchase was ultimately dismissed, but Jackson found that one easier to take: he loved the property, and in any case the previous owner had spent upward of $22 million buying and fixing it up. So even with the overcharge, Jackson figured he came out ahead.

While Jackson used his lawsuit as a platform to demand industry reforms, it also freed him to find a new bloodstock agent and trainer. A new team led by respected agent John Moynihan, trainer Steve Asmussen, and fellow trainer Scott Blasi didn't just turn Jackson's horse-racing ambitions around. The new team helped Jackson achieve a meteoric success unprecedented in racehorse history, as the brash promises he had made about focusing on quality and greatness when he had first swept into Kentucky started coming true. Just as he had used a winemaking disaster to create the world's most popular Chardonnay, his initially disastrous entry into the thoroughbred game allowed him to rise further faster than anyone in the history of horse racing.

JESS JACKSON'S HORSE-RACING fortunes changed on Super Bowl weekend 2007 with a phone call from his new bloodstock agent.

"Did you see that race at Gulfstream?" Moynihan practically shouted into the phone.

"I was just going to call to see if you saw it," Jackson said. "I've never seen anything like it. Let's get him."

This was how Jess Jackson came to see, meet, and own his first headline-grabbing champion, his latter-day Seabiscuit—a horse no one had heard of before named Curlin.

Gulfstream Park was a race course in Broward County, Florida. The race in question was a seven-furlong (7/8 of a mile) event with $38,000 in prize money for three-year-old "maidens"—horses that had never won a race. In Curlin's case, he also had never *run* a race. He had been held back and didn't race as a two-year-old because of a minor but slow-healing ankle injury.

By then Jackson had dived into horse racing in a big way, with a separate office on Alexander Mountain devoted to race records, breeding records, a DVD library of races, and a big-screen TV for watching satellite and cable broadcasts of races around the clock and around the world. What caught Jackson's and Moynihan's attention in the Gulfstream race was the way Curlin ran that debut. He was like a tourist on a stroll, looking around as if to see the sights, gawking at the other horses, zigzagging like the inexperienced racer he was. Yet he pulled away from the other horses even as he did so. He even pulled away going into the turn, where horses almost never gain ground. His powerful, easy strides left the other entries in the dust. He won easily by 12 3/4 lengths and looked as if he could have run twice the distance without tiring.

Moynihan was five hours away at a horse sale in Ocala, Florida, that day, horse-shopping for Jackson, when he caught the race on a TV monitor. He called trainer Asmussen, who was at Gulfstream that day. Asmussen said he not only saw the race but also saw Curlin during his cooldown. "He looked like he had hardly run," the trainer said and then echoed Jackson's comment. "We've got to get him."

Back in California on Alexander Mountain, Jackson watched the race again. "Basically we saw Curlin run in that maiden race, and we all fell in love. What an athlete!"

Discovering Curlin wasn't hard or lucky. But the circumstances that led to the purchase of Curlin were another story. As Moynihan raced to Gulfstream, Curlin's owners were hosting a Super Bowl party. They were not available to the various agents and horse experts who had seen the race at Gulfstream and knew a hot prospect when they saw one. But Moynihan had an advantage: Asmussen's second in command at the stables, Scott Blasi, had a brother who was dating (and would eventually marry) Helen Pitts, Curlin's first trainer. Normally, a trainer in that situation wouldn't do a thing to help a buyer attempt to steal a horse away from her, but in this case Pitts provided a number to reach the owners, a pair of Kentucky-based class-action attorneys who had won a $200 million settlement for a victims of the fad diet drug with potentially fatal side effects known as fen-phen. They had bought Curlin as a yearling for $57,000; he had good bloodlines, but there had been no reason to expect the performance the stallion turned in at Gulfstream. Moynihan reached one of the owners, Bill Gallion, at his party and spoke to him several times, coaxing him to consider selling at least a piece of the horse. At two in the morning, they reached an agreement: the two attorneys would sell 80 percent of Curlin for $3 million. Jackson, meanwhile, lined up two partners to go in on the $3 million purchase: his friends George Bolton, a San Francisco investment banker, and Florida software entrepreneur Satish Sanan (Jackson would buy out their shares by the end of 2007).

Moynihan visited Curlin the next morning at his stable and found him to be everything he had expected: fresh, beautiful, brimming with health, his coat a lustrous coppery brown. Soon Gallion showed up looking quite sour and said since their final telephone conversation, other potential buyers had finally tracked him down and he had been offered $5 million for the horse. Moynihan looked crushed, but then Gallion surprised him. He said a deal was a deal. He would honor their telephonic handshake deal, even though legally he could have got away with accepting the higher offer. It cost him $2 million, but he kept his word. "There's hope for this industry yet," an awed Jackson said when Moynihan told him what had happened.

Jackson had his dream horse, and he, Moynihan, and Asmussen started plotting what would come next: Curlin's first campaign. Jackson told Moynihan that plan would be a "Path to Greatness."

Moynihan liked the sound of that, though later he would come to view those words with dread, as they were usually accompanied by some demand from Jackson to do the impossible. And later still he would come to view those words as prophetic.

JOHN MOYNIHAN WAS the adviser and confidant—the horse consigliere—whom Jackson had wanted and needed all along. The freckled agent with the boyish face had risen quickly in the bloodstock trade. A computer science major who planned on becoming a stock trader, he was prompted to switch his career choice by an internship at a horse auction house. A season spent steeped in the mystique of the thoroughbred had him swapping the trading floor for stable hay and never looking back. His gift for picking winners was soon apparent: one of his first purchases for his first client went on to win both the Kentucky Derby and the Preakness. When that horse owner, Robert Lewis, began winding down his racing career, he introduced Moynihan to Jackson, and they began working together after the allegations against Stonestreet's first group of advisers had been exposed. Their first meeting after Moynihan's first big horse purchase for Jackson was memorable, a story the agent loved to retell, as it had cemented the bond between the two men.

Moynihan had come to Sonoma County after purchasing a very expensive yearling, which neither Jackson nor Banke had seen yet; they had both been in Hawaii for a Kendall-Jackson sales meeting when the auction took place. During a stay at one of the Alexander Mountain guesthouses, Jackson drove Moynihan around the mountain for a tour as the blood agent described the new horse. As they careened from one vineyard to the next in Jackson's Lexus, which he enjoyed driving fast on the winding, narrow roads of the estate, Moynihan kept his eyes open for a mountain lion. He had heard there had been a sighting on the property, and he badly wanted to see the big cat himself.

Suddenly, he saw a tawny flash near a bush, and he shouted to Jackson, "Stop the car! There's the mountain lion!"

Jackson jammed on the brakes, and the car skidded to a halt so fast that Moynihan's head banged into the windshield and another passenger in the car, who was nursing a bad back, slid off his seat and started howling. "Where is it?" Jackson asked.

Moynihan pointed at the bush way off the road. Jackson sped off through the grass, banging over hills, tearing through the vineyards, terrifying Moynihan in the process. Jackson grinned. They ground to a halt near the bush Moynihan had indicated, and Jackson shut off the car. They waited and watched. Nothing happened. Jackson honked the horn. Nothing happened.

Finally, the scrub moved a bit. They all leaned forward to see. And out from the bush emerged not a mountain lion but a jackrabbit. A very big jackrabbit, but a cottontail nonetheless.

Moynihan broke into a sweat. This was not funny. All he could think was how he had just spent a ton of money for a horse for this man he barely knew, a horse that Jackson had not seen yet, a man who, given his past experiences, hated to buy a horse without seeing it himself, talking to the animal, getting to know it. But this time Jackson had agreed to the purchase sight unseen based on Moynihan's good eye, the same eye that had just raised an alarm over a bunny.

Jackson looked at the rabbit, then turned to Moynihan and said, "I hope you're better at picking out my horses than you are with my mountain lions." Then his baleful look turned playful, and Jackson grinned again. Moynihan came to know that broad grin, as it was a very characteristic expression for Jackson, big and infectious, hinting of genuine amusement, boyish enthusiasm, mischief without irony. His grin made him look years younger, and it put Moynihan at ease.

They returned to the office and started plotting Curlin's path to greatness. They designed an ambitious and aggressive campaign that began with two stakes races in Arkansas, including the top race in the state, the Arkansas Derby, which Curlin won easily, after which they entered him in the Kentucky Derby, the first leg in the Triple Crown.

History was against him, as no horse with only three races under his belt had won the Derby since 1915, and the last horse to win without any races as a two-year-old was in 1882. The second-post position he drew was a bad spot for his style of racing, too. Curlin liked to take the lead from the center of the pack by going outside and using his superior speed and stamina in the later stages of a race. In the Derby the number two position allowed him to be boxed in by other horses for most of the race, though he was the only horse gaining on the leader at the end, finishing third.

The Preakness Stakes came next in the Triple Crown contests. It proved to be a thriller that began with Curlin stumbling out of the gate so badly his nose nearly grazed the ground, leaving him in sixth place during the first leg of the race. He came up strong but went wide in the stretch, which allowed the Kentucky Derby winner

Street Sense to squeeze by on the inside and take the lead. With only a furlong to go, Street Sense had a length-and-a-half lead and the race appeared to be all but over. But in a furious burst of speed, Curlin caught up and passed the other horse in the last stride before crossing the finish line, winning by a nose. Even though his stumble cost precious time, Curlin still tied the track speed record in that race, which he shared with three other horses, including a famed winner of the Triple Crown, Secretariat, considered to be one of the greatest racehorses of all time, second only to Man o' War.

Curlin came in second by a head in the third leg of the Triple Crown, the Belmont Stakes, then went on to win the Jockey Club Gold Cup at Belmont and the prestigious Breeders Cup Classic at Monmouth Park in New Jersey. The conditions were wet, sloppy, and slow after days of rain at Monmouth, yet Curlin's winning time was only two-tenths of a second off the track record set in 1962.

Curlin was named the American Horse of the Year in 2007 at the annual Eclipse Awards—horse racing's Academy Awards. At that point Jackson could have done what the vast majority of horse owners would have done: retire Curlin and make a fortune from stud fees as stables lined up to get their piece of champion DNA. Instead, Jackson realized several things. Curlin still wanted to run. He showed it every day, itching to train, to hit the practice track. He loved it. And Jackson loved planning that new campaign, scheming over which races to enter, whether to go abroad or stay in the States, whether to run on artificial surfaces or grass or stick to the dirt (Curlin ran on every surface, but it was dirt where he was king). The world needed heroes, Jackson said, and horse racing especially needed them. That would be Curlin's role: steady, strong, "the iron horse," Jackson called him.

He decided to run Curlin another year as a four-year-old. Many in racing thought Jackson mad. If Curlin was injured or died—and that happened all too often—then Jackson would lose tens of millions of dollars in stud fees. That same year a three-year-old filly, Eight Belles, shattered her ankles trying to win the Kentucky Derby and had to be euthanized right on the track in front of horrified spectators. What if that happened to Curlin? Or what if his record as a four-year-old was poor? If he lost too many races, his reputation and his stud fees would evaporate as well. It was crazy and risky to run him.

It also made the good old boys who saw their horses as ATM machines look bad, Banke told Jackson when he asked her if she agreed with his decision. "It's the right thing to do," Banke added.

Curlin won five major stakes races in 2008, including the Dubai World Cup and the Woodward Stakes at Churchill Downs. In the process he became the biggest money winner in racing history and was named Horse of the Year for the second year in a row, an accomplishment matched by only four other horses since the Eclipse Awards had begun in 1971 (the others were Secretariat, Forego, Affirmed, and Cigar). Jackson was celebrated as the ultimate sportsman, lavishly praised in press reports—and passed over by the Eclipse Awards when it came to Owner of the Year honors. The racing industry loved Curlin, but Jackson—not so much. He would never be one of them.

Jackson was probably hurt by this, though he behaved as if he did not care what anyone thought. He always found it ironic that so many of the central Kentucky elite had tolerated the abuses and double-dealing for so long but were outraged by Jackson's public airing of his experience. Meanwhile, the two sellers who had behaved most honorably toward Jackson were actually convicted frauds: Curlin's original owners. They had been offered $2 million more for the horse than Jackson paid, yet they did not renege when they legally could have. It turned out that those owners had defrauded clients out of millions of dollars in the fen-phen settlement, taking money earmarked for those whose lives had been shattered by an unsafe diet drug. The lawyers went to prison and lost everything; the courts took their 20 percent share of Curlin to pay off the clients. Curlin, meanwhile, retired in 2009, and every date he had with a mare—and there were many—earned Jackson $75,000 in stud fees.

And then, he told Moynihan, it was time to find a new path to glory. He began a new quest to reinvigorate the bloodlines of thoroughbreds in America, and he was certain that breeding practices abroad held the solution. There horses were bred for endurance and much longer careers, rather than the American emphasis on speed, on a lighter-boned, fast-maturing horse that reached its pinnacle as a three-year-old but was subject to far more catastrophic injuries. At a stage in life when European champions were just getting started, American thoroughbreds were already done. And to mask the breeding flaws, American horses were pumped full of drugs, which most other countries banned.

Modern champions in America run half as many races in their careers as was the case just a few decades ago. Most stakes horses have been bred to descendants of a 1950s champion, Native Dancer, who was renowned for speed and durability. But generations of inbreeding have weakened the line, and though this bloodline has a long list of champions attached to it—including Curlin, on both parents' sides—it has also produced fragile horses whose injuries have ended their careers, or their lives, prematurely. Eight Belles was such a horse. Their lighter bones and enormous muscle mass place too much stress on legs that are no larger than a human's. Given the much greater weight a horse must carry—its own weight plus a rider and tack—the stress on a horse's legs is equivalent to the bone stress a human would face by trying to run on index fingers.

Jackson put it this way: "We've bred horses that are unnatural, that cannot compete without drugs, and that cannot last. It's wrong and it's why champions are retired so fast, why the industry races to breed rather than breeds to race. They hate me for it, but I'm not afraid to say the emperor has no clothes. This inbreeding is wrong."

So Jackson started haunting horse auctions in Europe and South America. When the 2008 Preakness Stakes was being run, Jackson was in Argentina inspecting and bidding on horses. He spent more than a $1 million on six young stallions and three fillies. Breeding such sturdy, fleet horses who matured more slowly with the precocious but fragile American bloodlines should provide the right mix of traits—and some much-needed genetic diversity, Jackson believed. Such a hybrid, he hoped, could reinvigorate, even save, the sport of horse racing

But in the midst of this project, along with his advocacy for the creation of a horse-racing league modeled on professional baseball to provide some much-needed regulation and oversight, another female entered Jackson's life. And everything else went on hold for Rachel Alexandra.

THE FIRST THING to know about Rachel Alexandra is that she made Jackson say something he rarely said, hated to say, and didn't usually think he had to say: *I was wrong*. Up until then Jackson had no interest in racing fillies. He was interested only in the boys. In looking at the records of past champions and stake winners, he became convinced that mares who never raced produced better off-spring. But he had spent millions on a number of fillies with great potential. Instead of getting rid of them, Barbara had said she'd race them under her name. Jackson liked that idea: it got his wife heavily involved in the sport and business of racing, and it also got the fillies out of his hair. Barbara started a stable she named GRACE—for Girls Rule and Competently Endure—her way of telling Jess he was mistaken in his attitude about horses and gender. And sure enough Banke's stable soon produced a winner of multiple stakes races named Hot Dixie Chick.

But that didn't sway Jackson to rethink his views. It took Rachel to do that. As soon as he saw her dominate the Kentucky Oaks race in 2009, as soon as he saw her athleticism, her strength, her talent, he wondered just what he had been thinking, closing himself off from half the horses in the world based on their gender. Closing himself off from a horse he had loved on first sight. "I have to have her," he told a grinning Banke.

So he had paid $10 million to pry Rachel Alexandra free of her previous owner, a fantastic sum, and entered her into the Preakness Stakes with less than two weeks for trainer Steve Asmussen and his team to prep her. It was an audacious decision. Jackson had to fight to get his last-minute entry approved, and only public pressure and the willingness of another owner to step aside if necessary, volunteering to give up her coveted spot to let Rachel run, assured Jackson would be able to enter the race. He shrugged off the criticism. He was used to it; he already needed bodyguards in Horse Country, after all. He had been criticized for racing his living ATM machine, Curlin, for another year instead of putting him out to stud, risking everything, a sportsman who made his fellow owners look small and greedy as they did the safe and joyless thing. Now he was showing them up again with Rachel Alexandra, another path to glory, another big gamble, sitting there in the owner's box at Pimlico Park in Baltimore, his horse the betting favorite, one girl against all the boys.

An amazing horse, a fifty-to-one shot named Mine That Bird, had shocked the smart money and won the Kentucky Derby the day after Rachel won the Oaks. He was the other favorite this day at the Preakness. At the Derby he had been ridden by jockey Calvin Borel, who had been invited to reprise that ride at the Preakness. Instead, Borel had come to Jackson and begged to be able to ride Rachel instead of Mine That Bird. No jockey who won the Derby had ever turned down a chance to ride the same horse in the Preakness, not since the first Derby was run. But Rachel Alexandra had that kind of influence, it seems. "I love that horse," the young jockey had said. "She's the best horse I've ever ridden. I believe in her."

Jackson was moved. He had used Borel before, and he had ridden Rachel before, but he wasn't Stonestreet's top jockey. Still, something about his plea, about the faith he showed, the willingness to turn down the chance of riding a Triple Crown winner because of the love of another horse, convinced Jackson. The jockey was risking his career with that request, pursuing, Jackson realized, his own path to greatness. Why else would he turn down the chance to ride the Kentucky Derby winner at the Preakness unless he felt certain that Rachel would win and that he wanted to be part of it?

"Okay, Calvin, you've got the mount," Jackson said. "Let's go to the Preakness and win the damn thing."

From the start Jess takes to his feet, shouting over the crowd's roar, urging Rachel on, this impossible horse in an impossible race.

How does a filly beat the boys? Everyone at this track can see how now, Jackson thinks: she dashes to the front and stays there. If she can't see the boys, then there's nothing to give way to. The only instinct that kicks in is Rachel's instinct to run, and to never look back.

And he knows, even before she completes that first quarter mile, he knows no one will catch Rachel as she arrows around the 13/16th-mile course. For the first half of the race, she is flanked stride for stride by the number one horse, Big Drama, trying to stalk her, trying to intimidate, the stallion hoping to dominate the filly, the genetic imperative at work, the reason so few fillies compete in such races. But Rachel flattens her ears and presses harder, digging, refusing to look at the pursuer, and then it is the stallion who looks intimidated. Halfway through, Jess can see, Big Drama is beaten already, fading. But not his girl. Rachel keeps the pace and pulls a length ahead with the race three-quarters done.

And then, from dead last—the same place he had launched himself to victory in the Kentucky Derby—Mine That Bird makes his move, flying past the stragglers and mowing his way through the pack. At the final turn Rachel is running two lengths ahead, and it is her race to win or lose. Mine That Bird puts on a furious charge, passing every other horse, and finds second place. Jess resists the impulse to close his eyes. But Mine That Bird never gets closer than a length off the leader. Rachel never relents, and she crosses the finish line alone.

The cheers deafen Jackson. He sees Borel pumping his fist, standing in the stirrups and patting Rachel's neck. The girl has beaten the boys, another "impossible" wiped away, all the criticism, the doubts, the fears wiped away. Jackson is laughing and tearing up at the same time because, like Calvin Borel, he loves this fierce, beautiful horse. He has been wrong about the girls, and he is happy to say so.

In the winner's circle John Moynihan leans over and whispers to Jess in disbelief, "We won the Preakness again."

Jackson winks and smiles and says, "Of course we did."

RACHEL ALEXANDRA HAD a racing season for the ages, ending the year with nine straight wins, two more of them against the boys: the $1.25 million Haskell Stakes at Monmouth Park, where she won by six lengths with a speed rating that pegged her as the fastest horse in North America that year, and the prestigious Woodward Stakes at Saratoga, where the mayor declared race day "Rachel Alexandra Day" and the streets were decked with "Run Like a Girl" banners. Pink "Girl Power" T-shirts were in high demand as Rachel became the first filly in history to run the Woodward, a contest for older male stakes horses. Her win there cemented her place as one of the greatest fillies of all time. And for the third year in a row, a Jess Jackson thoroughbred won Horse of the Year honors, and that was a record, too.

Later Jackson said this one was sweeter than Curlin's. "No one criticized running Curlin in the Preakness. Rachel was different. She had to prove her greatness, and she did. And we had to prove the naysayers wrong. We had to show a generation of girls what their hero could do.

"And we did."

13

The Vineyard
by the Owl House

A S JESS JACKSON MADE HIS EXULTANT, DISRUPTIVE
mark in the thoroughbred world, then laid plans for the next
step—horses from overseas, a bit of matchmaking between Curlin
and Rachel, a horseman's league of extraordinary gentlemen—he
still devoted half his time to Kendall-Jackson. By his estimation,
that still amounted to a forty-hour workweek for wine, give or take.

What that meant was more vineyards and wineries purchased
and built—so much so that the *San Francisco Chronicle* pronounced
him one of the two most powerful vintners in the country, Ernest
Gallo being the other. It meant a conversion to sustainable winemaking and the $30 million construction of an experimental winery
to be run as a test bed by the University of California to pioneer
water, soil, and energy conservation for the entire industry. It meant
pushing for and winning a controversial fight for official designation
of a "California Coastal" region for wines, which many winemakers
thought was too generic but Jackson believed provided a clear distinction between the inferior interior and the cool coastal climes
that made the best wines. And, of course, that designation played

to Kendall-Jackson's strength, its coastal mountain *terroir* no other company could match. His opponents in that battle joined forces with him in the next, however, which was a truth-in-labeling battle for legislation that now requires wine with "Sonoma" on the label to actually contain at least 75 percent of its contents *from* Sonoma. "Anything else is lying to consumers," Jackson growled.

He also spent more than $100 million acquiring a portfolio of luxury brands and wineries to add to his already impressive collection, making him the undisputed king of premium wines in America. In secret deals and wild auctions reminiscent of some of his bidding wars in Horse Country, Jackson acquired the Murphy-Goode Estate Winery in Alexander Valley and Byron Estates in Santa Barbara. He also picked up Freemark Abbey, a historic Napa Valley winery more than a century old, whose wines had famously outscored the French in the 1975 blind tasting that came to be known as the "Judgment in Paris," which put California winemaking on the fine-wines map for the very first time. Owning a piece of that history was a "precious acquisition," Jackson said afterward.

While building up his collection of boutique wineries—with Freemark Abbey's addition, Jackson now had a collection of twenty-eight small, premium, highly regarded wine brands apart from the Vintner's Reserve cash cow—he and Banke were also spending increasing amounts of time on their dream home on the Alexander Mountain, the one place on earth he wanted to be more than anywhere else.

He used to think it was Hawaii he loved best and where he would retire, where he still had his old VW microbus waiting for him. Once, years before, he had even scouted out from the air Charles Lindbergh's burial spot on the islands, figuring he might like to go that route when he died. In later retellings Jackson claimed he had actually run into Lindberg shortly before the old aviator's death and shared a private plane rental with him. It was one of those unverifiable Jess Jackson tall tales, like the surf lessons he remembered having with Duke Kahanamoku, the five-time Olympic swimming medalist, actor, cop, and surfing evangelist who helped spread the sport from his native Hawaii to the rest of the world. It may have happened, and it may not have; Jenny thought he had lessons with Duke's brother, who operated a famous surfing school in Hawaii, and decided to embellish the story a bit. As for Lindbergh, it was unlikely but possible. Her dad had a way of running into extraordinary people without really trying.

Jackson also fell in love with his home in Kentucky, but he never felt welcome there. Any place where bodyguards were as important as air-conditioning wasn't a proper retirement home, Jackson said. And the villas in France and Italy were spectacular, wine and olives and history visible in every stride. He'd stand in one of the stone courtyards, centuries old, and marvel that the kid who had sold newspapers and worked the docks and almost had his brains knocked out lumberjacking in Redwood Country could be in such a place, could own such a place.

But none of it compared to his mountain, his Alexander Mountain Estates, a farmer's paradise, a veritable buffet of soils, where the finest grapes in his vast holdings grew within view and walking distance of his front porch. In some ways this estate in Sonoma County's backcountry is clearly a billionaire's nest: the main gate with guard shack; the seven guest cottages scattered around the mountain; the heliport and barn converted into a hanger and aviation center; the stables; the graceful, tree-shaded house dubbed the Redwoods where the Gauers once lived and that now serves as a central meeting, dining, and work space; and the family house, off on its own, with an eye-popping view of the valley below. Stand on the porch and an array of Jackson's most prized properties are spread out below in the distance, shrouded in cool, grape-nurturing fog in the morning, then leaping into view as the coastal mists burn off, the land embroidered with a patchwork of pasture, woodland, and ridgetop vineyards. Yet for all the accoutrements of wealth, the mountain remains a barely tamed riot of nature, of oaks and wildflowers and native plants. The architecture is simple, the cottages elegant but rustic, solid, all natural woods and stone and terracotta tile. The family home is spacious but simple, too, not a mansion but a white frame house. The living room is open and comfortable—and dominated by two large dog kennels where the family pets sleep. Dogs, cats, and other assorted animals roam as they please. This is not a showpiece, Jackson would say, but a place of comfort and family life. Jackson might have entertained presidential candidates and the Russian national orchestra and all manner of corporate tycoons here, and the hospitality may put a four-star hotel to shame—the wine racks and refrigerators and cupboards in the guesthouses are always filled with treasures, and those rustic cottages have broadband WiFi and HD TVs hidden inside the farmhouse furniture. Yet Jackson remained a blue-jeans-and-boots guy, and there was usually dirt caked on the boots and spattered on the denim.

His friend John Lasseter, the founder of Pixar Animation and the creative force behind *Toy Story* and a string of other animated masterpieces, said he figured out on his first visit to Jackson's home how a billionaire who lived on his own mountain with a helicopter in his backyard could seem so unpretentious: "I realized one thing Jess and I shared: we were both little boys who never grew up."

They had met through the Sonoma elementary school their children attended (and later the same high school that they had joined forces to create). Jackson invited Lasseter and his wife, Nancy, to dinner with the family after some school event, and the couple accepted. And though their intentions were to avoid drinking much wine at dinner, as they had a long drive home and Lasseter had to get to work early the next morning, Jackson proceeded to bring one wine after another for his guest to try. Lasseter saw his host was so proud of each vintage, and each had a story behind it, and when Lasseter started to wave off a pour, Jackson looked so crushed that the new friend had to hold out his glass for more. Pretty soon, it was very late, apparent to the Lasseters that driving home on dark, winding country roads was no longer an option, and they were being shepherded to a guesthouse.

They got up early and were heading to the car so that Lasseter could get to work, but then they heard a shout. Jackson was running out from his house with one boot on and he was pulling on the other boot while trying to run and hop, and one of his pants legs was caught crazily in the boot top—a common sight, Lasseter would soon learn—and Jackson called, "Wait, wait, wait. You can't go yet. You've got to see the vineyards from the helicopter. It'll be here any minute."

Lasseter and his wife looked at each other. Helicopter ride? The little boy inside Lasseter could never say no to a helicopter ride. Soon they were flying over Jackson's vineyards, over Sonoma, north toward the Edmeades winery, looping around and back over Napa. Lasseter would later say, "This was one of the most magnificent moments in my life. Jess from that moment on became one of my biggest inspirations." Eventually, that tour would lead to Lasseter's decision to start a small family winery, with Jackson as his guide and mentor.

But at the moment they were shooting across the skies of Wine Country and it was getting late. The next cut of *A Bug's Life* was waiting for Lasseter, deadlines looming, and Jackson said, "How about I just drop you off at Pixar?" The studio at that time was in Point Richmond on the San Francisco Bay, which was nowhere near the vineyards, but Lasseter replied, "Sure, that would be great!"

The chopper headed south, and the view was spectacular as they zipped over the San Francisco Bay, Lasseter smiling in boyish wonder. Jackson grinned at him, his big trademark grin, and said, "Hey John, you've got to get yourself one of these."

Lasseter started to laugh, then remembered something: Pixar had no helipad. There was no airfield anywhere close. "Are you allowed to land in Port Richmond?" he asked Jackson.

And there was that big grin again. "You can land anywhere," he said. And after a long pause, he added, "Once."

They touched down in a field near the studio, Lasseter piled out, Jackson waved, and the helicopter was gone before anyone noticed the less-than-legal landing.

While they were still on Jackson's mountain, he had brought the Lasseters up to the old Upper Barn vineyard, where some wine experts believed the greatest Chardonnay ever had been born. Lasseter saw that this was a beautiful hidden spot and that Jackson was particularly proud of the grapes here, their history, the rare *terroir* that made such fine grapes that his winemakers fought over them after each harvest. He gave the Lasseters a taste of Upper Barn Chardonnay, which at the moment was not a commercial wine, not sold in stores, just a special wine for special guests, and it was the most amazing wine Lasseter had ever tasted, though it no doubt was enhanced by the spectacular view from the small vineyard so high over the valley. And Jackson told them the story he loved, about the first grapes in the Caucasus, how the harsh conditions drove the vines to put all their energy and nourishment into the seeds and the ripening fruit—into the babies and the continuation of the line. Everything else shut down—leaves, vines, nothing else mattering but the grapes and their seeds.

Jackson had gestured at the steep landscape planted with vines, at the rocky, thin, volcanic soil. Here was his Caucasus, Lasseter realized. "This is why I decided to buy most of our prime vineyard land on rocky hillsides. This is where the amazing flavors of these world-class wines come from, when these vines are stressed. It goes back to the origins of the grapevine."

Lasseter never forgot that moment. On that hot day in the vineyard, he felt a shiver at the idea that his friend "was able to reach into history to find the answer for the present." He would later credit that story as inspiring him to incorporate historical context into his films, from the history of Route 66 in *Cars* to the history of industrialization in *Monsters, Inc.*

It was that same *terroir*, and the rare sort of grapes that grew there, that inspired winemaker Pierre Seillan to abandon his work in France and come to work for Jackson. Jess had challenged Seillan, who would be knighted in France for his winemaking in America—no small feat—to use his grapes to make a wine as good as Château

Petrus. Petrus is widely held out as one of the finest wines in the world, if not the finest. It is definitely the most expensive.

Seillan had given an answer guaranteed to make a lifelong friend out of Jackson: "Why not try to make it *better* than Château Petrus?"

Together they launched the Vérité Winery—Vérité for "Truth"—one of Jackson's most upscale labels and beloved winemaking projects, pulling the best of the best from Jackson's most rarified vineyards in blends of exquisite complexity. Though they started making Vérité wines in the late 1990s, these wines had to age much longer than Jackson's more mass-produced offerings, so rich were they in tannins from the volcanic topsoil of Jackson's mountain—which, Seillan liked to say, had more types of soil in a few square miles than all of France put together. These wines, priced as high as $800 a bottle, began to come into their own just as Jackson's efforts in horse racing began to gain traction with Curlin and Rachel. He and Seillan eagerly awaited the verdict of wine critics, particularly the world's most renowned, Robert Parker, who had been a friend to Kendall-Jackson for many years. Their ambition was for Vérité to secure Kendall-Jackson's place as maker of both the most popular wine in America and one of the world's finest wines. There were other elegant, expensive labels in Jackson's domain—Lokoya, Cardinale, the top tier of Stonestreet—but Vérité was Jackson's most beloved. Here, at last, he felt he was capturing the spirit of that first *vinifera*.

BUT FOR ALL the hopes for his vineyards, the new winery acquisitions, and his achievement bucking the system and conventional wisdom in Horse Country, these last years in the first decade of the new millennium were not the best of times for Jess Jackson. The economic downtown of 2008 and 2009 hit the wine industry hard as consumers cut spending across the board. Wine might have been the affordable luxury, but luxury it still was, and many loyal customers cut back their purchases. Jackson responded by cutting prices to maintain sales, but that meant lower revenues. In early

2009 Kendall-Jackson had its first layoffs in three and a half decades of operation. About 170 employees—nearly 15 percent of the workforce—were fired. Jackson also shut down an entire line of wines he had launched a year earlier, White Rocket, which was intended to cater to the millennial generation and entice its members to try inexpensive wines with such playful names as "Horse Play Rollicking Red," "Tin Roof," "Automoto," and "Dog House." They were a disaster. Nobody wanted to drink Dog House wine. Jackson had remarkably few marketing blunders in his career, but when he did stumble, they were as dramatic as his successes. White Rocket was a dud, quickly becoming a tax write-off and a topic best left unmentioned in Jackson's presence. It was a time to hunker down, cut back, and wait out the bad economy, Jackson told his staff.

He was also waiting out something else at this time, something much worse than an economic downturn. Jackson had developed cancer. He had a particularly aggressive form of the disease that started as skin cancer, then spread deep and fast.

Treated a few years earlier, he seemed to have beaten the odds. But remission isn't a cure, and the cancer returned in 2008 in a more virulent form, less responsive to treatment. In the winner's circle at the Preakness, standing next to Rachel, her eyes bright, Jackson, beneath the jubilance and the grin, looked old in a way he had never looked. Old and ill and tired. He wore a cap because beneath it he was bald, his silver mane stolen by chemotherapy.

At first he kept the seriousness of his condition from his children. It was bad, he said, but he would pull through. And because he had always been the iron man to them, they believed him. It was in this period he started pushing for his youngest to come home from college and join the business. Later, when conventional chemotherapy failed to slow the cancer and his doctors began experimental treatments at Stanford University Medical Center, there was no hiding the dire news from the family, though the kids were sworn to secrecy. The prognosis was poor, but Jackson still vowed to beat the cancer and still told them not to worry. Throughout 2009 and into 2010 he continued to work, splitting his time between wine and horses. At first there was improvement from the new treatments, but cancer is a cruel race course, and it reasserted itself as his eightieth birthday approached. He gradually reduced his hours, as he tired more easily, had little appetite, and had grown gaunt and weak, the clothes hanging loose on his big frame. Yet he continued poring over racing forms and pedigrees, formulating new strategies to bolster wine sales, and walking with Buddy over his mountain, more slowly than in the past, but striving to keep his body limber and his muscles working.

For a time it seemed that through sheer willpower and some very expensive and exotic treatments, he might just beat the odds. But by the holiday break in 2010, it was clear this was one battle he was not going to win. A disappointing second campaign for Rachel Alexandra ended prematurely, the horse retired by Jackson midseason because she was not running to her high standards, having never been the same after exhausting herself against the boys in the Woodward Stakes. And once he made that heartbreaking decision, Jackson began to pull back from his daily immersion in his company. Though he continued to work and meet with his people, he began to emphasize matters of succession, of perfecting his plan for his winemaking empire to continue after he was gone. The "two-hundred-year time horizon," he called it, or the "Antinori model." And he wanted to be with his family as much as possible.

Katie was home again and working at Kendall-Jackson in marketing and sales, blogging about wine, providing a new public face for the company, and she was engaged to be married to one of Jackson's sustainability specialists. Chris was rushing to graduate early so that he could get his degree ahead of schedule and be with his dad, but even so, he got home every weekend. Jenny and Laura were over every day. And Julia astonished her father by graduating with her art degree, then going to France to work the harvest for three months, twelve- and fifteen-hour days sorting grapes and doing pump-overs with the fermentation tanks—hard, manual, but edifying work, particularly for a young woman who had been courted by modeling agencies and had done some fashion work for them before rejecting the lifestyle. Then she told her father she was going to attend an intensive business program at Stanford when she got back. She wanted to prepare for work at Kendall-Jackson.

"Really?" he asked. "You'd do that?"

"Yeah," she said. "I want to." And it was true. She really did. After all the fighting and trying to strike her own path, she realized this was what she wanted. Her passion for art and her desire to be part of the family business would mesh somehow.

"I'm so proud of you," he had whispered into the phone, and she realized she had not heard those words in a while.

Once she completed the program at Stanford, Jackson told Julia to report to the office and get to work. That was it. No guidance. No assignment. No specific job. Just: go find where you're needed.

Julia knew well how sick he was by then. She had started riding with him on the long journeys for treatment at Stanford, keeping him company at his lowest. And yet there he was, testing her, seeing if she would flounder or find her way. But she found her niche in the long-suffering international division. It had slipped through the cracks again after Lew Platt left, and Julia though it was a mess. The Web sites were terrible. The Italian winery Web pages looked like missives from a faceless American corporation. Radically different wines with different consumer appeals—Chianti classico and super Tuscans—were being marketed together and going nowhere. The wines themselves were quite good, she thought, but the marketing and image were a disaster. The labels were terrible. There was no identity. The brand needed a complete repositioning. The company had invested $20 million in Italy and hadn't seen a return. Ninety percent of the Italian wine it made was exported to the United States, where it sat in warehouses, racking up huge costs with almost no sales.

She drew up a report and presented her findings and recommendations to her father. He was impressed. He agreed with her assessment. The company had been very foolish with international, he agreed. The good news, he said, was that it now represented a great opportunity. "So go fix it," he told her.

And so her life at Kendall-Jackson began.

AS SPRING APPROACHED, it was clear Jackson hadn't much time left. He was finding it hard to get out of bed and had taken to working with his laptop and two phones and the Racing Channel on TV in his bedroom. He wanted his family around all the time, and he told stories about his childhood and his family, some that were familiar, some that he had never shared before, some just fine tall stories, such as the time during Prohibition his teetotaling grandmother had cleared a saloon with a loaded six-gun, sending a crowd of heavy-drinking men home to their wives. He wanted to know if he had done enough to teach his children the value of hard work, of the need to earn things rather than simply receive them, and they had to laugh because if he had drummed anything into them, it was that the work ethic was everything. That, and family. Nothing was more important than family. The best wisdom he could offer, he said, lay in those most basic principles.

In February 2011, on Valentine's Day, Rachel and Curlin had their date. Jackson said he was glad he had lived to see that day. "I'd love to see their foal," he added wistfully, knowing that would be all but impossible.

In his last days he stopped seeing anyone but his closest family. He was so weak and tired, but he still had his pride, not wanting others to see him so diminished. Banke nursed him daily, rarely leaving his side. But one day in April Julia brought her best friend, Keiko Cadby, to see him. She was a gifted concert violinist, and Jackson had loved her since she was little, treating her as another daughter, another Linny. Julia had asked Keiko if she could compose her own rendition of Jess's favorite song and come play it. She said she would and worked on it feverishly for two nights in a row, feeling the pressure of time running out, and then she drove from Los Angeles to perform a recital for one.

Julia walked in first, and her father greeted his "Nurse Ratched," his *One Flew Over the Cuckoo's Nest* nickname for her because of all the green veggie blended drinks she had pushed him to drink. She had hoped it might help him as it had helped a friend's dad who recovered from colon cancer.

"I have a visitor," she said, and though he was upset at this violation of his wishes to see no one but family, she brought in Keiko anyway, violin in hand.

"I have a song for you," she said without preamble and began playing a sweetly haunting version of "As Time Goes By." How many times had Julia sat with her dad and watched his favorite movie, *Casablanca*? How many times had she heard her father say, "I love that song," as Dooley Wilson sat at the piano in Rick's bar and crooned those classic lyrics:

It's still the same old story
A fight for love and glory
A case of do or die.
The world will always welcome lovers
As time goes by.

When she finished, Keiko said, "I learned that for you."

Tears ran down Jackson's lined face, but he was smiling as he wept. "That's my favorite song. How did you know that was my favorite song?"

Keiko looked at Julia, then answered, "A little bird told me."

For the rest of that day he smiled. It was all he could talk about.

And though he had just a few days left to him, the next day he got on the phone and made some calls to Kentucky. He bought two foals. For the future, he said. For the kids. And every now and then he seemed to be humming or softly singing the phrase "as time goes by."

THAT SAME WEEK Julia and Chris went on a hike over their dad's mountain. Yes, it was their home, too. But it was their dad's mountain, they said, and always would be.

The spot he loved best, his personal retreat, where he built a small office with a spectacular view of vineyards and the valley, was called Bear Point. This was his escape. This was where he would go when he wanted to work and think undisturbed or just play the piano, surrounded by trees and silence. "That's where I want to be buried," he told Barbara. "Somewhere on Bear Point."

Julia and Chris had volunteered to go and find the right spot. They tromped for over an hour, unsure of the terrain or where to go, not even sure they wanted to perform this task, so final a thing, such a naked admission that their father was about to die. But it was what he wanted. He loved this place. And in the end it was a bird that led them to the right spot, which Julia found fitting for a man who loved and was loved by animals. She had spotted the movement of a bird through the trees above and out into the clear, and this led her to see an owl box, one of many nesting places scattered around the mountain. She and her brother walked to the spot and found it stood in a flat clearing on a natural terrace just below their dad's Bear Point getaway. It would need some leveling and an access road, Chris said, eying the slope, but it was the perfect spot. They took in the view and knew it was what he wanted, as Jackson had already described why he loved that place in an interview just a couple years earlier.

"I consider the view from the overlook one of the most spectacular on the Alexander Mountain Estate. From my perch I can see most of the Alexander Valley below, the Coastal Mountain Range to the west, the Santa Rosa Plain, Taylor Peak and Sonoma Mountain to the south, and most prominently Mount St. Helena in the east. On a late summer afternoon you are likely to spot a black bear, a flock of wild turkeys or a cougar walking through the brush. This is where I come to reflect on the power of nature and the exquisite flavors of mountain-grown grapes."

And that described the spot his children found for him. That's exactly what they saw. They came back with the news, and the estate maintenance staff rushed to ready the place, finishing just in time. Jess Stonestreet Jackson died April 21, 2011, at age eighty-one, surrounded by his family, with the perfect spot waiting for a man and his mountain to come together.

THERE WERE MANY remembrances of Jess Jackson at the multiple memorial services held in his honor, the letters and Web comments, the endless toasts—all reflecting on his kindness, his business acumen, and his accomplishments in law, in wine, in horse racing, in charity. Old friends volunteered previously unknown tidbits to his family, including how as a young man out of law school he had been tapped to serve on a committee that crafted California's groundbreaking master plan for higher education, meaning he had had a hand in designing the modern system of state universities and community colleges that made the state a world leader in education. There was Steve Miller, who had led such corporations as Bethlehem Steel and AIG, and who served on Kendall-Jackson's advisory board, who fondly described Jackson as "an extraordinary man and a regular guy." Fieldworkers recalled hauling Jess's Lexus out of ditches after his overly enthusiastic drives across his mountain. His entire workforce showed up at a convention center to raise a glass of wine and toast the man. The clinking glasses sounded like notes from a symphony, filling the space.

But how did Jess Jackson want to be remembered? I had asked him that, and he struggled with the question and the many answers he juggled. First, he focused on his winemaking. He wanted to be remembered for his commitment to quality and excellence. Then he said, no, that was important but not quite right.

He wanted to be remembered as a reformer, as a champion of the little guy, as an innovator who wasn't afraid to take on the big guys. That was good.

But no, there was something else, the secret of his success: the work ethic. A willingness to work harder than anyone else—that's what's important. And that may sound pedestrian, but hard work to Jess Jackson isn't just breaking your back or putting in long hours, though that's part of it. It's also thinking harder and longer and *differently* from anyone else, of looking at problems in new ways and rejecting the word "never" when it's pitted against your passion and conviction. Now *that's* hard work, Jackson said, and that's something anyone should be proud to be known for and remembered by.

But, he said, that wasn't it either. There was the matter of family—of building a family business that lasts. "We can't just be thinking about today or tomorrow. Mine is the one-hundred- or two-hundred-year time horizon. . . . That's what I hope my legacy is. That I built something that endures."

And still he wasn't satisfied. He thought, his brow knitted. He was getting tired. The cancer almost had him then, but he had wanted to tell his story. "They kept telling me I should do that, but I procrastinated," he said, "and now look at me." Then he shot me that Jess Jackson grin, infectious and heartbreaking in his gaunt, pained face. And then he had it, the legacy he really wanted to put out there:

I'm a farmer at heart. It was my first avocation, it was my first training, it was my first love, because just growing radishes in the backyard is a thrill when the damn radish finally gets ripe. And then I went through all my careers, the police, the law, real estate, computers. And then, after all that time, I had the opportunity to buy a farm again, just to get away. I thought it could extend my law career; that was the original idea. See, I'd drive up there, leave the rat race and the pressure behind. The place had no television. I had a radio, but I rarely used it. There was no access to civilization. And the next day I'd get on a tractor and I'd plow. Or I'd go out and pick or prune, whatever the season was. I thought I was back home, back to my childhood visits to the farm. I thought I was a kid again. Because farming, it's a spiritual thing to me. And when you restore your spiritual center for two or three days, then I could extend my legal career; I could go back fresh. At least that was the idea.

But what I was really doing was working my way back to farming. Because that's what I love best. That's what brought me my success. I'm a farmer.

So it's really a simple question, how to remember Jess Jackson: he loved dirt and hated debt. . . . If you stick with those guidelines in life, really, you can't go wrong. You can make it anywhere.

EPILOGUE

In Vino Veritas

O NE MONTH AFTER JESS JACKSON'S DEATH, WINE CRITIC
Robert Parker came to town to taste the late winemaker's
beloved Vérité. Parker was welcomed by Barbara Banke, who had
taken over the company, reassuring the workforce that her husband's
vision would continue, that the Jackson family would be here for the
long haul. Parker wept at the tasting, at not having Jackson sitting
there with him as he had so many times before. The critic spoke of
his enormous respect for Jess as one of the great figures of the wine
industry, a major force in the rise of California wines—not just
for his elite fine vintages, which rank among the world's best, but
for raising the bar on the quality of everyday consumer wines. "He
did something no one else has been able to do, occupying both sides
of the wine world successfully. This was an incredible achievement."

Parker is a plainspoken man, as was Jackson, who never much
cared for wine critics as group. But he liked and respected Parker
and had looked forward to his visits, eager to show off his wines and
to hear what this most eminent of wine critics had to say. Parker
enjoyed the strong, powerful, genteel vintner and observed that it
seemed fitting to him that Jackson had found his own mountain to

call home. "He always looked to me like someone who had been born on a mountain. He was formidable, bigger than life, yet when it came to the wine business, there was almost a spirituality about him."

This would be Parker's first tasting at Kendall-Jackson without Jess, and it would last all day at the Cardinale Winery in Napa. Parker sat down with Banke and several of her children, who were determined to carry on the family business of wine and horses and land. They reminisced and caught up and felt Jackson's absence because he had lived for moments like this, for being the proud host showing off his latest creations. And these wines had been his pride and joy in recent years, his link to that ancient vine in the Caucasus, his link to history and nature and the serendipity of science, art, farming, and taste.

And then it was time to taste. Parker had asked Pierre Seillan for a vertical tasting, meaning he would sample every vintage, top to bottom, of the Vérité line. And so the ritual commenced, the gauging of aroma and taste and feel of these Bordeaux-style wines built from the *terroir* of Sonoma.

Parker awarded five of the Vérité blends 98 points out of 100. Four more received near-perfect scores of 99.

And seven of these wines scored a perfect 100. Few wines had ever received so many perfect scores, and none from Sonoma ever had. Such scores put Jess Jackson's wine in the same category as the finest in the world: Chapoutier, Guigal, and, yes, Château Petrus.

And Parker, who spoke of the "great visionary genius of Jess Jackson" in his letter revealing these scores, said something else. These wines were not meant to be bought and poured but to be stored and saved. Because even with all those perfect scores, they would only get better with time. They were a legacy that would last.

ACKNOWLEDGMENTS

For sharing their time, stories, memories, and the unforgettable landscape of Alexander Mountain, I am grateful to Barbara Banke, Jennifer Hartford, Don Hartford, Laura Giron, Katie Jackson, Julia Jackson, Christopher Jackson, Randy Ullom, Rick Tigner, and the master of make-it-happen, Donna Stolz. I also must thank the many others at Kendall-Jackson and among Jess's friends and family who helped make this book possible.

Finally, I want to acknowledge Jess Jackson for trusting me with his story and inviting me into his world of wine, horses, and *terroir*. I miss our conversations—you almost always found a way to surprise me.

INDEX

EDWARD HUMES is a Pulitzer Prize–winning journalist and author of twelve nonfiction books, including *Mississippi Mud; No Matter How Loud I Shout: A Year in the Life of Juvenile Court; Force of Nature: The Unlikely Story of Wal-Mart's Green Revolution;* and *Garbology: Our Dirty Love Affair with Trash.* He lives in Southern California.

PublicAffairs is a publishing house founded in 1997. It is a tribute to the standards, values, and flair of three persons who have served as mentors to countless reporters, writers, editors, and book people of all kinds, including me.

I. F. STONE, proprietor of *I. F. Stone's Weekly*, combined a commitment to the First Amendment with entrepreneurial zeal and reporting skill and became one of the great independent journalists in American history. At the age of eighty, Izzy published *The Trial of Socrates*, which was a national bestseller. He wrote the book after he taught himself ancient Greek.

BENJAMIN C. BRADLEE was for nearly thirty years the charismatic editorial leader of *The Washington Post*. It was Ben who gave the *Post* the range and courage to pursue such historic issues as Watergate. He supported his reporters with a tenacity that made them fearless and it is no accident that so many became authors of influential, best-selling books.

ROBERT L. BERNSTEIN, the chief executive of Random House for more than a quarter century, guided one of the nation's premier publishing houses. Bob was personally responsible for many books of political dissent and argument that challenged tyranny around the globe. He is also the founder and longtime chair of Human Rights Watch, one of the most respected human rights organizations in the world.

.   .   .

For fifty years, the banner of Public Affairs Press was carried by its owner Morris B. Schnapper, who published Gandhi, Nasser, Toynbee, Truman, and about 1,500 other authors. In 1983, Schnapper was described by *The Washington Post* as "a redoubtable gadfly." His legacy will endure in the books to come.

Peter Osnos, *Founder and Editor-at-Large*